Collector's World

Collector's World

Stowers Johnson

ROBERT HALE · LONDON

© *Stowers Johnson 1989*
First published in Great Britain 1989

Robert Hale Limited
Clerkenwell House
Clerkenwell Green
London EC1R 0HT

British Library Cataloguing in Publication Data

Johnson, Stowers
  Collector's world.
  1. Visual arts. Collecting
  I. Title
  707′.5

ISBN 0–7090–3815–1

Photoset in North Wales by
Derek Doyle & Associates, Mold, Clwyd.
Printed in Great Britain by
St Edmundsbury Press Ltd, Bury St Edmunds, Suffolk.
Bound by Hunter & Foulis Ltd.

Contents

Illustrations

1   *Declaration and Display:*
J. Paul Getty

It was the day of days for me. I had that feeling of happy exultation, an enthusiasm which has brought imagined achievement into reality. Gathered over many years, my exhibition of paintings, sculpture and art miscellanies had been arranged in London's West End at Foyle's Art Galleries. One hundred and sixty-three items were displayed on walls, on benches and in glass cases hired for the purpose. There were examples of the Old Masters – Rembrandt and Hobbema, Wilson and Constable, among fine equestrian bronzes. Crowded together, they provided practical evidence of my triumphs, since I made no secret of the small sums for which each had been purchased out of the great sale-rooms of the metropolis.

That morning I had called in to see Michael Geare, who was handling the publicity for the exhibition. As he noticed my exhilaration, his face had hardened. He looked at me quizzically.

'After tonight,' he declared with an unchanging smile, 'you are going to be the most famous celebrity or else the biggest laughing-stock of London.'

I shrugged the threat aside with a grin and the rejoinder, 'Occupational hazards of a writer!'

'It is nice of you to take it so lightly,' he sighed, 'but I don't think my firm will, with our long tradition of publishing.'

This was something new I was doing. It was one thing to write a book of art criticism or on collecting, but to bring up a substantive body of examples as justification was a different matter, only to be done by folk of the stature and purse of such as Bernard Berenson, and I knew I might have to run the gauntlet of those journalists who tackle art fashions or collecting so glibly, wrapping opinions adroitly in verbosity without risking either their money or their reputation. It has always puzzled me how few are aware of that supreme enjoyment which possession of a work of art can bestow, and I confess I do tend to estimate the merit of a critic by the value of his collection.

Nevertheless, the publishers and Christina Foyle had shown their confidence by accepting all my list of invitees; only in one instance, the case of James Wentworth Day, had Michael Geare protested. 'Surely you don't intend to have him?' he argued. 'Everywhere that man goes, there's trouble!' Wentworth Day was a neighbour of mine and, despite his glorious successes in personal vendettas and libel cases, such as the Laski affair, Fleet Street could comment; 'His heart was always in the right place!' Moreover, he knew my collection, and I had advised him on his own purchases and disposals from time to time, so I had to insist, and more than insist, that his name be maintained on our list. As I had left Michael Geare, he had shaken his head and added the news, 'Your friend Mr Wentworth Day has accepted our invitation. Of course, as your friend, understandably, you had to invite him. I only hope he stays that way!'

'What do you mean?'

'As your friend, of course.'

At the appointed time everyone began to arrive. There were journalists, picture and museum experts and representatives from the major London auction houses, and in particular Arthur Lucas, the chief restorer of the National Gallery, was there. He had given me so much help and advice when I was a mere beginner with my collection that I was particularly glad to see his tall, dignified and bearded figure as he stood smiling like one of the old Renaissance patrons at the approach of a client. He always seemed to invoke some shadow of Titian, for whom he had a boundless admiration he never failed to impart. At that time I had no painting of this greatest of Masters, but years later it was recollections of what I had learned from him that led me to discover, outcast and forgotten in the back room of a Spanish shop, one precious example.

The picture experts from the larger auction rooms had drifted in unobtrusively, and I did not recognize any of these professional invitees – they seemed like new recruits to me. '*Singula de nobis anni praedantur euntes*' – 'The passing years plunder from us one by one' (Horace, Epistles, II, ii, 55). They wandered into a gossipy huddle in the corner and occupied themselves with rarified matters, nothing to do with the show on hand. I recall David Holloway of the *Daily Telegraph*, who did make a deliberate tour: tall and rather assertive, he moved around with, as it were, a bodyguard of lesser minions who united to scowl disapproval at me when on introduction I did not immediately catch his name. He was intrigued to see the smaller bronzes by Hamo Thornycroft and especially the *Salome* of Sir Bertram Mackennal, of whom he and his family had childhood recollections – interesting for me, since the Australian sculptor was then in the doldrums as far as sale-room prices went, whereas today his works have soared to their thousands of pounds and rightly so, passing even those of Gilbert.

Then, at the climactic moment, Christina Foyle brought in J.Paul Getty. I had written him a personal letter of invitation but no one thought he would come, despite his acceptance. And there he was, accompanied by his Art Adviser, a tall, capable woman as knowledgeable and erudite as the art world could provide. He himself might have been radio-active, for, as he moved around, the assembly moved back and he proceeded within a circle of space, making no comment on the pictures but more interested in their frames. A book had recently been published on that subject, only to be neglected and the edition doomed to be remaindered and become out of print. Neither he nor his Art Adviser knew of it, so I offered to procure a copy from a source I knew.

Like David Holloway, he fell to admiring my bronzes. Mostly Victorian, these were a new field to him whose purse ran to fine Pentelic marbles showing the splendour of Greece. As he left, he questioned the validity of my book's title and indeed that of the whole exhibition, asserting that collections like mine were not made by luck but by a combination of flair and knowledge. Choosing the title for any book was difficult but vital, and he had decided his own should be *Collector's Choice*. Since he could have whatever he wished, 'choice' was the determining word, and choice was indeed the decisive factor in the whole process of appreciation; therefore since in my case those exhibits must have been chosen out of many, it was not such a matter of luck. He thought, on reflection, he had the right title for his own book, *Collector's Choice*.

We stood in the doorway joking on the adversity of 'choice' or the benefits of 'luck'. I could not fail to notice how folk had been observing far from surreptitiously. Christina Foyle came forward and gracefully presented him with a copy of my book, and he left urging me to come and visit him at Sutton Place to see some of his own chosen collection, while his Art Adviser reminded me to obtain a copy of the book on the history of picture frames.

Michael Geare seized the moment as appropriate for me to make some formal address of welcome, so I uttered a few musings and platitudes about the life-enhancing qualities of a collection as not being confined to objects but magnifying the human personality on the one hand or if in reverse diminishing and impoverishing it on the other, suggesting that parallels could be found in the history of nations, whether progress reflected in Art or decadence shown in neglect and indifference or worse still in a pompous bombasity of the democratic many or the selected few.

Some time after I finished to formal applause, I realized how the audience, like myself, had been stunned by the departure of that presence. The richest man in the world, the collector with the largest-ever purse in history had been among them. He had crossed the threshold to visit the collector (as I had been wont to boast) with the smallest purse, and I could feel from the attitude of those listening that some glory had fallen upon me, as tactfully they sought to learn some crumbs of his conversation. I could not be forthcoming on this. For me it was a magnanimous and courageous gesture for such a world-famous collector, such a target of newspaper men, to come through the bookshelves of Foyles to the opening of my exhibition. As it was, William Hickey's column the very next morning carried a belittling paragraph asserting that he had come 'to get some tips on obtaining bargains for himself'.

Just as people were beginning to leave, there was a stir by the doorway. A large figure in wide, puffed-out, sporting tweeds swept in behind a huge red buttonhole and black-ribboned monacle. He greeted me in loud, grandiloquent tones, sweeping my companions aside and bowing to my wife.

'I have come,' he declared, 'to take you off to dinner. A table is taken! A celebration is called for! The Café Royal is the place for us!'

I caught Michael Geare's eyes, which had become baleful as his whole face drooped with foreboding. A celebration! A scene! Some public row. An argument in Churchillian style, with Munnings evoked. Someone possibly on whom assault could be provoked! Tablecloths pulled away at the least, clatter of broken crockery, headlines next day – infamy and glory wrestling together in print in some ugly championing of the true cause of Art. I shook my head!

'The table is taken!'

Gratefully and in as friendly a fashion as could be, I stood firm. The taxi was waiting. The table was taken. I pleaded fatigue: I must go straight home. Someone rescued me by asking about a picture. As I moved away, my wife stood by, astounded, while he grumbled: 'This is not the way to do things. No, it is not the way! Far from it!'

Safely, from the other side of the gallery, I saw him scrutinzing a picture or two, and then he was gone.

'You have escaped,' whispered a friend. 'It could have been worse, much worse.'

Next morning my telephone rang, and I heard the challenging voice of Wentworth Day. 'You did not tell me Getty would be coming,' he protested. 'Opportunity has been missed here. Why was I not told?'

As I placated him, he demanded to know which pictures Paul Getty had been interested in. 'What did he say then? What comments?'

'He was chiefly interested in the bronzes and especially the one by Sir Alfred Gilbert, *Homage to Hymen*, which I had bought many years ago for as little as £18.'

'What did he remark on that?'

'Oh, he laughed and commented, "That was a lot of money for you in those days, I guess!"'

Wentworth Day's voice rasped over the telephone, 'The mean individual! The world's richest man and the world's meanest! To say a thing like that!'

'Not at all! It was I myself who was boasting how cheaply I bought. The whole purpose of the exhibition was to show how Art could be purchased from the unappreciative public at these low prices, that anyone with discrimination could buy for himself.'

'Doesn't matter,' cried Wentworth Day as he hung up. 'He has said it.'

He must have been sore at his lost journalistic opportunity, for, journeyman bloodhound of Fleet Street as he was, he spent next afternoon loitering in the foyer of the Ritz, where J.Paul Getty was staying. No sooner did the great man enter than Wentworth Day was at his side.

'As I was commenting yesterday when we were both at the Stowers Johnson exhibition,' he began, when Getty's short, unobtrusive figure interrupted, waving him away with, 'I don't think so, no, I don't think so,' his eyes staring straight ahead as if they saw nothing, not even Wentworth Day's anxious moustache quivering with the protest, 'But really, I say, I say!'

With a shrug of the shoulders and another, 'No, I don't think so!', the quarry had gone, out of the journalist's sight for ever.

Not out of his mind, however. He was furious, and not just to me over the telephone. He had been passed by, mentally whipped away, and his blood curdled with wrath, wrath that was the one vital tonic necessary to rejuvenate his pen into action. During the coming months I had the mortification of reading articles accusing J.Paul Getty of being as mean as he was rich, instancing this by quoting that conversation on the price of my Gilbert bronze but with the accent shifting to portray lofty condescension. I was shocked and could only hope oblivion would soon cover such accounts. Getty's visit had been a noble gesture, and I felt nothing but gratitude for this, coupled with admiration for his courage in coming to the exhibition, which he surely knew would be frequented by publicity-making reporters capable of making news out of his very name.

My other guests were not so impelled, however, and had devoted their time as much to gossip and chatter among themselves as to any critical appraisal of the pictures. Arthur Lucas smiled benignly over them but he also was relishing the social atmosphere rather than making any appraisal. The one over-riding subject that caught everyone's imagination was the total value of the collection, the mathematical value measured in sterling, and this came as a shock to the establishment at Foyles when, as the public entered next day, calls from Fleet Street came in asking for estimates and how responsible were they for the premises. Security Express were hired to station uniformed guards, and a book was installed for a record of visitors.

In response to William Hickey's column referring to tips and bargains, a number of eager would-be customers arrived, prepared to make cash offers and take away instant purchases. An Essex MP entered to grace the exhibition with his presence. When I politely proffered the visitor's book, he demanded, 'Do *I* have to sign this?' Told it was customary, he picked up his case and took himself off in a dudgeon, leaving me amazed and holding the pen. Over 5,000 people did actually sign that book; some came specially, others merely because they happened to be visiting Foyles. One I missed, alas, who would surely have added some humour among those pictures, but Jimmy Duranti came and signed when I was away.

Sir Robert and Lady Mayer came during the first week and brought with them Erskine Childers. Lady Dorothy was writing a biography of Angelica Kauffmann and had been interested in collecting examples of her work. Her husband was tempted by the monetary rewards he envisaged suspended from the walls there. He had already advanced a successful publishing firm at Gerrard's Cross and dreamed up the prospect of founding a West End gallery, offering to promote it financially in a partnership with me. He raised the matter several times and again at his home in Essex but could not understand my impediment, akin to that of the miser, that I could never bear to part with the best I had. If I had lived with a painting, I would no more desert it than sacrifice a friend.

With my mother's Irish antecedents – the Devlins and the Chevalier Sheeran – and the book I had written on Cork and County Kerry (*Before and After Puck*, 1953), I felt it a great honour to meet Erskine Childers there, Irish Minister for Posts and Telegraphs as he then was, in 1973 to become the fourth President of the Republic of Ireland after a fierce contest with Terence O'Higgins. There was no air of a politician about him at all, only a certain melancholy wistfulness appropriate for the son of his father, the author of *The Riddle of the Sands*, whom he had visited in the condemned cell just before the Irish Free State Government executed him by firing-squad on that dubious charge of bearing arms in 1922.

The miscellanies in my glass cases astonished these new visitors, especially Sir Robert, who was intrigued by my silver Argentine maté cup with its platinum infusers. I also had a surprise for Erskine Childers, an Irish silver cup, eighteenth-century, hall-marked and with the inscription: 'For the cleanest and best crop of turnips' – a relic of those attempts to wean Irish farmers from eighteenth-century potato-growing, the failures and famines.

'Never part with this!' counselled Lady Dorothy. 'If ever you must, tell us, and it shall come straight back to Ireland, which it should never have left.'

Some days later I heard from Dame Laura Knight, RA, writing that she would like to have come to the exhibition but was not well enough to travel. I had been to her last exhibition near Grosvenor Square. A galaxy of magical lines, her work had spread across that gallery – water-colour drawings, quick crayonings of the circus life she knew and the performers whose transitory energy she had caught and made permanent on canvas or paper. She was wearing black then and sat by the entrance to her show, frail and watching, while the many visitors on their way to the pictures did not even pause to recognize the presence of the artist herself. Long ago, when

I was editor of the *Anglo-Soviet Journal* and concerned with arranging cultural visits, I had had the pleasure of introducing her to a party of Soviet circus and ballet artistes on their visit to Britain, an amusing thing to do, for it showed we also actually had the circus here, as Laura Knight easily proved with exchanges of anecdotes.

I telephoned to express my own regret that she could not come and offered to call for her myself at any time she felt recovered. Her housekeeper replied, and there was I, a day or two later, bringing her from somewhere in London NW into Foyles. She swept round the collection, artist that she was, coveting rather than the pictures of others the splendid frames themselves saving her great interest for the realities in the bronzes of Gilbert, Reid Dick and Drury. On the way back to her studio, she had reminiscences of her artist husband and their life on tours to circus locations but it was her studio that surprised me. She was still engaged as an active artist, painting not circus life nowadays but large water-colours, landscapes of forest and garden, bright with youthful colour. In her capacious, high-roofed studio they shone out in a reality of brightness. She poured the tea and we sat talking while they sparkled and seemed alive, as if it were not St John's Wood outside but the New Forest or Epping or far-away Cornwall.

One or two years were to pass before, in November 1970, I found myself sitting in Sotheby's. The frail artist had passed on and there were the contents of that very studio before the auctioneer's hammer. Some would say an artist's studio sale consists chiefly of left-overs, but Sotheby's were well pleased, for they fetched £10,751, with £700 offered for the picture *Self and Nude*, painted as long ago as 1913. The life she had painted had passed away long before her, but she had captured her view of it, and these days I cannot look at my own picture of hers – *The Ballerina's Dressing-Room* – without paying homage.

Before the end of my exhibition, I had begun to feel that surfeit of sudden publicity that first intoxicates and then nauseates. Friends had laughingly associated me with auction rings and the tale of the vamped-up purchase of the Duccio panel as it sped from auction to dealer and from thence into the National Gallery. Seizing the opportunity, I rang several news agencies and issued a press release declaring myself as a private collector with no trade association and angrily rebutting any suggestion of complicity in the Duccio auction, whether before or after.

A strong denial like this was calculated to make both Press and public believe the opposite, and so it did. Interest in my collection and my exhibition multiplied. I found myself on radio's *World at One* discussing an oil sketch on panel, a palette that may have belonged to Sir Joshua Reynolds. I taxied over to Alexandra Palace to show Noel Edmunds on television my bronzes, especially one I believed to be by Sir William Goscombe John. Showing influence of Canova, it created the spectacle of a naked lady balancing a butterfly on her arm and glancing with a curiosity that was both erotic and charming. When I had bought it, I read its incised title as *Sue*, but in maturer days I now read it as *Sin*. It was fun speculating on the lady's thoughts before those television cameras.

Next I was invited over to ITV and gave an illustrated interview showing a chosen selection of paintings taken straight out of the exhibition. The Van Hughtenburg picture of *The Battle for the Standard* at the Siege of Vienna was splendidly reproduced, and I was delighted to see how it was projected later on the small screen.

Perhaps my most varied experience was going to the old theatre at Golders Green to show some collector's items on Michael Aspel's television show, a pleasant occasion on which I displayed my *koro* with the Chinese Emperor's official seal stamped below it, embellished with 'elephants galore' shapely tendrils and leaves and peony flowers entwined the exterior of its bronze bowl. (It had been found in the ruined cellar of General Gordon's house, probably brought there from China to old Gravesend. I have since complemented it with a smaller, unstamped model found in a junk sale lower down the Thames.)

I seemed thoroughly out of place among the actors in that show, where Rolf Harris ran boisterously around, assertive and aloof at the same time, embracing and encouraging school-children to applaud him and where Cleo Lane warbled in some peculiar style of singing, serenaded and guarded by Johnny Dankworth, her husband. They behaved, each of these celebrities, as if they might be contaminated by mortals. Had they not descended from an Olympus to which they must return as soon as due tribute and applause was claimed by them? Only Sheila Scott, the courageous airwoman and world traveller, had none of this brusque haughtiness and showed a vivacious interest in the whole scene.

One of the programme secretaries had obviously noticed this hiatus between actors and present mortals, for she confided that the producers were everlastingly pestered by agents on behalf of stage and music personalities. These folk, by telephone, letter after letter and every possible means of soliciting, harassed the programme organizers to hire clients who, in actual fact, had nothing of their own individual creativity to give. Often they were merely representational, according to their stage training, whereas the public wanted variety of spirit, to see people from the real world rather than shadows of the Stage. Oh yes, she declared, these theatrical agents gave one no peace and could be a constant worry; yet the folk they supplied were reliable, and one knew exactly how they would perform, whereas with others, she continued, looking straight at me, one never knew, one could never be sure what would turn up.

These television interviews attracted attention not always welcome. A burly American arrived at Foyles with two suitcases and strap containers. He produced more than 'a fistful of dollars' and asserted he had come to buy. Tactfully he was directed back to the book-store, where there was a good display of illustrated art books. He was persistent and demanding. He had the right to buy! It was a shop. 'Right?' Anger replaced his eagerness, and he took himself off, slouching between his suitcases.

After one of the last of these media appearances, Michael Geare looked at me sadly, damping my exhilaration.

'In all this publicity,' he reminded me, 'you have never mentioned your book, and as for us, the publishers, not once have you breathed our name into the microphone.'

I was shaken. Of course, the book, its price, its publishers – that was the object of the exercises. What a tyro I was! And as for those friendly interviewers, they had not so much as thought of it! Crestfallen, I showed grief and contrition.

'Doesn't matter,' I was comforted. 'The book is so well known, they all know what to ask for.'

By this time, I was getting really tired. Everyone bleated about security. Foyles had Bow Street police station in touch with them. Security Express added another guard, with the firm's name even more prominent upon his uniform. Their photographer also came to record them protecting the collection. I would be sitting there warily watching the pictures and the glass cases, and necessarily so, for dealers kept trying to turn oil paintings round to read anything on the reverse; a trio of furniture men took out penknives and began to test the ivory inlay and the tortoiseshell veneers on my seventeenth-century Serbian cabinet; once a Thomas Cooper oil painting came crashing vertically to the floor, absolutely unharmed, with even its glass uncracked. Every day someone would come seeking advice, questioning attributions, begging me to assert their treasures to be precious, seeking proof they had some lost Old Master. Indeed, looking back, I can claim this brief series of encounters to be a one-man precursor of the famous '*Antiques Road Shows*' on television; but I had also found myself in the client stage, with everyone telling me how valuable my collection was, so that now I wanted only to get it safely home.

And home everything eventually came. In the removal process there was only one casualty, and that involved Pluto's trident. When one of the hurrying removal men tripped and fell headlong across my hall, Pluto saved him in his staggering collapse but the bronze trident broke into the stairs as he crashed. It was some time afterwards before I managed to locate a metal craftsman skilful enough to re-arm the King of the Underworld. The price charged seemed exorbitant, as might be expected of work for royalty.

A letter arrived from Paul Getty's Art Adviser acknowledging and paying for the illustrated book on the history of picture frames I had obtained for him. She repeated Paul Getty's invitation to visit his collection at Sutton Place and urged me to come as soon as possible.

At the time arranged, I arrived and came past the security station beside the American-style notices on converted stable marked 'Livery', from where flunkeys telephoned to the house.

Though it was known I was coming, I could detect some anxiety. Was I alone? The house was protected against intruders, as much against publicity as against thieves and bandits. Did anyone know I was coming? Were any friends meeting me? The threat of publicity seemed to radiate around me and haunt the whole establishment. Of course, I had come unattended except for the taxi-man and unheralded except for that telephone call.

Paul Getty, summoned by complications in his oil interests, was now in America, but he had left instructions that I should be shown all the treasures, though his main collection and indeed his art interests had now been centralized at Malibu, which he hoped I would see next time I came to America.

In the great hall before the stairway, larger than life, was a fine marble of Aphrodite at her bath. I knew it as similar to the Roman copy of a Hellenistic original in bronze by the sculptor Doidalus, found in Rome in 1760 (listed as in the Vatican Museum, (815)

H.0.8 m). Now I also realized why Paul Getty and his Art Adviser had been so long examining the little bronze of the same subject in my exhibition.

I had bought mine for 12 shillings from old Mr Wheeler in Cecil Court, London, where it lay without a plinth with the rubbish on his dusty shelf. All Aphrodite's back had been seared in bronze droplets by some breath of devastating heat by which the right hand had melted into a withered form. The droplets of bronze were easily filed away but I could not bear to look at that hand, so I had persuaded a Greek colleague who was a skilful potter to model a sponge of clay and fire it so that, by fitting over the up-raised wrist, it would hide any damage. Had the bronze received some blast from a high explosive during the London Blitz, or perhaps as likely been taken out of the lava at Pompeii by some nineteenth-century traveller? Today I can compare it with a photograph in *The Erotic Art of Greece* (Eugenio la Rocca, John Murray). Mine is no exact copy: the hands are more in proportion, the hair-style is more detailed, as Aphrodite looks definitely over her shoulder, and the feet – both of them – are more delicately moulded. I think my Pompeii theory is more reasonable, the bronze perhaps fallen with the hand supporting and the back lying on old lava within some hillside villa. Standing by the splendid marble, I began to tell my theories and the story of that discovery made in the middle of London, but broke off, for the Art Adviser was now on her own ground in the presence of treasures she had assisted in acquiring and was daily researching.

There was something cute and American overlying that old English manor house, more than mere electric light and telephone communication with the 'Livery' departments. No great Tudor fire blazed in the hall. My admiration for its owner had been based not on his being by far the richest man in the wide world but on his intermittent quests for anonymity, so that, for instance, he could buy for some £50 at Sotheby's a painting catalogued as a pseudo-Raphael and sit down cheek by jowl with all the literary hacks and academic drudges in the British Museum Reading Room to prove its authenticity and succeed in establishing the *Madonna di Loreto* for loan to the National Gallery, overstepping the art historians by his own researches. This, to me, was a greater feat than when he bullied his way with millions of wealth through all the auctions of oilfields, tycoons and corporations.

But that house seemed cold, almost frozen. Beyond the Art

Adviser, there seemed no one within. When, between 1521 and 1526, Sir Richard Weston built it as an unfortified manor, he exulted in his status at the Court of Henry VIII. Then it must have been full of people eating in public, thronging galleries and corridors, as if in a village on some noisy market day. Now a silence had come down, and the air seemed heavy. Great pictures, not apparently expressive of anything but grandeur, and tapestries hung everywhere, huge tapestries and weighty, which the Art Adviser explained were extremely rare and priceless. But tapestries are allergic to me, and I more so to them. When new, gleaming with bright hues, sparkling in clear lines direct from the ancient weaving factories of the Continent, they had their purposes, they brightened the barren walls of medieval manors and castles with a new perspective that could lighten men's spirits through gloomy winters. Now, however, they seemed to hang heavily, their colours faded, perspectives vanished, and only the detailed history the Art Adviser narrated seemed to justify their presence as they overlapped and obscured the beautiful Tudor panelling. She must have noticed some gloom upon me, for she hastened to answer my queries by explaining how all Paul Getty's great collection was in America. Everything of greatest character had gone to Malibu; it seemed there was nothing left but the bare bones of splendour – no whimsies, no secret loves or delights, not even a collector's laden table of treasures.

None of the tragic chain of disastrous fortune that bore down on the old collector, nor the demons of litigation that pursued all his family beyond his death seven years after my visit, may be a part of this book, but, looking back, it seems as if the shadows were about that house when I left it in 1969.

Nomad as he had to be, Getty had bought Sutton Place 'to get out of hotels', and he reckoned that its upkeep of $100 dollars a day would cost less than his bill at the London Ritz, though, as he had admitted, 'I spend only a limited amount of time in England. My chief home is in California. I also have a house on the coast between Rome and Naples. I spend some time in Scotland. I live in Paris, too, from time to time – in a hotel.'

When he came into Sutton Place, he had brought to it a costly sparkle – a £16,000 Paul de Lamerie old English silver service complemented with a solid gold service of thirty-seven pieces; the house-warming had 2,500 guests dancing to three orchestras, with four champagne bars. The complicated burglar – and fire-alarms, so anachronistic in a Tudor dwelling, were supplemented by three resident detectives and four alsatians, while in the beginning it was customary for a dozen or more friends and associates to take meals at the long Tudor table.

As I waited for the taxi to come out of the town and take me to the railway station, there was never a remnant to suggest all this spending and celebration, yet, from all I knew, I felt the presence of a man reaching out with both hands for immortality, building for it, planning for it, buying for it, for something the world says one cannot buy. Yet he did buy it, even more magnificently than Maecenas bought it in the days of Horace and Virgil, and now, despite his personal disasters, the magnificence of the Getty Trust protects his name and preserves the art he loved beyond his death in that cold Tudor manor house in the summer of 1976.

2 Importunities

Blessed anonymity. No writer seeks this today, nor do publishers welcome it on his behalf. Certainly I had no wish for it at the crowning time of my exhibition, however much real friends might advise and caution.

One particular letter I recall came from the last of the Gaiety Girls, Gabrielle Ray. At the age of twenty-two she had become famous overnight from her début in *The Orchard*, when in those days of picture postcards the image of her style was sold everywhere in the land, and now, nearly ninety years of age, she was living on the south coast in peace with her recollections. Kind as it was, her writing carried an earnest remonstrance. She drew from her own memories of the footlights and the obliteration that can follow their momentary blaze. Especially it seemed to her that I was inviting all the rogues of London to become anonymous shareholders in my collection. In her opinion, the guarded gallery, the dark strong-room or the bank vaults were the only suitable places for works of art. As she had grown older, the safekeeping of possessions, security, had become an obsession. I had sought publicity, and now I had it for what it was worth. She knew and was urgent in illustrating the dangers.

With my treasures now safely re-installed, at last I expected some calm and relaxation, satisfaction and the easy mood in which to continue with my next book. Far from it!

The very next day the doorbell at my home rang. Then someone grasped the knocker with commanding raps. There were two cars in my drive. Unframed oil-paintings were being propped up beneath my veranda. A little team of four or five people were arranging them to best effect. Would I value them, please? Two pictures belonged to them, the others came from some undisclosed source from whom they did not wish to buy without advice. They would buy, if advised.

It was early morning. I stood there unshaven and non-plussed, feeling no sort of expert whatever. Flattered by their deference and eager expectation but hurt by the necessity to tell them they held typical eighteenth-century copies of known Italian Old Masters, I hesitated. A recurrence of this sort of experience would be inconvenient and embarrassing. Neighbours on their way to the railway station were pausing to glance at huge canvases being juggled on my doorstep. I advised that Sotheby's be visited for such an opinion. But the pictures were too high to take down those narrow approaches, they protested.

Well, then, Bonhams would surely tell them.

No, no, they had come specially to have me see them.

Bonhams was the place, I insisted.

But they all shook their heads at my stubbornness. They had already been there! I dragged the admission out as they pleaded they wanted a real opinion. They nearly got it!

However, memories of my early struggles in collecting had conditioned me, and I began to let them down lightly – that is, until the real truth emerged. They wanted to sell me those wares. They were antique-dealers. Those canvases bore the recent chalkmarks of London auction-rooms. My book, my recent exhibition, had led them to believe that I was omnivorous and would buy anything.

It was beginning to rain as they struggled down my drive, but I felt no compassion, no, not even when one ran back to ask if I could recommend another dealer, offering me a commission on sales achieved.

Letters that were almost as tiresome continued to arrive. Many required, practically on demand, a statement authenticating a painting from photographs – an impossible task – but more often an expert valuation, and they seldom enclosed any postage for reply. Some thought it my duty to go and visit their picture for this purpose. and I came to realize that I must have given some impression of altruism in my writing; how else could people think it was my delight, my hobby, to renovate pictures and prove them valuable?

The hall of the manor of Stubbers had been acquired by the Local Authority for Youth Service purposes and was hung with grand Tudor portraits, as large as from floor to ceiling. The warden asked me would I approach the County Council to seek the opportunity to restore and clean them – gratuitously, of course. It would be such a good opportunity to make use of my hobby!

It must be the lot of many a collector to see things not in his possession go mouldering into oblivion for want of publicity that would follow their recognition. I think of the old red-brick tower of Great Warley church, all that remained of the edifice under which the bones of aldermen of the City of London lie, centuries after the pomp of their imposing funerals. Fine alabaster Renaissance busts stood here in a splendid celebration, but ignored and dirty. Though I called attention to their importance, they vanished entirely and are today perhaps deteriorating as suburban garden ornaments. Then again, when I used to drive every day past the estate of Stubbers, I would catch a glimpse of a remnant of Champion Russell's collection, a fine bronze figure with flying robes ascending and descending, having become part of the garden rockery of a labourer's terrace cottage. I had no money at that time and would pass it by until, pressed on by some temporary affluence and overcoming my English fear of intruding on privacy, I resolved to knock upon that door and buy it, whatever the cost. But I found the garden empty and the rockery gone, nor had I the initiative to call and ask after it. Lucky I consider myself over this failure, for I can still, even today, boast that I have never bought any art object or collectable from any private individual, and everything in all my collecting life has been acquired from auctions or from shops as goods exposed for sale.

Alone with my collection, I could feel a new exhilaration. In my early days as a collector I had tried to assert the advantages and joy of acquiring works of art by offering to lend my pictures to some particular public exhibition. Every time, on each and every occasion, my offer had been turned aside. I realized I was only an author, a pen-pusher: maybe I had written some verse, a book or two, but I was not one of the titled gentry. My things, so far as was known, had not come down from a mouldering castle wall nor from the glittering splendour of a millionaire's sale – celebrated neither by ancestry nor by the fabulous use of an unlimited chequebook.

Now I had defied convention, had my own exhibition and glorified my *trouvailles* not just by a catalogue but by a well-illustrated hardback volume. Now I could enjoy myself happily, back in possession of the whole collection which hung safely suspended against secure walls to render once again that delightful, life-enhancing measure of instruction and beauty. Interviews on the radio *World at One*, on BBC Television's *Town and Around* and *The Monday Show*, as well as on ITV's *Today* had celebrated them, while the run-of-the-mill tribe of reviewers followed suit, some admiring, others from a distance incredulous, even mocking. I was learning that there are two kinds of scribe, one positive in the strength of hard-won erudition and skill, the other carping and critical, concealing ignorance by supercilious mockery. Fortunately they both struck at the same time.

From a telephone call I gave permission for David Hodgson to come and take pictures of the collection. He also wanted to illustrate a typical antique-shop of the 'hidden treasure' variety , so I met him in London and took him to see old Louis Meier in Cecil Court. Beside the narrow corridor in the back shop he took photograph after photograph while the old man looked on, bewildered at such instantaneous publicity, as he held up a pseudo-Egyptian jackal and some glass and Etruscan objects and showed many pictures, hoping, I knew, for a sale. Alas for him, photographers and journalists are seldom buyers. I recall Louis protesting about being photographed with the phoney jackal and showing some much more promising drawings and water-colours.

On another appointed day, David Hodgson arrived at my house with a more complicated arrangement of cameras and lighting. He had seen the exhibition and he had read my book. He was easy to talk to, and the upshot of his visit was a fine centrefold in colour for *Ideal Home* magazine. I had theories that modern furniture sets off and displays ancient treasures and paintings much more spectacularly than patinated mahogany or old oak can, and long ago, in the thirties, had been fortunate enough to buy straight out of Gordon Russell's Wigmore Street showrooms a fine rosewood and elm writing-desk with chairs, a gunstock table and other examples of his individual designing. Now, when Sir Gordon Russell had come to be recognized as the prince of craftsmen, I had reason to congratulate myself on having personally salvaged every article from under the broken bricks and mortar when a German parachute mine had demolished my Romford home.

Long since I had disposed my collection to a contrast of modern design against the gold frames of Old Master paintings and recently had accented this by buying the finest dining-room suite in teak straight out of the front window of Heal's in Tottenham Court Road. Made by Muller from a Danish firm, its straight, clear lines and strong definition of colour could sweep any room to provide harmony against whatever arrangements of wall space. Though David Hodgson listened to my eulogies on eye-catching uses of furniture, my words drifted away from him as he reeled under the differences between my original purchase prices and the present value of the collection, so that his pages in the *Ideal Home* magazine were captioned 'The Shoe-String Millionaire'.

While I was talking, a telephone call brought me the news that a representative of the *Observer* newspaper wanted to do an article and was actually on his way with a photographer: great apologies for short notice, pressure of time to meet a deadline etc, etc. Of course, I agreed, but was a little surprised to find he arrived in half an hour or so.

In spite of his urgent protests, he had to be told to wait while I continued with David Hodgson. This exasperated him and, perhaps fearful of being upstaged by another journalist, he came forward to interrupt from time to time, demanding to know the identity of my visitor and whom he represented. The latter took no notice of his presence and went calmly on with his project.

As he paced to and fro across the front lawn outside, my wife took pity on the new visitor, who had introduced himself as Mr Barrie Penrose. She asked him into the small front room. Little knowing how her words were 'to be taken down in evidence and used' to her dissatisfaction, she answered his questions on security with the frank innocence with which one might reply to a friend. Blissfully ignorant both of his motives and of his methods, I myself came like a lamb to the slaughter, for neither of us knew we were in the presence of that menacing phenomenon of the modern press – the 'investigative journalist'.

David Hodgson was just departing when Penrose thrust forward carrying a copy of my book open in his hand. He had been going around the hall checking pictures hanging there against their reproductions in the book. 'Time is important,' he asserted, nodding in the direction of David Hodgson. 'You can't waste time on people like that.' We moved through the dining-room into the lounge; it seemed a trifle offensive that he paused to check pictures with my illustrations as if he had doubts as to whether I actually possessed them. Of course, nowadays everyone knows that the purpose of an 'investigative' reporter is to probe fraud and prove guilt rather than establish glory.

I found a chair for Jane Bown, his photographer, and we moved to a place beside my desk. He only wanted one photograph of myself amid a cluster of paintings. As soon as I afforded him this, he began to ask questions. He had avoided or parried any discussion on art or on painters, much in the way that a man devoid of knowledge or culture will. What he wanted was answers to write in his notebook, and he began as philistines do: 'How much would you say your whole collection is worth?'

'Impossible to estimate,' I replied. 'Even by adding up individual pictures, one could say a million pounds, but optimists and auctioneers might say six millions or more!'

I felt the photographer draw her breath. She looked at me with sad, wide-open eyes. She knew. The lamb had been slaughtered! I had earned the headline the *Observer* was to carry: 'COLLECTOR CLAIMS: I MADE A MILLION.'

Other questions followed – in particular, a definitive one. 'Has any art scholar authenticated any of these paintings?' By this time I had found the atmosphere of inquisitive suspicion tantalizing to my sense of humour, and I replied, 'They have all been thoroughly researched and authenticated.'

'All of them?'

'Yes, every one of them!'

'May I ask by whom?'

'By a very well-known scholar and collector.'

There was a long interrogatory pause. Before it could be broken by another question, I added triumphantly, 'By Stowers Johnson himself, of course. Who better?'

The face of Jane Bown, the photographer, was a picture. The lamb had slaughtered himself. No use wasting any more pity here. Barrie Penrose sniffed and rose to go. Not a man of any humour, he was not having his visit turned into a joke.

'Do you mean that none has been verified by art galleries?' he blustered.

'Why should I carry all these around to officials at art galleries? Read my book and you will see the story.'

'Not one of them?' he persisted.

'Read how the Turner was cleaned at the National Gallery and the Constable assessed at the V & A. Read the book!'

This was enough for him. He thumbed the book in his hand, sniffed again and took himself off, refusing my offer of a lift to the railway station.

He had given the impression that he thought it was illegal for the owner to style a picture with the title and full name of the artist before finding some panjandrum to certify accordingly. He was absolutely ignorant that such panjandrums do not exist and that the certificates of many others have been proved mistaken, false or actually venal. (Even Berenson, these days, is occasionally accorded post-mortem accusations of this kind.)

A quick telephone call by him to the National Gallery was enough to illicit from the 'spokesman' in the office that the Rembrandt they remembered was 'by an unknown contemporary or later'. Something about a van Balen was remembered but quoted by Penrose as *Three Graces*!

I read his *Observer* article on 10 November. My publishers were delighted but not so I. In those days I would resent an insult to my collection, though now, its fame established I can afford to smile at such whimsies of juvenile ignorance.

My wife, however, was angry at casual words taken out of her mouth and quoted in a section that could attract burglars. She was reported as saying, naïvely enough, 'I don't think burglars would bother us, you see.'

I regarded the article as flagrant misrepresentation. 'There are no burglar alarms or grilled windows,' the article had said, 'just an ordinary Yale lock on the front door.' Was this reporter saying just what he wanted to say? Not only were there Crittal steel windows everywhere but a grill and a mortice lock on that front door.

I wrote a letter of protest to the *Observer*. It was ignored.

I reported this to the Press Council, as a result of which the *Observer* melted enough to publish the following letter from me. (15 December 1968):

Readers of my book *Collector's Luck* will at once recognise the inaccuracies in your article of 10 November. The pictures shown in the photograph are not those mentioned in the caption: the prices paid are misquoted; even the number of rooms in my house is not correct. If you choose to assert my things are worth £1 million or £10 million, yours is the responsibility.

With regard to my Rembrandt, circumstantial evidence shows this as probably from the collection of the Second Earl of Arundel, the great collector rival of Charles I. All the time it was on exhibition in London it had a Security Express officer standing by it. The Trustees of the National Gallery have been unable to confirm that it was examined, and it never has been examined at the National Gallery. The 'Rembrandt' that actually was 'examined' at the Gallery, years ago, and pronounced as 'by an unknown contemporary or of later date', I showed on BBC Television (18 November, 1968. *The Monday Show*) beside my authentic Rembrandt, so that viewers could judge.

The published remarks about my house security were also quite

inaccurate and remain more so today, after police, smiths and burglar
alarm specialists have been to check the premises.

STOWERS JOHNSON

Such tardy publication was all very well now, but I had reported
the matter to the Press Council and, in spite of their expostulatory
telephone calls, insisted they obtained an explanation from the
editor. This they eventually did, evoking the weak defence from Mr
David Astor replying in April, months later, saying: 'Mr Astor said
that one would not normally draw public attention to unprotected
wealth. But as a visiting reporter "Sturt" Penrose had talked openly
to the Johnsons about this question. Both had told him there were
no burglar alarms. They seemed very proud that nothing was
insured and there was specifically no request that the security angle
should not be mentioned.'

However, it was not for the mighty Press Council to flagellate the
mightier *Observer*, so after a full report which that paper had to
publish (13 April 1969) came the termination, 'The complaint is
rejected.'

Even these days nothing in my collection is insured, though the
assembly remains intact, greatly increased in numbers and value. I
never fail to marvel at the constant association in the public mind of
monetary insurance values with works of art. As if any financial
compensation could ever balance the loss of some life-enhancing
possession! No doubt the constant advice on insurance during the
television *Antiques Road Shows* reinforces this, but for me,
independent as I am, to pay such premiums would mean either
selling from the collection or seeking some employment – and who
would engage a man of my temperament?

Of course, I could not leave the matter without picking a bone
with the National Gallery. I received a firm assurance from the
Trustees that it was never their policy to make public comments
unknown to the owners about objects in private collections and
that no such comments were ever made. More satisfaction I could
not expect.

By now an American edition of my book was called for, and I
began to receive copies of reviews from all sorts of periodicals
across the United States. This had its concomitant disadvantages,
however, for they promoted an interminable sequence of letters
which came from addresses as far away as Idaho and Texas, as well
as the larger cities, asking for advice on collecting, demanding

itineraries for treasure-hunting collectors travelling to Europe, some containing dimes to pay for return postage, some, the most tiresome of all, enclosing photographs of paintings in expectation of detailed historical information coupled with a signed and guaranteed authentication. For most of these correspondents, the pleasure of a work of art was only relative to its contemporary monetary value. They were failing the test of a real collector, who esteems art only for the life-enhancing delight it gives, never contemplates re-sale calculations and never thinks of separation from his treasures.

I became self-conscious and nervous of frequenting my old haunts in the London auction-rooms, where I would encounter such quips as this from the clerks at Bonhams where I faced the pseudo congratulations: 'I hear you are going to be elected a City of London Freeman. Let us know when you are in line for Lord Mayor!' Bevis Hillier had pointed me out in the *Times* as a ceaseless collector, 'a galloping case unconcealed by sophistication or pedantry' (7 October 1968). Such publicity, of course, destroyed the 'blessed anonymity' under which I had succeeded by quietly bidding in the larger sale-rooms, and I found it advisable to transfer my collecting urge to places far from London. Even there I could not be always fortunate. In one East Anglian sale-room I found one individual ruthlessly outbidding me. He stood in front of the rostrum and fixed me with his eye wherever I stood. Afterwards he confused me, distilling my anger as he made a bee-line in my direction to produce a copy of my book and beg my signature on it.

'You have been a great help to me,' he gloated. 'Yes, I watch you like a hawk!'

Another acquaintance (and I write 'acquaintance' precisely) only dropped his voice into a sinister whisper. The matey individual ran with his cronies between the gallery dealers and both the London and the provincial sale-rooms. His throaty whisper declared, 'Lucky you are not to have mentioned any of us. If ever you do, and you know who I mean, you'll get what's coming to you!' I watched him go back to his friends after this little passage and realized he was obviously repeating his words to his expectant group, for they smiled grimly and nodded with satisfaction.

3 Rembrandts

Time was when my collecting confessions were issued as a paperback and I rejoiced in the wider circulation of readers such a cheap edition could reach. To my surprise, interest flared around the one picture hardly noticed in the first hardback edition.

Long ago I had bought that picture at Coe's on a busy day, ages before those premises were taken over as Christie's South Kensington. Old Coe was the auctioneer then, quick and ruthless, more accustomed to dealing in goods left by pawnbrokers. One had to be alert and quick to bid to him – a picture would be sold almost before the lot number was called and the porter lifted it into view. That summer I had been touring England and Scotland with a caravan, visiting the great provincial galleries, and now, there in that South Kensington sale-room was lifted a sketch that caught my attention, for I had seen the large completed oil in the Russell Coates Museum at Eastbourne. It was *Jephthah's Vow*, painted by Edwin Long at the height of fashion when his biblical pictures such as *The Babylonian Marriage Market* were sold for hundreds of thousands of pounds to the accompaniment of thunderous applause at the fall of the hammer. This picture had no such erotic undertones, as it depicted Jephthah's daughter fully clothed being the first to greet her father, who, in exchange for God's bargained gift of victory, has vowed to sacrifice the first individual to meet him on his return from battle – a subject calculated to appeal more to relishers of the Old Testament than to us today. I noticed the monogram E.L. Despite its being a mere sketch, the artist had initialled.

No sooner had I blinked and noticed the monogram than the picture was knocked down to me for £2.10s.! When, after the sale, I paid and was collecting my pictures, the old porter came towards me.

'There is another bundle in that lot, sir!'
'So there is!'

'I don't expect you will want them?'

'Oh, yes. I take everything I buy,' I replied and threw them, a bundle of dirty, unframed portraits, into the boot of my car.

Not imagining they could be any use, I cast them into the coalshed at home and not till months later, experimenting with wax varnishes and solvents, did I happen to pick out the oldest portrait. The varnish was dark and had aged upon it. Some time ago it had been re-lined and mounted on to an expensive mid-Victorian stretcher. Carelessly I mixed a strong acetone solution and tested its strength on the actual painting before diluting. To my surprise, the paint stood firm, only the yellow varnish moved, leaving the hard seventeenth-century paint immaculate and the canvas firm upon its nineteenth-century liner. An old picture, firmly but surely painted, the light glow shining from the browns and the dark with a sureness of delineation characteristic of the seventeenth century: a sketch with no finesse of finishing, the face built up, with clear, thoughtful eyes, and the hand hardly drawn, as if finger and thumb were moving along the strands of beard.

A Rembrandt? My cottonwool pad swept away any trace of solvent and rinsed all with pure turpentine. The surface had dried when I returned with my copy of Bredius' *Rembrandt. Complete Edition of the Paintings* (revised by H. Gerson, 3rd ed., 1969). Still shaken at my temerity in so recklessly handling the old picture, I went carefully through the pages until there, on page 152, I found an oval photograph of a painting symptomatic of my very picture and captioned: '*An old man with a beard* 163 (4) Panel 70 x 56 cm Paris Louvre (Br 182)'. Apart from being an oval inset on a panel, the photograph showed serious differences in the treatment of the hair, the facial expression, nose and lips, while the hand in this Louvre painting seemed purposeless, the shading of the old man's cloak massed and unreal. My painting seemed to have the greater vigour, with more definition of character and thought expressed in the features.

Were they both sketches of some particular character known to Rembrandt and his circle? Certainly the sitter had been depicted out of interest for his own intrinsic attraction, never surely by himself commissioned. The Louvre picture is noted as 'signed Rembrandt f 168 (3)', but though in my picture below the beard something like Rembrandt's initials could be made out, dark upon dark, I dismissed the impression as mere optimism, that bane of the collector – wishful thinking.

Nevertheless, a Rembrandt it was, without a doubt, and a better example than the Louvre had. No imagination can understand the care with which I varnished that picture. The old paint needed no attention – the whole surface had survived intact. Sometime some folk inheriting must have disliked the subject and turned from it so indifferently as to take away its old contemporary frame and, with a bundle of other old unwanted portraits, also stripped of frames to provide immediate cash profit, consigned it to Christie's, and then, perhaps rejected from Christie's, on to Coe's.

Of course, I found a sturdy, plain oak frame and a pleasant situation under glass with a north light, where the Old Man could meditate undisturbed, and I also could speculate and sometimes research, hoping that some Renaissance scholar, such as Sir Roy Strong of the V & A, would one day find some evidence to associate it with that drawing (which he has written about in the Royal Society of Arts Journal) once in the possession of the second Earl of Arundel, or, indeed, better still, known to his rival collector, King Charles I.

It was only later, when my book was republished as an inexpensive paperback, that public interest flared up and attention focused upon the painting that had been almost ignored when it hung in Central London at Foyles Art Gallery. The *Daily Mail* sent a reporter to take down the story. Previous experience had made me wary of journalists. A story was all in all to them, positive or negative. Richard Lay was neither optimist nor pessimist and took down the account meticulously, so I let him have a photograph. Off he went, and to my surprise the *Daily Mail* immediately sent a man over to the Louvre Museum in Paris.

Three years before, in 1969, Horst Gerson, the world's leading expert on the painter, had said he was not convinced that the Louvre example was an original Rembrandt, and now, faced by the *Mail* reporter, the Louvre admitted that theirs was a copy. Jacques Foucard, Rembrandt expert at the Louvre, was quoted as saying: 'We would dearly like to see the picture you have in Britain. We obtained our *Old Man* some time before the French Revolution when it was believed to be in the possession of the Duc de Brissac.'

A letter came from Mr Gerson himself later, offering to give his opinion free of any fee if I would bring the painting over to the Continent. Grateful as I was for the offer, I have seldom been able to see the advantage of hawking my treasures around to be scrutinized by others. I myself was quoted as saying, 'You have only to compare the *Old Man*'s hand to realize the Louvre version is obviously a copy.' And I went on to declare and the *Mail* quoted: 'My picture has the dominating quality you only find in true Rembrandts, and the sitter has that look of serene wisdom which could only come from the Master. I will never part with my picture. It hangs in my breakfast room in the corner out of the sun and that's where it will stay.'

News travels fast this century, and a Bulgarian friend sent me a magazine photograph of myself looking infinitely less wise than that *Old Man* as I held up his picture for Bulgarian readers!

Excited by the *Daily Mail* illustrated pages, BBC Television's *Nationwide* telephoned to ask if I would show my Rembrandt on their programme, offering to send a car to bring me to the Lime Grove studio that very day. Mindful of the advantage to my publishers for their sales, I agreed.

I was shown into a studio where I found Bob Welling rehearsing to himself *sotto voce* the part of auctioneer, repeating his lines over and over again.

One can imagine how displeased I was to find that the the TV producer had already planned to arrange a controversial discussion about the picture – and a one-sided one at that, for he had already invited a West End dealer, Ed Spielman, whom I had often seen about the London sale-rooms. He was late. I was inclined to think he would not so expose himself, but there was no deterring the over-confident self-assurance of Sue Lawley, as BBC interviewer, and after telephone calls and delays by some traffic hold-up, there he was in the studio, looking taken aback to see me there in person.

'The picture must come out of its frame!' he declared.

'No, it mustn't,' I replied.

'Of course, it must!' he insisted. 'I can't be expected to examine it under glass. I can't see craquelure if there's glass. And the back is covered as well! That must come off.'

'Nothing comes off! It is my picture, and it stays as it is!'

Nevertheless, he got down on his knees and peered at the painting. Next minute a call came and we went before the cameras, listening to a preamble by Sue Lawley quoting a few naïve words from me about the story, before, as announcer, she introduced Ed Spielman:

'Now Mr Spielman, I expect a great many Rembrandts have passed through your hands.'

'Yes, a great many,' he averred. (I was astonished. A great many Rembrandts, from hand to hand, as if they were ready-made suits!)

'Then you feel quite competent to judge whether this is a genuine Rembrandt or not? You really feel you can decide?'

'Oh yes, quite certainly!' came the reply.

'Would you look at the picture please and tell us?' Going through the motions, he turned to the announcer. 'Well, what do you say?'

'No, it is not a Rembrandt,' he asserted.

'Why do you say that?'

'There is no craquelure,' he declared, and much more triumphantly, 'and it is not old paint!'

'That settles it then!' declared Sue Lawley with utmost conviction. 'We shall now have to wait till the real one turns up!'

'This is the real one!' I interrupted, and repeated, 'Here is the real one!' But like a flash we were off the air!

'How can you say that without really looking?' I complained to Spielman.

Taken aback by my confidence, he murmured, 'Well, we shall have to see what the Louvre says about it.'

Obviously he did not even know what the Louvre had already said!

This was not the end, however, for insult was added to all by the miserable cheque which arrived, awarding me only £10, when for each of my three previous television appearances on collecting topics the fee had been £20. After angry telephone arguments about time and rate, I demanded £10 also for the other performer.

'I suppose that's all right,' agreed the BBC official. 'Who was the other performer?'

'The Old Man in the painting.'

'Yes,' said the BBC. 'That would be all right.' The cheque came for £20. The Old Man had justified himself by BBC standards!

By this time once again my long-suffering publishers had reminded me that neither my book nor its price nor they had ever been mentioned. It seemed to hurt some newspapers as well as the media to refer to authors or to mention their books as being currently for sale, as if they grudged unpaid publicity, and maybe it is sometimes feared they might steal a march on the actor, who, after all, is only mouthing some writer's words of imagination.

While I ruminated on these unsatisfactory matters, another call came from a staff member of the television programme *Pebble Mill At One*. They would send a car for me to bring my pictures all the way to Birmingham. No trouble! Bring as many as possible. It would be a large car, and they would bring both myself and the pictures safely back.

So there I found myself in that modern studio beside the open lawns with my Turner *Sunset at Sea*, a Constable, *The Battle for the Standard* by van Hughtenberg and two or three others.

I was met with dismay. 'Where is the Rembrandt?' The producer was holding a copy of the *Daily Mail* and I recognized the page. But I had not brought it, since they had not so requested. In any case, I would have been quite unwilling to have the *Old Man* bantered about by another fortuitous dealer or gallery official who might also be reckless enough to come forward and advertise that he had had 'many Rembrandts passing through his hands'.

The absence of the Rembrandt threw the staff into some dismay: there were hasty conversations in corners before I was allowed to outline a few suggestions – understandably so, for *Pebble Mill* goes out live. All was well, however, for there was a story to each picture and I managed to show each in good order. Bob Langley in his bluff and hearty manner carried the dialogue through, concluding with the question, 'How would you recommend anyone to make a start towards a collection like yours?'

Without hesitation, I stepped forward, waving a copy of my book and naming it clearly: 'No better way than can be found in these pages. Buy it and you will know how I have collected.' Bob Langley's mouth opened in surprise at this unabashed sales-manship. His good humour closed that advertisement down as effectively as I had promoted it, but the job had been done before the cameras came off me. He shook his head with a reproaching grin while they wheeled in the champion fishmongery ovens and set going a competition between fish-and-chip fryers.

As I sat down and watched, two or three telephone calls came in to ask about bronzes, obviously relating to some of the multitudinous copies of the *Horses of Marly* after Cousteau. I looked up from the telephone receiver and found that some generous person had dumped a paper-wrapped sample of cooked fish and chips for me! *Haute climax* as it was, I took it as some kind of Birmingham testimonial, but the producer who had been relying for text on her gleanings from the *Daily Mail* indicated that the hire-car driver was waving his peaked cap and looking at his watch. I smelt fish and chips in his car and noticed he had acquired a couple of unsavoury-looking parcels from the champions. 'They will hot up!' he remarked several times on the way to London. 'Oh yes, they will hot up all right!'

Of course, a library could be built up entirely devoted to publications from all the world's languages in appreciation of Rembrandt, and for that matter an entire gallery from the reproductions, the forgeries, the fakes and the skilful copies of Rembrandt's work; even pictures of the aged companion from my collection and myself were now appearing in periodicals in Sweden and Germany and even in far Bulgaria. From all the books of photographs that abound, the one I have at my side continually is that definitive volume of Bredius, edited by Gerson.

Unleashed by the *Daily Mail*, letters continued to arrive in my post demanding verification of some picture the writers possessed, earnest letters, not all activated by greed. I think of one from a Canadian self-styled 'expert' who sent pages of newspaper cuttings from over there demonstrating his life's work, which had been to illustrate how every picture painted by Rembrandt had a concealed Master signature woven and mingled in the brushwork. He had obtained a photograph of my own picture and indicated several signatures upon it. He wrote imploring me to give maximum publicity to his theory, so that the whole world should have a yardstick by which to measure the authenticity of any such painting. Squiggles of paint strokes, infilling of shadows or a line above a garment for him became the genuine signature of Rembrandt himself, sometimes by full name, sometimes by a mere imagined letter or two!

There is a favourite book of mine: the Rijksmuseum's *Catalogue of Rembrandt 1669-1969*, celebrating the commemorative gathering of select paintings and drawings from famous international collections for the Tricentennial Year Exhibition. In a few sentences it dispels the legend of his neglected reputation, for in the year of his death ' ... there were plenty of Amsterdam people alive who had had their portraits painted by him, who had bought his drawings or who had known him personally.' And again, it gives the clue to that mystic aura which surrounds the great painter, for he had stepped beyond the fashion and departed from the rules of the classicists to realize things as he saw them rather than through the collective eyes that measured the appropriate style by accepted tradition. So he makes his direct appeal to us without the formality of that contemporary manner of his day and stands himself above the centuries.

Andreis Pels, friend of Rembrandt's pupil de Lairesse, went right to the heart of appreciating this when he warned other artists not to follow such an individualist:

> The great Rembrandt who did not go to Titian nor Van Dyck,
> Not Michelangelo nor Raphael:
> Who rather chose illustriously to wander,
> To be the foremost heretic in painting,
> Than to subject his famous brush to any discipline.
> A shame it is for Art
> That such an honest hand
> Does not make better use of gifts inborn!
> In painting, who would have surpassed him?
> Helas, the nobler be the spirit, the more it will run wild
> If he build not on common ground nor recognise the rules,
> But try to know it all out of himself!
>
> P.J.J. van Thiel (trans.) Cat. Rijkmuseum Amsterdam, 1969

How significant was the demand Pels formulated for the artist to conform and thereby lose his genius!

As I read on, I come upon a quotation mentioned as by H.E. Greve, signed under Albert Hahn's caricature of the famous Rembrandt connoisseurs Bredius and Hofstede de Groot:

> Do not discover any more Rembrandts for us.
> Bring Rembrandt himself nearer to us!
> Hail then to your Rembrandt knowledge!

This jibe against Bredius and Hofstede de Groot is true only in part, for they learned to know the Master by their own discoveries. But it hits me also! For I can declare not one Rembrandt discovery but two – and, even more, a contemporary portrait of him.

How can I dare, especially when I recall the wisdom of old Arthur Kay, who asserted: 'If you find a Rembrandt, never attribute it so! Call it Bol. Let someone else determine it as a Rembrandt, someone known as an expert, someone not the owner. Else you and the picture likewise will surely be damned and the work will never be approved or recognised.' (*Treasure Trove in Art*, Oliver & Boyd, 1939.)

'Do not discover any more Rembrandts for us!' commands van Thiel in his essay for the exhibition's introductory essay. Alas, *mea culpa*, since my original find of the portrait of the *Old Man*, I have discovered another of his masterpieces, a remarkable little landscape on an old Dutch panel, 24.5 x 38.5 cm, the seventeenth-century paint, when unveiled from ancient varnishes, making one as surprised as if it were painted yesterday, so vivid and clear does the sunlight show falling upon the riverside village, while storm clouds move away overhead. I kept the picture some time before I cleaned and re-varnished it, almost afraid to admit I had acquired it for a small sum in Birmingham. In a dialogue with Jack de Manio on his radio programme *Today*, he told me how he had seen a Rembrandt in an old mansion in Switzerland, forgotten but hanging plainly on the wall there: yet my picture had been on view in a public auction and ignored by picture-dealers.

Why should I respond to the warning of old Arthur Kay? Truth is truth. I seek no profit for my pictures, and I have had that picture some twenty years now, so it is almost a part of me. Hardly anyone has seen it, for I detest both the caution of connoisseurs and the scrutiny of sceptics. But there is the Rijksmuseum version of this very picture illustrated in the Bredius, page 352, and note 440: '*Landscape with a stone bridge*. HdG 939. Bauch 543. Cleaning would probably result in stronger "Baroque" contrasts between the light and dark areas. A sensitive appreciation has been written by H. van de Waal (*Openbaar Kunstbezit* 2, 1958, no. 26).' This note is doubly interesting, for my picture had already been partly cleaned, and now I had completely cleaned it, so 'the stronger "Baroque" contrasts' were revealed between those light and dark areas!

But there is so much more to my picture than is in the Rijksmuseum version: not only in the darkening storm retreating from the whole landscape, the old carriage and the village architecture on both near and far sides of the bridge but in the light that chases across the woodland before which a multitude of workers pursue their labours and a ploughman directs his ox. Of course, the Rijksmuseum picture as shown in the photograph is uncleaned, but I do not gather there is the same disposition of human action, and it seems there can be no doubt that mine is the superior and the first version. Were I my Canadian correspondent, I would have cause to be delighted at the pseudo-authenticity some seek, for along the river bank, the far shore and by the bridge can be imagined a good supply of squiggles that very little wishful optimism might translate into the authentic handwork of Rembrandt initials.

The old panel comforts me, for it contains the leisure of a time gone by, when there was no hurry and not a great deal of need, where the river supplies and the woodland shelters and the village, with its few houses and the church spire, is home.

How strange is life! I know I could take, and actually for a trial have taken, this picture into a typical London sale-room without betraying background information or any attribution, only to have some youngster peer through the glass, shake his head sadly and direct me elsewhere! Archibald Russell's words often come to me when he advised, 'Collect the greatest Masters. Dealers, critics and buyers do not understand the great and are afraid of genius. They have not the time, or they dare not lose money.' I think of the well-publicized sale of Rembrandt's *Juno*, which had disappeared for 200 years to be resurrected in 1935 under the cloak of 'style of Rembrandt' and sold for $214. On 29 September 1936 it was bought by Armand Hammer, head of Occidental Petroleum for $3,250,000 (then £1,900,000), and bequeathed with his collection to the Los Angeles County Museum. The long history of Rembrandt sales contains examples similar to this, indicating a hiatus in understanding of the Master (*The Times*, 30 September 1976).

Not so with drawings, however. This had become a more specialized matter, more *recherché* altogether. In the greater London sale-rooms are handled the portfolios of the great collectors – sheets of paper that have wandered the Continent and gone to sleep in bureaux or attics of the bygone wealthy, relics perhaps from some noble ancestor's Grand Tour, perhaps even having crossed the Atlantic now and again to pass connoisseurship and prestige from tycoon to tycoon; for those who shuffle such collections, some marked with the stamp of Reynolds or Lely or indeed, of gentlemen of the Diplomatic Corps, this is a different matter, and each London sale-room treasures its own experts upon whose infallibility its reputation rests.

For the collector like myself who is likely to find an unknown and unattributed Older Master drawing only once in several lifetimes, the expertise from actually enjoying such works can never match the insight of folk who live with them and daily compare and admire them. Such as I must hesitate, seek the advice of friends to build up that association of knowledge which constant reference to Master works will afford. One needs to develop a sympathetic eye so as to be reluctant to acquiesce in doubt and above all nervous about parting rashly with one's possessions.

I had bought a number of old prints and etchings – old they were, but crude. On the basis of age, I thought them saleable. There were one or two in nice colour by eighteenth-century artists, and I took them to Sotheby's for sale. I called the attention of the man at the counter to one in particular, as it bore the monogram of Adrien van de Veen, was on seventeenth-century paper and seemed built up in a marvel of the finest etched lines. Rembrandt, I had thought. Probably a print of some known portrait. The expert at the counter held it to the light and gave a superficial glance across the paper.

'I must take this in for consideration,' he said, and off he went with the little framed picture in both hands as if it were a treasure, holding it carefully, though it measured no more than 18.5 x 15cm.

When he returned, he gave me a very respectful, straight look.

'This is the wrong department,' he declared. 'It is a pen-and-ink drawing, and the Old Master Drawings department would like to take this in. They are extremely interested.'

'Pen-and-ink? Did they say it was pen-and-ink, and a drawing?'

'Yes, yes, of course. You take it down the stairs and to the other counter.'

I was staggered. I had only decided to sell thinking it was an old print – something like the others, whose sale would bring in more wherewithal to buy other treasures.

'A pen-and-ink drawing?' I repeated.

'Yes, yes,' he said impatiently. 'You can take it there straightaway while I deal with these other items. This is not the place for that drawing.'

'I don't want to sell this now,' I pleaded, as if there were some objection against which I had to contend. 'I have changed my mind. I thought it was only a print! It must go into my collection now.'

'Collection?' he echoed, dully. 'But they want it at the other counter. You will have to tell them.'

I shook my head, restraining the impulse to jump there and then and shout for joy. With that dead-pan expression learnt from years in the sale-rooms, I slipped the picture back into my case, signed the chit for the sale of those other prints and came away as the expert pleaded once more: 'They want it at the other counter!'

Well did I now know what I had. A drawing! On an old print the monogram of Adrien van de Veen would have been something, for he was noted as both painter and engraver. Born at Delft in 1589, he was older than Rembrandt, whose birth was in 1606, and he had outlived him until 1680, Rembrandt having died in 1669. But here was a pen-and-ink sketch, a portrait of Rembrandt by one of his seniors, an older and more established painter: a contemporary portait revealing how another and more experienced painter saw him. Dressed in a fur coat fastened with a clasp, he stares boldly and wide-eyed at his senior, who has drawn him seated but in a pose of unconcealed bravado, his face surmounted with flamboyant, fur-topped turban.

There is self-confident, almost grasping ambition depicted, as if van de Veen knew that the younger man thought himself better, good enough and ready indeed to step into his master's shoes in a direct challenge of almost defiance, the pen-and-ink lines denying what Shakespeare has asserted, that 'There's no art to read the mind's construction in the face.' It was an unscrupulous face van de Veen had sketched in his fine, delicate lines, one that might have been the face of an emperor or of some tyrannical judge: perhaps professional jealousy provided a spur, as if van de Veen realized that here was the man who would surpass them all. Certainly none of that life-enhancing benevolence is here drawn, but Rembrandt's severity and the swagger of moustaches and turban indicate his desire for the achievement he wished his contemporaries to recognize in his person. For all that, van de Veen has allowed in his eyes and demeanour none of that mellow, reflective thoughtfulness Rembrandt painted into his own self-portraits, such as either of the two panels in the Louvre, dated 1633 (Br.18) and 163(4?) (Br.19). By comparison, one could well imagine that van de Veen's drawing was earlier than these, especially if the self-assertion depicted be taken as no more than is apt to cloak the insecurity of youth.

Does the drawing of van de Veen – to quote Greves' sigh under Albert Hahn's famous caricature – 'bring Rembrandt nearer to us', or is it the unfeeling work of another, jealous practitioner? Everyone knows that Rembrandt 'comes nearer to us' not by words but by his own art. Such a studied drawing as van de Veen's can show only how he was seen by a contemporary, not how he wished to be.

To know Rembrandt, one must make more than mere acquaintance with his pictures and the humanity of which they tell. Other painters of his age may have painted objects with exquisite definition and reality, but within the tone, the shadow and the drifting light of a Rembrandt painting lie the wanderings of the human spirit itself, and in such a painting as my landscape panel, the comfort of the homestead, the serenity of accepted religion surround the local activities of man, despite the wild, darkening sky above that rising flood of the river.

There it lies, this message stable as a classic verse – *monumentum perennius aere* – but yet so perishable and transient to the eye of the beholder lacking kinship of that spirit. So, yellowing with dirty varnish, so old it had fractured from the paint, and shorn of its frame, that oaken panel had come to me from the debris of the auction-room, a touchstone before which connoisseurs, auctioneers and valuers, avaricious collectors even, had been tested and failed.

Dr van Schendel, Director of the Rijksmuseum, tells how in 1807 the Rijksmuseum authorities declined to buy the famous Rembrandt portrait of the Clothmakers' Guild (*De Staalmeesters*). The connoisseur who had spent so much energy recommending the purchase, anxious no doubt not to forfeit the museum's approbation, wrote to ally himself with their decision, asserting, 'Should the purchase not be made, you need feel no regret; the painting takes up a great deal of room and shows nothing but five gentlemen sitting down'!

Times change, and perceptions and values also. Today *De Staalmeesters* is one of the museum's great treasures.

4 Taste and Decision: Fashion and Indecision

In the post-war years I stepped through a door in Lisle Street, then a dingy part of Soho, to listen to William Coldstream talking to a small group of artists. That particular society has long vacated those converted shop premises. Coldstream, since knighted, departed this life at the mature age of seventy-eight, but I well remember his crisp energy of thought as he gave his attention to the gathering in that small, half-empty room, his neat grey suit seeming to outline the decisiveness of his speech. One or two questioners tried to pin him down into some statement defining and admitting the conflicts between current schools, between Impressionism and tradition and also the developing modern trends. But for him, progress was wide open. It was the structure of a painting that mattered, and that could be resolved by consideration of the works by such as Cézanne.

I well remember hearing repeated in several instances that evening the words by which he divided artists into two categories by which their personalities and their styles were resolved: the man who could paint out of his head, and the man who could not and for whom structure was all important. Cézanne being one of the latter, his art became more monumental and therefore, he asserted, greater. In a way this was a tilt against Impressionism, though I doubt if his audience realized.

The division as detailed by Sir William Coldstream has significance also when applied to the quest for criteria in the mind of the collector. The art-dealer in his search for reality depends on value expressed in finance and goes for the immediately attainable by cash and vision, whereas the true connoisseur has built up a memory of pleasures, of photographic images often out of many years, and can criticize to make a decisive purchase 'out of his head' without recourse to current fashion or auction prices.

47

The search for criteria so numbing to the beginner is really a demand for a touchstone for which printer's ink is no substitute. The determination of 'good art' depends upon the rules of taste. Before the nineteenth century these were made by a plutocracy of fashion, but during the nineteenth century 'taste' became the universal fashion of so many that it vanished. Writers like Tolstoy (in *What is Art?*) strove to show how the 'best' could be winnowed down by the decision of the majority. He decided that art survived as great by 1. its function promoting humanity's progress (by religious intentions;) 2. its significant form; 3. its sincerity. Thus it appeared to him that any work answering these criteria must inevitably be judged good and accepted by the masses.

How strange that such a perceptive genius should not have room in his definition to deplore the time-lag for those sensitive plants of humanity ahead of their age who are cast out until 'The multitude make virtue, Of the Faith they had denied.'

However, the sale-room auctioneer, the dealer or my reader himself plaintively waving his catalogue towards the uplifted hammer has neither inclination nor money for such philosophies. The touchstone they can use is either the flair of inherited genius or experiences stored in memory over long years of trial and error. Letters have come to me from all over the English-speaking world pining for advice and insisting there are some such arcane rules. And rules there were in the eighteenth century, when fashion governed and people like Horace Walpole could say: 'Nothing is so ill bred as to persist in anything that is out of fashion' (projected *History of Good Breeding*, VIII).

But today 'taste' itself is out of fashion!

One must remember the dictum of the Bard: 'Nothing is either good or bad but thinking makes it so,' or as expounded by John Steegmann: 'It is customary to deride fashionable taste, but since there is no permanent canon it follows that all taste is an affair of fashion, whether a given vogue be long or short-lived is immaterial for though it may last a decade or a century or simply be the rage for two seasons it will vanish in the end.' (*The Rule of Taste*, Macmillan, 1936.)

Here then is the decision before a collector. Taste and fashion are detailed in the auction-room prices. Is he to collect for today? The dealers know about that. For tomorrow? This is speculation.

'Go for the Great!' that distinguished collector Archibald Russell, Lancaster Herald, once advised me. 'There you can succeed. The dealers never understand the Great!'

We may convince ourselves, but I am afraid doubtfully, that only the Great can outride the tides of changing taste and fickle fashion.

How to discern the Great, indeed? For this discernment is the criterion of the true collector. As in the making of friends, it can be acquired only by acquaintance. Some will brush success aside by the term 'flair' or 'experience', ignoring the wide field such words cover. Where is the connoisseur who can pluck the answers out of his head better than by describing his own adventures and instancing the causes of his pleasure? For most collectors there are many questions to which he can hardly give answer. In a long life I have taken on board thousands of artefacts, all purchased when presented for sale at auction or in a shop window. It gives me great satisfaction to claim that nothing have I ever bought from any private individual. Many the giants that have dwindled as acquaintanceship deteriorated, discarded as tedious, some thrown overboard in disgust, some providing me with the wherewithal to make further purchases, but never a true friend have I parted with or forsaken. And that is the true touchstone. Live with a work of art and it may become your friend in a revelation over the passage of time which the passing years cannot plunder and, moreover, in a way you will probably not perceive until much later, part of your own personality; on the other hand it could distance itself from your own sentiment and become your enemy, in which case for these days of inflation you may find a profitable way of dispensing with its company.

Those rules which the Augustan Age of the eighteenth century applied to test excellence and define the 'Great' have long ceased to hold firm and, presumptuous as it now seems to prescribe definitions, the struggle between assertions of the sublime or the picturesque has gone, but the financial criterion of the market value remains accentuated by the esteem which rarity gives to attainment. Tolstoy's maxim that the universal verdict of mankind's majority opinion must be the final judgement now appears a doubtful prescription for the would-be collector who, chequebook in hand, knows the variation of industrial returns and the instability of commercial fashion. Only the great family collections, where they survive, can survey the vicissitudes of fashion and taste across the generations with a history of rise or fall in market prices.

If there are no longer rules, if there is the test only of universal approbation, there can be seen only one genuine path for a collector's choice in art – the pursuit of pleasure. And so it has seemed to me as, travelling through opportunities of acquisition, I abandon Archibald Russell's advice of 'going for the Great'. No wreckage from two world wars today drifts through the sale-rooms, and education of a visual nature through television alerts human perceptions, so that few can immediately achieve possession of the 'Great' without resources sufficient to buy items distinguished by the publicity of world approbation. It is only long acquaintance that will identify the best by sharing that original experience recreated and bestowed by hand and eye of the artist. Rarely, rarely can this immediately give the fanciful or fearful reality that summons the majestic sense of the sublime. For the most, only such long acquaintance with a work will determine its true and lasting merit, or its veracity of authentic picturesque to justify a place beside its fellows in a collection.

So if one has not the finance to buy a place among the great collectors, one must live long, travel far and see much by which the test of time and the renewed delight of each viewing can bring that empathy with long-dead genius to recognize the dexterity of hand, the truth of eye, an awareness to strengthen first experience or shatter it to pieces as acquaintance palls.

Even after all my years of collecting, I will neither pronounce upon the 'Great' nor associate with the 'critics', for rules comfort me not at all, nor important names, nor provenance. I seek in my collecting only delight and the enhancement of pleasure by continued association; and it is this continued rapture that a work of art can give its owner in algebraical progression, as it were, with longevity. The severity of any break is well instanced by the words of Cardinal Mazarin, who, with death impending, went the rounds of his collection, muttering: 'And must I then leave all this?'

Often folk chatting to me suggest the advantage of winnowing one's assembly of works, of selling some for profit-taking to buy again, staging the art market to enrich and magnify one's collection in a triumphant array against others. No such advisers grasp even the beginnings of real pleasure, for it is delight a collector seeks, enduring enjoyment rather than such transitory amusement or grasping profit, though, as everyone knows, the latter tends to come tumbling along.

There is no doubt that these days the wrong people have been drifting into authority in museums and art galleries, whose governing bodies should not be a refuge for the elderly nor the titled nonentities but consist of energetic members who are prepared to put their backs to the wheel and raise money for gallery upkeep rather than acquiesce in the sale of donated works of art for that purpose.

Some years ago, at a Royal Society of Arts talk by Lord Eccles, himself a collector and then a responsible Minister, I brought up the matter of the sale of the Dulwich pictures by the trustees to pay for building costs. Unprepared for the question, the Minister brushed it aside. Despite public protests much more powerful than mine, the trustees had their way. What collector would now donate to Dulwich?

In November 1987 Brian Sewell challenged another Arts Minister, Richard Luce, in no way famous for cultural sagacity, concerning this matter (which I myself would term 'privatising works of art'). This he followed up by a powerful article in *The Times* on 21 November headed 'Art Outbid by Avarice'. I can do no better than quote Sewell's letter to the *Evening Standard* of 18 November 1987:

MUSEUM'S MISTAKE

It is a mistake to give museum trustees the power to discard the works of art in their charge.

In 1958 the gallery in Port Sunlight sold at Christie's for a few thousand pounds nearly 200 unwanted unfashionable pictures. The list includes Burne-Jones (by the dozen), Alma-Tadema, Etty, Fantin-Latour, Laura Knight, Lord Leighton, Millais, Soloman and Wilson, all now at renewed heights of popularity and worth many millions.

Your leader writer's arguments in favour of Mr Luce's measure to enable sales can carry no weight if he supposes that the cluttered basements of the National Gallery support them.

Were he even an irregular visitor he would know that every picture owned by the National Gallery is on permanent view.

BRIAN SEWELL, VICTORIA ROAD, KENSINGTON

Happy is the private collector independent of the democratic consensus of desirability or value! I have the cast-iron head of a bull, reputed to have come from the old bull ring in Chelmsford Market. Maybe one of my distant relatives leaned against it when selling cattle there in the early nineteenth century. I doubt if it was worth the few shillings I gave for it years ago, but without price are the pauses when I stop to imagine how the country blacksmith who had cast the molten iron from his mould would stare into the large, melancholy eyes so evoked.

A week or two ago, in Wales, I drove towards Rhuddlan Castle through the High Street and there in the bric-à-brac of a shop window was a standing effigy of Nelson. To my eye it dominated the scene. No, it was not bronze but cast iron and, as seen through the window, crude; but it dominated that street as now it dominates me. When I returned through Rhuddlan, the shop was closed, so I had to return on some future occasion. Should I buy it? Most probably, for I was hypnotized.

When I actually did buy this lump of cast iron, ignoring the more decorative flower bouquet cast with tendrils and iron blossoms which the shopkeeper lauded so highly, it was for a trivial sum only, perhaps its market price, but far below its treasure of worth to me personally.

Shall I keep it? Therein lies the great test. Will its spell upon me last? That will depend upon the delight which it has power to bestow or withhold — delight neither diminished nor increased by anything friends or visitors may say, for this delight is intrinsic and the basis of true collecting, whether from it arise awe, humour or laughter, even.

5   Making a Collection

For some, making a collection involves choices of excellences, selection from the best into a series of themes, literary fancies or history, perhaps the set purpose being to complete a period or fill a serial of subjects. Something that everyone wants can be bought in triumph, leaving rivals disappointed and envious. And the merit of such an effort depends on whether it is merely an accumulation based on the recommendation of others or a selection illustrating one's personal interests, even the changes and development of a particular taste over the years. The inherited traditions that fettered the activities of the heirs of great inheritances are quite startling in this respect. When one visits a stately home – especially some National Trust property, there is usually little to show for the acquisitions of recent owners, as if the presence of those grander works, souvenirs of long-past ancestral European tours, had dwarfed the present owner and cramped his contemporary taste, an insinuation which, of course, can easily be brushed away with the words 'Wall-space!'

Today it can seem that the good chances have gone by. Art books full of photographs tell their readers how to make an attribution, price lists in many a guide or art dictionary give an indication of values, television is an educational medium unsurpassed for all the visual arts, bringing the Great Masters into every home, while local auctions and, in particular, that parade of their auction experts known as the *Antiques Road Show* bring the pleasure and excitement of collecting in samples to all, though its educational effect is limited, for, by never showing anything poor, it illustrates things of museum quality only, by which the public learns to admire rather than discriminate as it would if miscellaneous things of less quality were also shown.

A visit to any provincial sale today indicates the change that has come about. Once these sales were solemn enough, attended by local folk anxious to 'get something from the big house' and by a representative group of dealers whose numbers would swell mysteriously in some nearby field or pub after the sale to share out their plunder by that mutual inter-sale known as the illegal 'ring'. Now a sale audience takes care to note the dealers, to catch some estimate of their reputations and spending-powers and, far from being quelled, attends the viewing-days with little printed pocketbooks of sale-room identification and price indexes. In a cosmopolitan rush they go searching for bargains, for 'finds' and discoveries, looking under tables, turning over packs of items deliberately thrown by the auctioneer into grouped lots, and plunging both hands into boxes as if real treasure were within – so different from those pre-television days, when it was regarded as unwise to show eagerness and just not done to covet openly the possessions of someone deceased, days when dealers were to be avoided and even the advice of the auctioneer actually trusted.

In those days, just as now, everyone would mourn how opportunities had vanished: the confusion of two world wars, the passing away of ancestors accumulating death duties, the fall of prices in some slump, all great opportunities of which few availed themselves when neither art nor learning could be turned into money. And now, of course, everyone could commiserate, saying that after all these years of peace since 1945 everything had been bought, taken off the market, vanished utterly. *Plus ça change, plus c'est la même chose.*

But this is an old story, and I like to think the luck of the opportunity is still about. Of course, there is one difference. This little island of ours into which, besides our own indigenous art creations, the vast treasures of Europe and the further world came pouring, is surrounded by the former colonies and dominions with rising populations and good universities, all thirsting for a share in the precious things and with money, ample money, to buy them. South America, Brazil, even the Land of the Rising Sun and indeed all the new countries wish to give their multiplying populations a share in this civilized delight, a delight which requires no laborious learning and which can be obtained merely by a glance of the eye, as at flowers in a garden.

At present the young countries and, in respect of Western art, the Oriental ones, have not the traditional discrimination and are in the hands of dealers, but while the money is theirs, no impeding state legislation will be wholly successful in restraining art exports, for works we now consider 'minor' will go to them, while for the collector more and more opportunities must be fated to decline, save for those impetuous enough to collect against the trends of fashion, finding some forgotten joy from the older time.

I see the secret of success as going in search of delight and being satisfied with sheer pleasure, regardless of the dictum of others or some general amalgam of theoretical conclusions. Pleasure must satisfy a need one has, and the artefact must declare satisfaction to one by the appeal of its own intrinsic merit. Indeed, personal assertion of one's own will, dominating over true emotional impulses by intelligence alone, and commanded by mere convention, can lead to unhappy decisions.

I remember how, as a young poet on my way to my first publishers in the Belgrave Road, SW1, I would often pass a shop window full of clothing tumbled with bric-à-brac, antiques and odds and ends. The proprietor, a middle-aged woman, had tantalizingly glorified her establishment with that blatantly alluring title 'The Delightful Muddle'. A couple of old Indian ivories could be seen through the window, so I stepped inside and enquired their price. They were £9 each, but as one handled the figures they seemed cruder and insensitive, the colour much yellower in the hand than as viewed from outside. Intelligence suggested to me that the India Museum was not far away, and the advice of the Victoria and Albert museum would also have been available to that shopkeeper. In the hand those ivories lost their appeal, so I uttered a few pleasantries and took my leave, apologizing.

But beside the door I had noticed a little bronze bust of a man in a skullcap. The charm of his jacket, the thoughtful pose of his head enchanted me; yes, the image haunted my memory day after day: no miser ever had such desire, for the soft brown patina, kind and seductive, contrasted against the secondhand clothing. A victorian work maybe, some Catholic eminence possibly.

A month later I had to make another visit to Belgravia, passing that shop window, where the 'muddle' was as 'delightful' as ever, but those Indian ivories had gone. There, however, behind some cardboard on the windowshelf stood that little bronze bust. Anyone could see it now, thousands might come by and crave it even more than I. But the shop door was shut. The shop would not be open for some indefinite time, as the scribbled 'Closed for Holidays' notice declared.

It must have been nearly another month before I came that way once again, looked in the window and tried the door. The little brown bronze, posed just as thoughtful as before, had not been moved. Casually I enquired about the Indian ivories. The shopkeeper remembered me.

'Sold,' she said curtly. 'Almost a day or two after you came. You need to make your mind up. Things don't stay in my shop! Everything goes. Everything!'

What frightening words for a collector! They certainly motivated me, though I managed to appear as indecisive as ever when I enquired the price of an odd piece of china and then pointed to the bronze.

'£5!' she declared.

'All right, I will take it.'

Surprised, almost disconcerted at my decision, 'You haven't seen it!' she snapped as she reached across the bundles of clothing and handed it to me. 'You can't bring it back, you know. I don't change anything here.'

'That's all right. I like the colour,' I explained.

'The colour will be all right when you clean it,' came the mollifying reply. 'I like customers to be satisfied.'

I had not examined that bronze. Communication with it had been almost telepathic in the memory, but now I saw that the left-hand bow of the tie had been merged into the left lapel. She must have thought it broken and a defective object. Perhaps it came to her as such marked 'a.f.' ('as found' or 'all faults') in some auction. But now it was mine, signed 'A Gilbert A.R.A Sc 1890', and a fine portrait bronze of George Frederick Watts RA, the Victorian painter and himself a sculptor, adding a third to my two Alfred Gilbert bronzes – *Winged Victory* and *Homage to Hymen*, the latter the one so much admired by Bernard Shaw. In 1987 another casting of this very Watts portrait bronze appeared on the *Antiques Road Show* to be chosen for display to the millions of viewers who heard it valued by a Sotheby's expert at £1,000.

The incident is significant, as it illustrates the changing opportunity for the collector. The visual educational effect of television is enormous. It is not just the knowledge, the awareness that is imparted but the desire to possess, for some to acquire and grow happier beside life-enhancing objects, for others the mere greed for safe and quick wealth.

I have the little bronze still, for it came to me by its own genuine assertion of merit to satisfy my own desire, regardless of 'What is art?', like a beseeching 'Voice of silence' (to use Malraux's phrase) that spoke to my own heart. Time may change fashion, taste or sentiment, and the masses may dictate their required uniformity, but choice is for the individual to satisfy his own needs, privately to answer to his own yearnings. And in choice, by the acquisition of a collectable object, he replies to the need of his own spirit, so that unanswerable question 'What is art?' resolves into another and ultimate interrogative, 'What is man?' A man's possessions – the *Lares* (household gods) around his hearth – his own collection, be it whatever, is some reflection, some answer to this and can resolve into a dream of hope or a battle with reality, whether history of the past or exultation in the present.

Not all collectors will feel this underlying urge to be 'in touch with the absolute', but in their pursuit of pleasure such is what the sub-conscious will dictate, however in one's own collection it be interpreted. So, oblivious to such pyschology, I collect the things that pleasure something within myself. Conditioned as I am by financial stringency, since I will not part with any object which has asserted its place in my collection, I must wait for opportunity, gathering the while a knowledge which allows me to find what others may have missed or to take some path in a wandering search which will provide a new zest for my collecting.

So I found that objects made, almost visibly made, by the hand of man enchanted me, especially in bronze. Maybe I had become fascinated by that phrase '*perennius aere*' by which Horace implies that only structured thought in words can be more lasting than that most durable, most indestructible medium for an artist. Certainly, when the poured molten bronze solidifies within the mould, the artist's inspiration becomes more evident, the metal hardens over that easy plastic shaping and the fluidity of the clay translates into the severity of the metal to take on a patina with the passing years. Yes, bronze has undying appeal: the play of light over the shapen surface conveys messages almost superhuman in a plastic dream that, whether within walls or out of doors, is never cold as stone.

Fortunately for me when I was beginning collecting, bronze, except for the museum-inspired demand for attested Italian Renaissance examples, was out of fashion and almost unsaleable in the larger auction-rooms. I clearly recall Hawkins of Phillips Son & Neale brandishing an auction bill of sale above a beautiful Clodion group. This had been sold for over £1,000 between the wars and was now returning to the same rooms with the effects of the deceased after house clearance, posed for re-sale.

The auctioneer's reading of that invoice met with stony silence.

No one wanted to buy those waving maidens, for all the grace of their nudity. (I myself had a larger version, splendid upon a green marble pedestal.) Mr Hawkins tried again and looked at me, but to no avail, for I knew there was no profit in duplication here.

'This is what the times have come to!' he muttered, as his hammer came down and those lovely dancers hardly reached a price of two figures, there off Bond Street, in the centre of London's art world. Some time before, he had been kind enough, after some sale I had been unable to attend, to arrange my purchase of a bought-in lot. There had been no reserve, but no buyer either. I was the only admirer of the master sculptor, the doyen of the eighteenth-century French Court, so my offer of a mere £3 was accepted for a charming Clodion plaquette of nymphs enslaving a satyr.

Fortune's wheel erratically turning has changed the markets today. Prices are always ascending when the treasures of the eighteenth century are never short of buyers, but in those days, going by my star, my touchstone, delight, I bought and bought, and kept my *trouvailles*. I would walk out of Phillips with a heavy statue under each arm and folk staring as if I were crazy. Often, when short of money, I had to keep the auction house waiting. Nothing makes one better known than if this is done.

On such an occasion I was attracted by quite a large bronze of the Duke of Wellington (totally unidentified in the catalogue). He was mounted upon a rearing charger tied all around which were little parcels of items broken off his accoutrements – pistols in brown paper, harness wrapped and loose as his sword and whip, quite enough to make him viewed as a damaged object and unattractive. I had no money then, absolutely none to spare, but I bid nevertheless, and the Iron Duke was knocked down to me for £17.10s. At once my dilemma became clear. There was no chance of my writing a cheque until the end of the month. If I left that statue in the sale-room to be pushed about between sales, the parcels might get torn away from the saddle, the charming little pistols could fall out of their brown paper, the statue become bare, unfinished, faultful even.

Without hesitation I went directly to its stand, brushing aside the porter who was leaning against it, with, 'Yes, I've bought this one,' while I cut away the strings and put pistols, paper and harness into my pockets. The Duke of Wellington was stripped, but no one else should steal from him, and at least he was now not re-saleable!

This was not the correct thing to do. Emergency as it was, my collector's ambition sought to justify it. Nevertheless, as I made my way home to Brentwood, a feeling of guilt arose until I telephoned my intention to call very soon to collect, pleading the size and weight of the object. As I was a known and regular customer, no difficulty was raised.

At the end of the month, when I arrived to pay up and collect my treasure, there was an atmosphere in Phillips' office. Obviously some porter had noticed the mounted horseman divested of his gear, for no sooner had I paid than someone came forward to treat me to a terrible lecture. I had bought the statue. I was responsible, not they the auctioneers. I must take it as it stood. It was my risk. It had been left in the sale-room. They had no storage for it. I must take it away. They did not want to hear any more about it. Neither I nor that office mentioned the little paper parcels. Of course they knew, but not of my involvement, so grateful were they for my acquiescence, and my obvious delight mystified them and the porter, who was not expecting his tip, so friendly and pleased he became on receiving it.

I have that equestrian bronze to this day. With the help of my craftsman colleague Mike Hunwick, skilled metalworker as he is, it was taken to pieces and reconnected, the contents of those parcels installed, the pistols to the saddle, the whip in hand, the harness in place.

A little research and identificaiton show it to be a work by the contemporary Portuguese sculptor Joao Pauo da Silva Pelvides, born at Mafra in 1751 and living near Lisbon until 1821, member of the school of Portuguese sculptors founded by Alessandro Giusti (1715-99) to execute the marble statues made at Mafra Monastery near Lisbon. The bronze plinth carries the date 1815, so that it was probably made after Wellington's triumph at Waterloo, possibly for Portuguese admirers, mindful of their long struggle at the Lines of Torres Vedras north of Lisbon.

No more does the bronze endure my unjustified neglect, the charger fully equipped as he rears in my dining-room, making such a contrast to the more polished equestrian bronze by Baron Carlo Marochetti RA in my neighbouring room, showing the Duke less war-like now, hatless as if taking a salute to royalty on his well-trained charger, perhaps indeed the famous 'Copenhagen'. (And this was bought just as neglected by fashion and even more cheaply in the same sale-room.)

Those were lucky days when bronzes were in the doldrums. The larger sale-rooms would not give them space, and even Phillips sold them downstairs. Once under the furniture down there, hidden behind two flamboyant nineteenth-century spelter figures of Louis XIV and Peter the Great and listed together in this same lot, was a splendid equestrian lead statue of King George III. Contemporary, smaller of course, but as good as any in the royal collections, it fell to me for a few pounds. Dealers had cunningly scraped the tips of the horse's ears to reveal the lead shining below a beautiful brown patina. Such tradesmen thought themselves too clever to bid for such a deceptive object, regarding it as painted to imitate bronze. The auctioneer had failed to identify it, merely listing it with the accompanying two spelter statues. Even they later had their use, for I was able to re-sell them to get a profit which more than paid for the eighteenth-century equestrian King George. This I have still, though the sculptor is not yet known. Everywhere I have sought an attribution without success, actually going to the trouble of leaving it at the Wallace Museum for Sir Francis Watson to show it to the Keeper of the Queen's Pictures.

The statue is precious indeed. Lead is more difficult to cast than bronze, less durable also, and I do not know of any other English eighteenth-century equestrian model made from the medium in such detail.

Easy it would be for my pen to run on, giving a list of such triumphs, but I am telling how my collection has determined itself by pursuit of sheer delight rather than making a mere inventory of possessions. In sculpture, however, the pleasure is so strong that I have to bridle myself, for with pictures even one's friends can look puzzled, visitors sometimes can hardly fail to conceal a prompting to suggest some alternative attribution, mindful of the raging interest in fakes and forgeries. With fine patinated bronze of the kind I have garnered, combination of the foundryman's skill coupled with a forger's avarice would be preposterous to imagine. Never could so expensive a deception be achieved, and any Doubting Thomas who might seek to bug a collector's happiness must perforce pass by.

In making a collection without the assistance of unlimited resources, one has to take advantage of the neglect of others. Nowhere has this neglect occurred more than for sculpture this century. London is the characteristic example: great masterpieces in bronze, superb memorials in carved stone abound in churches without very much admiration. Even when works are placed so as to become known as important London landmarks – Boadicea, the Quadra over Wellington Arch, Nelson on his Trafalgar Column or that magnificent equestrian of Charles I west of the square – the sculptor is neither appreciated nor mentioned: Reid Dick may be remembered for his royal statue, Epstein on Broadcasting House and, of course, Gilbert for Eros, the latter only for the spectacular arrow-boy of love rather than for the sumptuous and magnificent water pedestal from which he takes aim. It is as if modern taste has discarded them as mere solid objects, a materialization to stare at without perception of the artist's vision that has dreamed them into existence. No wonder I found opportunities facing me in the back-street shops in Central London as well as in the sales dispersing great collections.

I went down to Burnham for the sale at Dropmore on a March day in 1969. The collection of the late Lord Kemsley was being sold by Sotheby's and splendidly displayed in that grand mansion. After viewing, I drifted back into the entrance hall and was surprised to see my wife walking round a central table from which a fine equestrian bronze commanded the scene. She went slowly round as if in a trance, for the bronze was exactly the same as the one in our own lounge and actually was not even as good, for it was only on a '2½in. mounted base' whereas mine was majestically placed upon a concave, ornamental plinth of Boulle inlay work, twenty-five inches high, with elaborate ormolu acanthus mounts surmounted by female heads at each corner and a facing ormolu plaque of the 'Sun King'. This, the pride of Lord Kemsley's bronzes, had been granted the honour of a full-page illustration in the catalogue and (as Lot 389) was described as:

A FINE FRENCH EQUESTRIAN BRONZE GROUP OF LOUIS XIV on a rearing mount, *in the manner of Guillaume de Groff* (1680-1742), the king in classical armour beneath a draped cloak, holding a baton in his right hand, the horse with fringed saddle cloth, chestnut patina showing beneath reddish black lacquer, 22in. 18th *Century*, on later ormolu-mounted black wood base.

 This present equestrian group would appear to be closely related to two others versions of Louis XIV on a rearing mount the first illustrated by Weirauch, *Catalogue of Bronzes*, in the Bayerisches National Museum, München, pls. 227-9, the second exhibited in New York, illustrated *The French Bronze* (M. Knoedler and Co.) 1968, no. 52.

The auctioneer's hammer duly came down upon the lot, and it was sold to a dealer named Patch for £1,000. Today this would be considered incredibly cheap, for times have been changing and prices with them. In the 1950s I had seen my version, covered with dust and rubbish, at the back of a shop in Seven Dials. I had seen it for weeks and weeks before I made up my mind to go and make an offer to the dealer. Firstly I had to persuade him to come and open up that deserted shop. Heavy dust enveloped the ormolu; nothing in that place had been disturbed for years. I had offered £25, but the old dealer wiped over the boulle inlay with his hand so that the ormolu shone upon the red tortoiseshell like old gold.

'What? With all this?' he protested plaintively.

'£30 then,' I grudged with feigned reluctance, and the deal was done.

How much he had paid for it I never knew, only that he was very pleased as he helped me carry it out of the shop into my car; so I have no feeling of guilt, for I sought to make no profit and have the statue to this day. He would have sold to anyone if he could, his shop was only five minutes walk from the National Gallery, even nearer to the Portrait Gallery. It was just that no one had the eye, no one wanted these solid objects. Either they had lost their special power to impose a spell upon the spectator or the latter's imagination refused to respond to any evocation of dignity or spirit, an extraordinary contrast in times when some kinds of painting were becoming unreal and lumpy and more solid calling themselves 'cubist'! I bless these esoteric modernists, for it is their dicta and corrupting notions that have enabled me to get in, as it were, between the showers and buy regardless of critics or so-called experts.

So here I have this royal group, this grand work from some Parisian palace of the eighteenth century, snatched from where it lay unnoticed in the shadow of our own great galleries – galleries which no doubt the public thinks brimful of experts! Apart from the sculpture, the pedestal indicates the supremacy of my version, made perhaps to the order of Louis XIV himself, who had made Boulle his premier cabinetmaker. The veneers remain perfect still in ebony and tortoiseshell, with intricate inlays of brass. This André Charles Boulle, (1642-1732) was a Parisian who became famous after becoming a member of the Academy of St Luke in 1664 and taking up work on the royal palaces, engaging in sculpture and architecture as well as decorating. Though he commanded the highest prices, he became a collector almost to distraction, for he fell into debt and could seldom pay his workmen on time. His workshop caught fire and everything he had was destroyed – castings, stock and completed work. Yet he recovered and lived to see his four sons continuing his tradition as cabinetmakers to the King, paying that time-old compliment to an artist, the copious imitation of their father's work.

Archibald Russell had been a diplomat, and his duties had necessitated residence abroad. His collection of Old Master drawings was important enough to merit a separately catalogued individual sale at Sotheby's when later in life he chose to sell a selection from it. Well-travelled as he was, I remember, often his surprising advice on where to go for treasure-hunting in works of art. 'London's the place!' he never had the slightest hesitation in declaring. He maintained that the greatest bargains were to be found in the two major sale-rooms, because their employees never really understood the Great Masters that would find their way there, and neither did their clientele. Among the masses of the smaller sales, he would say, great works could be smothered and lumped together or else, perceived as outstanding among minor works, could attract the more attention and fetch absurd prices. A poor work, even by a great master, was scarcely comparable with the best of a minor master. Any advice he gave would always carry the recurring refrains 'London's the place!' and, more specifically, 'Always go for the great!'

To a Londoner this does seem unreal, yet though the odd corners of the world, the derelict squares of old European towns may appear uncharted treasure caves, theirs is a false promise. I have travelled, and no one has searched with greater hope and optimism: the back streets of Spanish cities, the antique-dealers of Hamburg, the medley of stalls along the Seine banks, odd cellars in old Stockholm. I have pored over tattered bric-à-brac with a bespectacled artisan selling copper armlets engraved with St Christopher in Bulgaria's Sofia: I have tangled myself in these and many others, only to find opportunities for buying small decorative artefacts. In northern Greece, for example, in Yanina, I recall a window full of excitement behind the caged birds there, but within I could find nothing to delight the eye except an ancient carved bone shoehorn, hardly treasure trove, and a shepherd's crook that was beautiful indeed but quite undatable.

Coins are a different matter; these one can buy, but only for the standard prices known worldwide. My old Sicilian silver and the big coins of Alexander the Great were bought years ago, like my other coins, off Bond Street in the old Puttick & Simpson rooms. For anything I was able to buy, the flea-markets of Europe might have been combed with the small-toothed combs of most efficient antique-dealers. In Portugal, for example, after rushing to the Lisbon open-air trading pavements, I could only get a little cast-bronze dish showing a wild boar, and as for Turkey, in that city of the Grand Bazaar, when I had visited two or three stalls there, the little wild boys running between the booths always seemed to have spread the word that I was no buyer, for the Turkish dealers would have none of me, nor even bring out their more precious wares to a tourist with such an empty purse.

In Spain also one must look hard to find a really spirited original representation of Don Quixote or Sancho Panza, and owing to religious fervour, ancient pictures of the saints have become more expensive. Here they do not throw away old things, but I have always refused to give up and gone on doggedly searching the back-street shops, for it makes a pleasant holiday diversion: the dealers are inquisitive, the shops always empty and time for everyone cheapest of all. Even rubbishy domestic objects of such a foreign country provide a bizarre interest if one can stomach their must and mould.

In one of many such shops in Granada there were crude paintings on the walls – of toreadors, of the blood of the bull-ring spattering tormented animals beside saintly virgins berobed and praying safely within gilded frames. A young soldier had brought out a picture and was holding it up to the light, doubtfully staring at the holy face, upturned eyes and long, powder-blue drapery. I could not more than glance in case it were thought I coveted his intended purchase, so during the trading dialogue I wandered around. There were old beds and clothing tucked between mattresses, rubbish packed out of sight of customers. The soldier changed his mind and decided not to buy the picture, leaving without any discussion of its price. With the shop deserted, in a moment of freedom I had seen a broken stretcher protruding from the blankets and bedding. After a little care it came to be extricated, though one arm of the stretcher had been torn away. I held it up by the broken wood upon which it survived and brought it casually forward to the proprietor. A glance told that the canvas was seventeenth-century beneath its

A Japanese pavilion
Josiah Conder, 1879

Salmon fishers on a rock above the river
David Cox, 1783–1859

A cottage in a cornfield
John Constable, 1776–1837

Sir Richard Steele's cottage, Hampstead
John Constable, 1776–1837

The cottage door
Thomas Gainsborough, 1727–88

The cornfield
John Middleton, 1828–56

The horse show
Sir Alfred James Munnings, 1878–1959

Scottish washer-women
Sir Edwin Henry Landseer, 1802–73

Sandling's Ferry, Norwich
John Crome, 1768–1821

Sweeping his studio
Joseph Mallord William Turner, 1775–1851

The Price family
William Say, 1768–1834

The Vale of Narni
Richard Wilson, 1714–82

Dr Samuel Johnson
Sir Joshua Reynolds,
1723–92

John Milton
English, 17th century

Percy Bysshe Shelley
Amelia Curran, *ob.* 1847

Lord Byron
James Holmes, 1777–1860

A vase of mixed flowers with a bird's nest
Dutch, 17th century

dirt, where could just be glimpsed the cloaked figure of a holy saint extending her arms above smaller figures to whom she afforded her protection.

The price? The shopkeeper was decisive, but I could not conjure enough mental energy to change his pesetas into pounds. Was it £50 for this unframed piece of old canvas pulled out from musty, tattered blankets and mattresses? I put it down and shook my head sadly as I went out of the shop.

Outside in the clean fresh air of summer morning my wits returned. That was no ordinary saint but the patron saint of a particular village or town. That was no ordinary badge she wore upon her breast but the crest of her village or community, and her arms were spread out in protection over those below – no ordinary figures they, but souls in Purgatory surely, for the flames of Hell were rising and burning there below that decayed varnish.

I stopped in the passing crowd on that street. A smiling flaxen-haired woman came down like a huntress from a side turning, flashing the red paint upon her lips. Behind her in a window sat a chemist, his posters offering instantaneous 'cures', his shelves stocked also with means of protection from disastrous ailments and other accidents. Somehow the vision of that outstretched cloak took significance. I could restore that canvas!

Back into the shop I went and offered the equivalent of £40 in pesetas for it, expecting to have to bargain upwards to some settled intermediate price. My offer was accepted without question. So pleased was the shopkeeper that he would have folded the canvas and rolled it round the remaining arm of its stretcher, had I not prevented him and instead accepted a paper cover.

When returning to Britain, I came by Madrid that time and stayed a couple of nights at the Hotel Moro opposite the Prado, happily walking round the magnificent collection that still shines as bright as ever, a galaxy of the Old Masters from the Holy Roman Empire and the glory of Charles V. I parked my car just by an established police car-park in a side street there. Spanish friends had entrusted me with a child's First Communion dress as a present for their relatives in London. It was complete with embroideries beautifully hand-worked, and there were also a couple of sacks of native chickpeas for their London restaurant. I had packed them carefully with my precious canvas, protected as it lay on the floor by layers of haphazardly gathered Spanish periodicals – some indeed, of an unsavoury kind, portraying samples of Spanish nudity.

On the morning of departure, I humped my luggage from the Hotel Moro, but, as soon as I laid hand upon the car door handle, I knew something was amiss. Within, all was confusion.

Thieves had been there! Both sacks of chickpeas were gone! Every garment of the little child's communion dress had been stolen. My German ciné-camera had vanished.

The impact of cognizance of a thief's visit is shocking. Humanity suddenly presents itself like the wild fox in a poultry house. A few chickpeas were about the floor, scattered idly, but marvel of marvels, under the pornographic pages of those newspapers lay the canvas image of the holy saint peacefully undisturbed by those searching intruders.

The police had gone from their car station. The street was empty. Back at the Hotel Moro, I was told that a car theft was nothing unusual in that district. The year before, a film team from a British television company had lost all their cameras, their equipment and their film, the product of months of work for some television programme, all stolen. Tears there had been on the part of the women, anger from the men: all were of no avail. Nothing could be or would be done, and back they went to London, their venture ruined. The implication of the story was obvious.

'Nothing could be or would be done' was to me a challenge. Unkind as it may seem, I suspected the police on their car station. At the least they were guilty of negligence, and I would see that it was recorded.

Off I went to the central police station in the Plaza Mayor. The great doors of the entrance hall were open as I marched in but immediately the whole place sprang to attention. Doors closed upon me, armed police confronted me. Once inside – easy enough; but to get out, every door and passage, every glance indicated impossibility of egress. ETA had been active in Madrid. Bombs had been recently thrown from the Plaza Mayor thereabouts. No one was going to be allowed any possible escape in an emergency; a delivery man for explosives would be trapped there and then.

A most efficient young woman was quickly brought to act as my interpreter, and a long statement taken down for signature in a locked room. The morning had gone by now, and I asked what was going to be done.

'When we recover the camera,' I was promised, 'it will be given to your ambassador for return to England, but for the other things, as you cannot give any details of identification, what can we do?'

I came out of that central police station, glad to be in the Plaza again with no doors closed upon me. What could they do? But at least I had made my protest against camera-stealers, robbers of children's ceremonial dresses and eaters of chickpeas. No doubt the details would be circulated to worry any potential malefactor in uniform, a comforting thought but tiring, for during the whole of the previous day I had treated myself to that exhausting feast of Prado masterpieces, to enjoy which not one seat had been provided, not even in the cafeteria or refreshment rooms. Extensive building operations had been in progress, causing the noise of pneumatic drills to add to one's fatigue.

In the Plaza Mayor there were seats in plenty, vendors of refreshment everywhere and the pleasant spectacle of Spanish idlers going by. I lounged and watched them, counting my good fortune in having taken my main travelling goods into that hotel and my greater good luck that the thieves were not connoisseurs of their own nation's art. For that canvas on its broken stretcher proved to be a rare painting by Alonzo Cano, painter and sculptor architect, native of Granada, perhaps the only one now in Britain, for, as I write, not even the National Gallery had an example: the patron saint treading the clouds on that canvas, serene and kindly, stretches out her cloak to cover souls tormented while her face expresses the fulfilment of the hope she offers.

I have mounted the picture upon a panel of marine plywood and found a pleasant frame, but it was cleaning and refreshing the old paint that threw me into trouble and confusion. The bacon rind with which peasants used to brighten up church paintings before festivals and processions is bad enough, but this picture needed even more forbearance. It had been regularly dressed with olive oil, which had soaked and dried within the canvas. Most things in conservation yield to consistent and repeated effort, however, and now *Souls in Purgatory* by Alonzo Cano shines like a fine star among my Spanish paintings, equalling in importance the picture of children, *The Good and the Evil Soul*, I had bought in Birmingham.

So my experiences come around to proving Archibald Russell right, for the only other painting I have ever bought abroad is an oval Slavonic panel depicting *St Nicholas in Prison*, which I chanced to find in Athens' Hephaestos Street when I came ashore from a cruise ship. 'London is the place!' Yes, and the foreigners know it, but they are often nervous of their knowledge and not so keen to load themselves with speculative works that might get themselves laughed at when back home in their fine show-rooms in Hamburg or Paris. Spanish painting is a field few understand, else I could never have bought my three little Goya pictures, one in Pulborough, another at Sevenoaks and the third actually at Christie's.

It is easy to rejoice at opportunities taken and yet still easier to regret opportunities missed when one looks back. One snowy winter day I found myself at Syon Lodge. Bert Crowther was having a great clear-out sale preparatory to making extensions to the premises and achieving a better display of architectural furniture. Some vicissitudes had hit the firm since they were prosecuted for removing Adam-style marble fireplaces from London buildings by arrangement with employees of building contractors. Now there was to be a turn for the better: land was to be developed for road-building, premises altered and anything surplus put up for 'auction on the premises'.

I had walked by the lots as they lay out in the open: pieces of sculpture, broken friezes, statues torn way from buildings, perhaps even survivors of London's bombing. now and again a gap in the lottage, items 'withdrawn from sale', indicated that a knowledge-able eye had overseen the whole exhibition. Some adviser from one of the London auction houses or official of a museum had perhaps been engaged to check that nothing went away for less than its market value. I refrained from bidding as the prices seemed to rise and rise, and was standing at the back on some raised planks from which I could overlook the market. The snow continued to fall and a chill destroyed the usual optimism which I seldom fail to conjure.

'Look at these prices,' I grumbled to a neighbouring onlooker. Now well known in Bond Street, I don't suppose these days he leaves a comfortable office to climb planks and barrels in the snow, but there he was, shivering on that platform, bidding nevertheless.

'These are not competitive prices,' I declared. 'They are too high! None of these can be sold in the West End.'

'Yes, they are,' he agreed, ' much too high now, but in retrospect it will not seem so.'

In retrospect! Serious words for this part of the century when prices rise and rise, when those who prophesy that prices cannot endure are confounded.

'I suppose you know, Mr Johnson, there is a recession in pictures!' commented a rival collector years later, staggered at seeing me buying for the first time at a sale far from London, but nearer his home.

'Aha!' I replied, 'that's what they tell me when they want to see me unhappy.'

The bogey of a change in art prices is often seized upon by newsmen, of course, but it seldom comes violently enough to be noticed as permanent, for it steals through coming generations step by step in a balancing game against new aspects of market interest either to diminish inheritances or, more often, to exalt them.

6 *Opportunities and Estimations*

When, from one source or another, it has happened that I have had money, and money to spend, I have gone into the auction-rooms with a care-free joy to obtain some object of excellence worthy to take a proper place in my collection, something to give prestige and enhance the value of the old companions there. For such a prescribed purpose, reckless buying of some object favoured by the market has always proved a disaster. It might be that in its exalted place in some auction-room, enhanced by the skill of the auctioneer, the work could take on an aura of excellence, yet beside those old companions on my walls such a newcomer would often dwindle and have no right of place.

Once I bought a fishmarket scene for several hundred pounds at a London auction. An old carved frame gave it distinction, and the varnish seemed old. Age had fogged the painting and concealed how many artists had been at work replacing parts fallen away from the copper panel. 'Restored' by me, or rather cleaned, the fish lost their glitter, which swam away with solvents so that the corpses flopped lifeless upon their trays. No fisherwoman would ever display them so, nor exhibit her wares with so forbidding a smile. Some hack artist had portrayed her, and I had revealed her posture as stiff as her wares.

No place certainly for this, the most expensive picture I had yet bought, among my possessions. Cleaning had evoked all its defects into the light of the twentieth century, and I had to resort to ancient methods urged by da Vinci and other Renaissance artists to cause my own new paint and shiny varnish to slip back beneath a false bloom of age. Urine, vinegar even, was not sufficient; only a layer of foul mud proved really effective and enabled me to hand the reprobate to a far-away auctioneer. Imagine my horror when he licked his hand repeatedly and used his fingers to rub away at the surface. (I have noticed some dealers in London sale-rooms use their saliva similarly; perhaps they need a little reflection on the

71

health aspects of such a practice.) After several more licks, the
auctioneer delivered his verdict. 'Yes,' he remarked, 'like you said,
it is only a pot-boiler.' He could not get my reserved price, so that
piece of old copper travelled around several sale-rooms before it
was finally sold, though how many 'experts' licked it I never
wanted to know.

My best possessions seem to have come to me almost by chance
and accident rather than by deliberate searches. Those foreigners
who come to London each spring and summer to buy in quantity
appear to be reckless rather than knowledgeable. It does not
surprise me to see them disappear after a season or two: they
increase or decline according to particular market pressures and are
far from being real collectors, searching as they are for mere
commodities, some indeed exchanging Mediterranean soft fruit
proceeds for pictures.

One could say that success is just chance, the luck to be moving
round and among opportunities where works of art are exposed
and offering themselves for sale. They abound in plenty these days,
not merely in London sales and street markets, such as the
Portobello and Caledonian, but further afield in antique fairs, even
that new phenomenon the 'car boot sale'. It is true that one can go
to dozens of these and not feel compelled to buy, but compulsion
urges to travel wherever opportunities may lurk, else how can
discoveries be made? To look and to find is surely not quite a
matter of chance; persistence of motives – in fact, endurance – is
the requirement. The lesson is to avoid going anywhere with the
intention to spend, as I had when, with a few hundreds to invest, I
had bought that old copper panel of the fishermarket.

'That's right!' commented Christopher Weston once from the
rostrum at Phillips, as he knocked down a rather slow-selling and
pathetic picture. 'One must take away something.' Unconsciously,
perhaps, he had noticed that the buyer was buying for the sake of
buying, merely justifying his presence at the sale.

There is an intrinsic quality in a work of art which will make its
own appeal to the eye, but one has to be present when it is on offer,
and the eye that sees it must not be blinded by the quantities of
printer's ink on which it has been promoted. Never am I impressed
by the erudition of art critics *per se*, always being inclined to assess
their ability by their own personal art acquisitions. Most of them,
alas, have a non-existent art collection. In my early days, moving
among old-timers like Schidlof and Dr Hildeburgh and wondering

at the persistent group of buyers around the rostrum at Christie's or Sotheby's, I would marvel at their style. Neither in demeanour nor in conversation did they use to have anything in common with the exemplified university don, all being practical, uncomplicated men, and I came to know that they were educated not by words alone. The magic of the recollective eye had shown them the way. All had that quality of which I myself became conscious, the photographic gift of complete recall. Constant association with the pictures or treasures coming before them, stored in the memory bank, provided experience that could answer on demand and make a decision upon attribution or value. From the strength of the pleasure these special memory banks gave, came their individual power. Of course, their weakness lay in that their eyes were knowledgeable only as far as the current auction-room traffic would allow and were regulated by an equation between fashion and cash with which taste seldom interferes.

Here a true connoisseur has the edge. To him taste and refinement have been made the touchstone, over-riding fashions of all times. In the sentiment of old Southey, he can feel, 'My friends are with the dead', and make his acquisitions regardless of contemporary thought, independent of fashion. Dealers, however, pseudo-collectors and the auction-room personnel are ruled by the iron hand of estimated values and never so controlled as today. Objects presented at a sale-room counter or for advice to a *Road Show* tend to elicit some pause for reference to records. Only then, after recourse behind the scenes to the *Benezit Dictionary* or one of the standard art price record books, will the oracle speak and each article receive its contemporary valuation and grade of merit. This I find as a collector not so much an annoyance as a triviality – that each object has, as it were, an employment testimonial, a reference to the cash value it could make on re-sale. I claim to have collected and to hold my collection independently of this, valuing my things as I have bought them, on prospects of pleasure alone.

At a sale in Clare village, Suffolk, some ten years ago there was a little piece of wood lying on the old furniture and depicting a woman bathing by moonlight. A Rembrandtish quality was about the naked figure, and I bought the oil-painting unframed, neglected as it was, for only £3. The stencil marks of Christie's on the back, when subsequently traced, proved it to have come from the artist's special patron, David Price, passing through the sale-room in 1875. How had it come to be passed over in Clare, so neglected? Had some amateur painter coveted its Victorian gilt frame and thrown the panel away? Now attributed, re-framed, re-varnished, it takes a different place, valued not for its cash assessment, for perhaps it would not fetch a great sum today, but for the pleasure it gives daily and for that greater pleasure, greater than all, the delight of having rescued a work of art from the dust, from oblivion: *The Bather Alarmed* by James Falconer Poole, RA.

In this salvage of thrown-away works, of things cast out by ignorant owners or careless inheritors, I have had the companionship of long-gone geniuses, the thrill, the exhilaration of travelling worldwide across the centuries. This is so far from what many consider collecting, that is, completing some serial by filling a gap or hunting for rarity alone. Such is the empty side of it all, when, failing to achieve acquisition of the great, a collector is seduced and descends into the trivial pursuit of rarities, looking for printing errors in postage stamps, for example, or, harder still, errors in the striking of coins. What a sight is that at the Royal Mint when coins come down the rollers! After being struck they pass over shallow moving trays keenly watched by teams of men looking to take out any mis-stamped items. None ever slips through, as they assured me on my visit, though any that did would fetch their price, could they escape that surveillance into the hands of collectors.

To my mind the most trivial of all mankind's fantasies is this garnering of mistakes and accidents, and yet in terms of value it conjures astonishment and illustrates that primitive desire in the heart of man to possess something unique, so rare that it will cause his fellows to marvel and envy, and lift him by mere possession of it into an admired position far higher than any personal quality of his own could attain. And, of course, such admiration is rooted in cash values which come or provide themselves with a necessary label attached.

The current *Road Shows* lure minor collectors to bring along their treasures for exhibition and assessment. Their success in enthusing real cultural appreciation cannot be over-estimated, and they take the surest way by telling clients the value of their possessions, thus protecting them from the vultures that come knocking at doors. Sometimes the urgency with which they tell clients to insure their possessions, naming cash figures, seems a little suspect, not that there could be collusion with the great insurance companies, of course.

In contrast to this, the determination with which certain public galleries decline to advise on values seems reprehensible. Naturally they should not be the minions of the art trade, but objects brought to them are mostly from domestic sources; national institutions have some duty to advise fully and protect the public. They have a responsibility to come forward and not shirk a knowledge of market values. No one has ever suggested that museums and art galleries put a price label on all their own exhibits, marking up or downgrading according to the drift of world prices. What a challenge that would be, a stimulus to the security arrangements and something more to interest visitors, especially if a history of price rises and falls were attached here and there – but even writers of art monographs are inclined to baulk at such an unacademic venture as recording prices.

It has been said there are two kinds of art collector: one will at once declare the value of each possession, emphasizing mostly those for which he has paid the greatest money, while the other prefers to stress his sagacity and prove he has outwitted dealers and the entire art market, boasting of low purchase prices and of attribution triumphs.

Attributions in a collection may strengthen as the collector's knowledge and wisdom grow or indeed may vanish entirely, and here perhaps I should make reference to one picture in my 1968 exhibition that was styled 'Zoffany: *Portrait of an Oriental*'. Mr Krystena Wuccen Saling noticed it reproduced in my book and was kind enough, writing from San Diego, California, to send me Polish art books and a published photograph which clearly indicated that my picture is a portrait of King Jan III Sobieski by an unknown Polish painter. His granddaughter Klementina Sobieski became the consort of James, Prince of Wales, in 1719. A book by Peggy Miller, entitled *A Wife for the Pretender, Clementina Sobieski* (George Allen & Unwin, 1965), told of the Stuart connection. Of course, this explains how I found the picture where it lay at Cobham Hall, the former residence of the Earl of Darnley, with its many echoes of the Stuarts!

Jan Sobieski cultivated the appearance of a fierce Oriental potentate for his campaign against the Turks but he began his campaign by taking his troops on a pilgrimage to a rather obscure Virgin Mary shrine. He was deeply in love with his *intriguante* French wife. (Prudish nineteenth-century historians found his letters to her most shocking!) He became exceptionally fond of a tame otter presented to him, which, when it strayed from the palace, was shot by a gamekeeper ignorant that it was a friend of the King. The King's response was characteristic. The gamekeeper was executed forthwith.

Only a few months ago, a famous London gallery sought me out, having accepted my 1968 attribution, hoping to identify the sitter with an Indian celebrity, to acquire and publicize the painting with a view to its sale for the growing cultural interest in that sub-continent. They were shocked and disappointed by my insistence on a Polish source, and I sensed that their respect for Polish art had a very matter-of-fact basis!

7   Authenticity

Lucky is the man who can avoid the auction-rooms and the dealers, avoid the tyranny of the past altogether and go straight to the artist of his choice, make him an acquaintance – indeed, possibly a friend – and have the pleasure of his personality permanently and visibly placed before him in the form of a purchase from the artist himself. There are the galleries of the West End, not so well advertised, it is true, as of yore, but accessible even to windowshoppers around Bond Street. The pleasures of being a real patron of art are inestimable; the presence of works of art commissioned from a living artist seems to have something more intense and immediate than the silent awe of Old Masters.

When, in pre-war days, furnishing my first house, I remember going to Wigmore Street and chatting to the people in the Gordon Russell showrooms. The simple, functional design of their furniture attracted me. Gordon Russell, an eminent innovator in design, and his brother Richard Drew Russell seemed to have an originality possessed by no others then. I persuaded them to sell me a fine large desk in rosewood, held by one chromium bar and with drawers cut from a single and solid elm panel surmounted by birmabright handles, a simple, modern design that came to dominate my room with an accompanying pair of chairs, also in rosewood. I had to persuade them to separate it from an enormous sideboard which could have grown overbearing in my situation. (Some months later they told me with relief that they had sold this to a visiting foreigner who had taken it abroad.) Attracted by their catalogue, I came back and bought a circular table with gunstock-type legs and two adaptable easy chairs, all in natural Honduras mahogany. I have always liked to see as much wood as possible showing in furniture: a plethora of cushions and soft upholstery is anathema to me. Captivated by the style, almost at the same time, I bought a Murphy radiogram. In blending of veneers and singularity of form, it seemed to demand a place with me, and no wonder, for I learned later that Richard Drew Russell had joined Murphy Radio as staff industrial designer. Some years later he was in the RNVR and during the 1939-45 war engaged on ship camouflage and serving in India and China.

In the mid-evening of 24 November 1940, protected by that rosewood desk and supported by a sturdy oak dining-room set purchased from Heal's, my wife and I crouched down listening while a heavy German mine drifted overhead, its torn parachute cloth flapping, mysterious and threatening, till it exploded just beyond the back door, shaking the earth, making an enormous crater. After a terrible moment, it seemed, of static silence, in some kind of recoil it brought down all the houses that side of the avenue. My wife was unhurt, though five neighbours were killed and eighteen injured. As for me, a piece of metal had gone right through the house, passing me so near as to take the right arm from my spectacles without my noticing.

Next morning the demolition men came to pull down the remaining bits of wall as a dangerous structure, but my desk, that precious desk, a real 'collector's piece' was underneath.

'Leave it to the Government!' the men urged. 'They will pay! You can get compensation in plenty!'

They refused to help extract the desk, demanding that it be sawn in half. After a horrid argument and much shouting, they eventually agreed to pull out the metal window and some of the wall underneath, through which I carried that desk, that precious desk, on my back, and a real back-breaking task that was, but I have it even today, surrounded and covered with books and writing-papers as it was then. The veneers were undamaged, the birmabright handles of the elmwood drawers all unscratched. Every morsel, every wooden relic of my aesthetic furnishing was saved to be re-assembled in days of peace time, though a close friend has commented, comforting me about an oak sideboard, 'Honourable scars, honourable scars!' And well it was so, for the Government assessed furniture replacement 'War Damage' at domestic pre-1939 secondhand prices!

Elsewhere (*Collector's Luck*) I have told the story of my refurnishing from Knight, Frank & Rutley's auction-rooms in Hanover Square, with the auction-room room on fire and embers dripping sparks, with sirens blaring outside and bidders as non-existent as prices. As the furniture van I had hired was approaching Grays, it had to pass the spot where two children had just been killed in the day-time raid. There was no thought of collecting *per se* in those days, and of collectors there were none.

Looking back, I remember how my taste in furniture used to be severely modern, so much so that years and years later, after the success of my exhibition, I went again to Heal's and bought from their front windows the best dining-room suite they had on show, a teak assembly made by Muller, one of the finest Danish designers, a suite I deliberately chose to offset the gilded and carved frames that had come to hang upon the clean white walls of my new house.

It takes a lifetime to understand how transient is individual taste operating in one's career with influences unrealized that must flourish there within the personality, quite apart from the changing fashions of the multitude. When we were guests of my wife's aunt in North Wales, she would remind us of the cabinet she had presented to us. In those days it seemed vulgar ostentation, with its great ebonized door, its semi-precious stones that made bold designs of fruit and flowers, and above all the mighty gilded ormolu, over-emphasizing wealth and splendour. Though it had been a wedding present, it would not agree, we thought, with either Gordon Russell or Ambrose Heal. At each visit we renewed our thanks but delayed the task of collecting. When the war intervened, though thanks were in order, apologies for non-collection were unnecessary. Only when she had passed on did we deem it appropriate to possess it, together with the Welsh seventeenth-century long-case clock made in Denbigh town by Thomas Jones around 1696.

By then our eyes were wider. Aunt Peggy had bought that cabinet in one of her sale-room forays, for she was a compulsive bidder. She had gone in the late twenties to the Gwrych Castle sale of the Earl of Dundonald. There it had attracted her as it stood in the full glory of a castellated dwelling, the flower design intact, the gilded acanthus and emblems of the Sun King shining gold. The signature of the famous imperial eboniste was there, and then there had been a label, proving its appearance at a famous Paris exhibition. The marble top would detach; beautiful little bolts would undo so that the whole piece would disintegrate to be packed panel on panel, shelf upon shelf, in order to travel by coach with the equipage of that Glorious Majesty as he pleased himself going from palace to palace about his domains.

Today, as it stands facing the seventeenth-century ebony and ivory cabinet in my lounge and against the paintings and bronze acquisitions made long since that gift was proffered, it seems not a whit pretentious, so much have the years changed one's taste. Indeed, unless the big door is open to show the china and silver within, it takes quite a diffident place.

With superb craftsmanship revealed in furniture, there can be no doubts concerning authenticity, but with regard to other works of art it is a different matter. The great Duveen would advise constantly: 'Beware of *scavi* (objects excavated) never buy them!' In our day, Arthur Negus confessed, after his firm had passed over a celebrated little Holbein: 'Pictures terrify me!'

After the elation of my own exhibition, contented with my picture collection and perhaps paying too much attention to friends who would admire yet comment: 'Nothing like that can be done today,' I resolved to collect objects in a medium where doubt was impossible.

Silver!

Authenticity was clearly definable by silver 'hallmarks', indication – indeed, proofs – quite easy to commit to memory for identification. By avoiding purchases that came under the heading 'marks rubbed', one could gather a collection that would show history of style and also, one hoped, give opportunity for choice in making a display of refined craftsmanship.

I bought the reference books. I learned the silver marks. Shapes and outlines gave a clear definition of historical development. The Victoria and Albert Museum had excellent showcases full of shining examples, and easy-to-read books of photographs explaining them. Shop windows in the City of London, the London Silver Vaults, the Broad Street emporiums had examples almost as good. I had money now from my writing – easy come easy go – it burned in my hands. I would make an astonishing collection, without the dreadful risks of using chemicals in cleaning and restoration, without the labour of carpentry, repairing panels and making frames.

I went to a provincial auction of silver wares. A sheep in wolf's clothing was I, for the personnel there had the appearance of pawnbrokers, and the goods when handled had mysterious scratches upon them, quite apart from authentic hallmarks. Nevertheless, I reckoned I could outbid the Trade. I could learn by re-selling in London, where values were known, the weights of each object in ounces and even makers and silver marks clearly set out in the catalogues. One had only to inspect each object for damage or repairs, check the hallmarks and bid!

I decided to go for the best, only the best, and bought the dearest article in that sale, a George I coffee-pot, intact, with the hallmarks clearly on the base. £750 seemed a great deal of money in a first venture, for that was in the late sixties before inflation had begun to gallop, but I comforted myself that I had something incontrovertible, a good weight of eighteenth-century silver with clear marks, a pot in the clean-cut style of that mid century before florid embossing of designs became fashionable.

I came away from the auction happily. The market price for such an article was then from £2,500 to £3,000. I placed it full in my view at home, where I could admire it constantly, and that is how temptation came to me. If profits could come so easily, why should I not follow the same path I had with pictures? Sell! Take the profit and buy again and again – profit and buy again till I had a collection to rival any other, all built out of that one coffee-pot! The prospect was attractive indeed. There would be no mixing of dangerous cleaning-solvents, no testing and trying of colours in restoration, no re-lining of canvases, no glueing up of old panels, no carpentry with frames or toning away new gilded surfaces, and above all, no tedious picture research from photograph to photograph, from library to gallery and museum to gallery, working through old catalogues to confirm and prove a painting's attribution. My beautiful volumes of Sir Charles Jackson, newly purchased, contained every necessary reference, with photographs of almost every known type of obtainable English silver as well as details of owners and collectors. I had bought them at once with my resolve to collect and they stood handy upon my book shelves: *English Goldsmiths and their Marks, A History of Goldsmiths and Plate Workers of England, Scotland and Ireland* and also his *Illustrated History of English Plate, Volumes One and Two,* wonderful picture-books with a text that seemed to contain not just what one needed to know but everything that could be known about Britian's national silver, in a tradition acknowledged to be the finest, the most collectable sequence the world can show. As I turn over those attractive pages today, more sophisticated though I have come to be, I can still appreciate how, by a careful study of them, I thought myself competent, supremely competent.

There were things illustrated in Sir Charles Jackson's books far better than this coffee-pot of mine. Temptation gripped me and I coveted them. I would become a dealer to make real progress, but on a different path from my picture collecting, for once an object is known as silver and the marks are seen, it is seldom neglected like an old painting in some attic. Up to now I had collected only one silver object – a little medieval figure balancing a silver clock within a star, making an outline as significant as a monstrance, neglected and thought worthless because it was corroded black and having no silver marks, so being considered no more than pewter.

I wrote out a ticket for my precious coffee-pot and presented it at the silver counter at Sotheby's. Its sale would increase my spare capital, which could go on snowballing in a great silver chase.

The face of the expert there did not expand in any congratulatory smile.

'We can't sell this,' he declared severely. 'I'm sorry.' He turned away to leave the counter.

'What? But why ever not?' I demanded.

'Because it is a fake!' The severity in his voice softened as he understood my astonishment.

'A fake?' I echoed incredulously. 'Is it a copy then? A modern copy?'

'No, it is just a fake!'

I held my breath. Perspiration stood out upon my forehead. Surely the ghost of Sir Charles Jackson might have taken pity on me.

'How can that be?' I persisted. 'Look! The silver marks!'

'Yes, on the bottom,' he insisted. 'The old trick, the bottom cut from a smaller genuine period piece and inserted. To be right, the marks had better be on the sides of the pot, not just on the bottom or the lid.'

'Had better be? Whatever does that mean? Suppose they chose to put them just where they wished?'

But the interview was becoming tedious for that expert. 'Doesn't matter how much you paid for this,' he affirmed. 'We can't sell it here. It could only be sold in America, where they don't bother about the legal aspect of silver marks. Here, if it came into the hands of the Goldsmiths' Company, they would put it under their machine and crush it down, as they are obliged to. Its value is only the silver content.'

Ah, one straw! Here was a straw I could clutch! 'Well,' I pleaded, 'send it to America, then. Sell it in your auctions there. It is a good copy at least and well made. I will pay expenses in advance.'

Commenting 'I shall have to ask', he disappeared within but came back shaking his head. 'It would be too much trouble and not the kind of thing they wanted to handle over there. Oh no, no.'

'Steady,' said a voice at my elbow. It was a silver dealer I had often seen in the sale-rooms, yes, and always with a group of them, even at that very coffee-pot sale. He picked up the coffee-pot from the paper I was wrapping round it, repeating, 'Steady, now, steady.'

He turned the pot round and smelt it, held it up to the light and tried the lid and the handle. He looked down the seams of metal and stared at the base.

'There's nothing wrong with this pot,' he asserted in slow, measured tones. 'Nothing. And nobody can tell why those silver marks are there. Lots of true coffee-pots and the like never had any marks, never, providing they were made to order and not for sale. How can you tell the marks have not been put there, put on the pot just to confirm its date and prove it's a good pot all the same.'

'Just so,' said Sotheby's expert, 'and that's why it won't sell, not by us at least.'

'It's a good pot,' confirmed my new-found supporter, 'and it's right, yes, period, no doubt of that, period. How much did you say you gave for it?'

'Of course,' he continued when I told him. 'It's a nice coffee-pot. You don't want to be in a hurry. It will pour well and look grand on any table. If it pleases you, take your time. No, it's kind of you to offer me the chance of buying and I would buy it, definitely I would, but I've overbought lately and my capital is tied up. But you go steady. You'll get to like it. With all this nonsense about marks on the bottom! Who turns up a coffee-pot if it's full of coffee?'

'But there are no marks on the side,' I complained.

'Ah,' he commented knowingly. 'Not on the side.'

He was about to make a suggestion but checked himself with, 'That's a good place, the side, yes, a good place that.'

Perhaps he was trifling with me. I clutched the pot in its paper and made off. He must have been trafficking there somehow, entering his wares maybe. If I had waited, I might have found out; but he had raised my hopes. That expert might have been wrong. He was certainly in a hurry and a bit abrupt, as if at first he imagined that I myself had put a new bottom to that pot. I would go to Phillips, only a five-minute walk up Bond Street, and at the same time ask them about a heavy silver Russian caviare dish I had with me but had forgotten in all this despair.

Disaster never depresses me for long. I wiped away the perspiration from my forehead and came into Phillips sale-rooms smiling and hopeful. Nothing there in that kinder location sweeps a visitor into submissive deference, and no high-faluting voices pitched a half-octave above assert the authority of a Bond Street location. The silver sale-room office was upstairs, off the auction-room, where the director was always approachable. Sympathy and friendliness radiated from his anonymous dark suit. He would always take trouble to make sure he could really help one, for knowledge to him was for passing on and he would give freely to all comers. He was one of the few I have met among sale-room workers who never played any esoteric card to justify his status. A week or two before, he had recommended me to an old family firm in Broad Street to which I had brought one or two broken pieces for repair. There I had taken Mrs Smith into my confidence, for she and her husband had seen my television interviews on pictures. As she listened to my optimism, she had warned me to be careful with silver, and as I took the lift at Phillips, I remembered her words, 'Well, I hope you make a great deal of money!' But now the intonation in that remark as I recalled it hid some kind of admonition, even foreboding.

Though there was no one in the outer office of the silver room, at a touch of the bell the expert came to the counter. As he picked up the coffee-pot, not a shadow of hesitation came over his face.

'You've been done!' he advised. 'Get your money back straight away. Take it back! It's a bad thing to have!'

I gave him my little preamble, the tale of the silver dealer waiting at Sotheby's. I read the catalogue description: George I Coffee Pot..1725.. maker Wm. Darkeratt 28½ ozs.' All produced nothing more than a suggestive grin.

'That's what they do, these dealers,' he laughed. 'They'll take anybody up the garden path to keep things to themselves. But you take this back to where you bought it. Whoever sold it knows what it is, and it is dangerous. The Law allows the Assay Office to seize anything like this and smash it up. Get your money back before that sort of thing happens.'

Not wishing to lose face so rapidly with an acquaintance who had previously been so helpful, I produced my heavy Russian caviare dish engraved with Russian scroll work and proud with its heavy silver lid. He read the Cyrillic silver marks instantly: 'And that's no good to you either,' he declared.

'Why ever not? You can't say this is a fake!'

'No, but look at the date mark – 1876 – not one hundred years old, so not an antique and cannot be sold as such for a few years. Keep it and hang on. That's one way of making money.'

I explained that I collected Russian articles and had no intention of selling, but he shrugged his shoulders.

'Oh, you'll change your mind,' he grinned. 'Everyone does. Bring it along in ten years and it will be a different story then!'

So it is, but I have not changed my mind and treasure it still, for every year it seems larger and heavier and more valuable.

I left that office with a note about Continental silver marks: *Poinçons d'Argent*. Tardy, a guide to the silver marks of the world, for which I immediately placed an order. The clear and easy-to-read listing places any collector streets ahead of those without it when contemplating foreign silver.

But now I had another haste to make and literally hurled myself towards a telephone booth to ring my bank manager and command that my auction cheque be stopped. A week had gone by, a whole week! The cashier demurred. To stop a cheque after a week, on a telephone request! Along came the bank manager to listen to my enjoining. Was not I a lifelong client and my father another such, also a lifelong client? With a good balance in the current account, the emergency demanded action, immediate action! Yes it did, and the job was done.

After a day or two to recover from this shock, I travelled to the provincial auctioneer's office and proffered that coffee-pot to the chief clerk there, placing the offending object in its attractive glitter upon the counter.

'That sale has been over for more than a week. A whole week! We don't want this. People can't bring things back. Nothing comes back! The cheques have gone out! I've sent out all the money and paid the vendors.' Then, slamming a cabinet door to emphasize finality, 'The cheques went out yesterday,' she snapped.

'Stop them then, like I have stopped mine!' I advised.

The effect was quite electric. The other clerks stopped work. She came right up to the counter and broke the silence.

'You can't do that,' she protested. 'It's not allowed.'

'Two London sale-rooms say the pot is a fake,' I argued. 'Here it is now. Prove it is not deceptive and I will take it back and pay. Best for you to return it to the vendor when he comes with the cheque after you bounce it. I expect he will.'

I wanted neither to hear nor to say more, and indicated that unhappy coffee-pot in its loneliness on the counter. She reached out and began muttering over it, but I shamelessly took myself off.

I liked that provincial sale-room and always enjoyed the sales there, so I did not cease attending and was actually at the next sale when one of the partners approached me sadly.

'You stopped that cheque without speaking to us first,' he complained in a tone of mild reproof. 'Such action causes complications, even if you had cause. As a matter of fact, the vendor was glad to get the coffee-pot back and declared we had sold it too cheaply; in fact, he said we had almost given it away! There was no unpleasantness with him, so it turned out all right.'

I was staggered to hear this, suspicious, however, at the same time.

'Was the vendor a dealer?' I asked. 'Does he come to the sales here?'

'Well, yes, and we do know him, but I'd rather not say anything about that. Not now, please.'

Suspicion only needs a link or two to race ahead in this small world, but suspicion and reflection travelling as far as may be are not conviction. The helpful grey-suited client waiting with me at Sotheby's, so kind he was, so anxious for me to have faith in that coffee-pot, to keep and enjoy· it. Did it belong to him? Was he that mysterious vendor? I have never known. I did see him later, not in that sale-room but buying silver in Kent and never associated with any coffee-pot. Perhaps his fingers had been burnt with it as badly as mine might have been. I shall never know.

I had learnt a severe lesson. Authenticity and condition are never very far apart: repairs, damage and interference in metal objects can be just as detectable as the age of a panel painting, the craquelure of paint or the weave of a canvas. Over-painting and the presence of modern paint I could easily discern, but repairs in metal work, the subtraction of little plates with genuine silver marks from small, inexpensive articles and their insertion into larger artefacts to pretend age and magnify value, to detect these needed close examination. Of course, nowadays the pocket ultra-violet lamp soon betrays an alteration, but only a tyro would use that in the sale-room where the dealer knows by experience alone. I recall a bewildered client asking the famous dealer Schidlof for an opinion, showing him a great silver tankard that might have been Renaissance, and Schidlof pulling at his moustache with the words, 'It takes more than one look, this. But don't be mistaken. These things always look new, they always look new. They make them look new to send into a sale.'

With the Trade it is a different matter: nothing pleases a silver man more than to see a chest of blackened silver, the crust of oxidation indicating not only authenticity but hope that no centuries of polishing have obliterated the crucial silver marks. One hopes to find such silver in old house sales, preferably executors' sales, where representatives have not had their 'family division' pick, for relatives always go for a choice of silver. Many, idly fashionable, will aver they like to have their silver collection daily in family use, taking pride in tableware and domestic ostentation; unaware how soft a metal silver really is, they never protect the marks and ignore the fact that the beautiful, loving shine which pleases them is proof of the wearing away of their treasures. This made me tire of collecting silver utensils for everyday use. Either they become dull or someone insists on polishing them out of their status.

So I came to the conclusion that folk who polished antique silver for their table were misguided and gave my own objects one final polishing so they could shine in a few country auctions, for I soon resolved to abandon such a trend to acquire antique English silverware for display as utensils and, led by the same motives as in my other collecting, decided to acquire only objects that could justify their presence as works of art or, even on a somewhat lower basis, as curios.

Fortune favoured me, for the 'recession' in silver prices was over, so that the pendulum had swung to my advantage. Auctioneers photographed several objects for their catalogues, and the sums obtained were many times my previous expenditure.

There was one item with which I could not bear to part, utensil though it is, and I have it still, a silver cruet with attractive ball-and-claw feet, George II clear hallmarks. Alas, when I bought it, one bottle was missing! There had been so much to see in that auction at Kentwell Hall in Suffolk that I had not noticed this lack!

That old red-brick mansion with its moat had been often used for film sets. The late owner had stuffed the house with stage props and scenery, armour and oil paintings, period furniture and anything to bring the Tudor mansion into some historic reality upon celluloid, so that all those contents seemed far from the height of excellence, all except that cruet which caught my fancy until, as I took it away, an empty space showed it was minus its castor. Even today I am still enchanted by the design, well cast and solid, with the cut glass of the bottles throwing silver shine around the group, and do not wonder that I kept it, utensil as it was and deficient. Then, one day, years later, I attended a sale in a barn beside the red-brick Hatfield House. It was Derby Day, and a television set adjacent to the auction was distracting us all. I had intended to add some large and decorative Irish silver potato rings to my collection but noticed under the exuberant and bouncing leaf decoration modern silver marks betraying the distance from the Regency period. Nevertheless, their weight and mass of cast silver lifted the price of all four of them into more eager pockets than mine. Then the sale prices fell, as they often do following anything spectacular, and I bought a silver castor for £45.

On checking after the purchase I realized I had bought as nearly as could be that missing castor from my George II cruet! The castor's circumference fitted into the cruet, the hallmarks fitted the period in a lucky coincidence. Perhaps I had the actual individual that had neglected to wander when its fellows travelled in their frame! This is something that experience teaches. The best things for collecting do not always become finally anchored but will travel on and on until they come to the web where the serious collector waits.

I had thought to give up any hope of making a collection from a profitable turn-over in silver objects. The values were all known, computed and characterized by weight, dated hallmarks and listed silversmiths. The little pack of dealers that turned up everywhere seemed to settle market prices. The only way to profit would be to buy in the depths of a recession, hold – and tightly hold – to sell at the top of some rising market, as I had by disposing of my tableware in Kent, treating a collection rather like stocks and shares, verily a doubtful way of making money or enhancing a collection, for, although it is successful financially, when objects have been disposed of at a profit because the market has risen, how can they be replaced or bettered? When the market has fallen again? But the art market moves in far less calculable ways than the stock markets, and more slowly, and lifetimes can go by before taste and fashion change. Already pension fund investors and other financial wizards have calculated that a comparison between art-price rises and regular investment return at compound interest gives the advantage to a balanced Stock Exchange portfolio.

Despite these ponderings, I had the vacillation of purpose that affects so many collectors. The attraction of silver-collecting seemed to have enmeshed me. I resolved to try at one more house sale. I had been impetuous, had jumped off on the wrong foot and been rash and over-confident in collective sales, but silver that had been long cherished in the possession of old families would hardly have remained there if spurious.

So I went to the Depperhaugh in East Anglia. Not far from Sandringham, the house had hosted the Kaiser in pre-World War I days. The chair in which he was wont to sit was listed in the catalogue. There might be imaginative Continental silver there. it was snowing on the day of the sale, and items were carried out into a marquee on the lawn. Porters held them up for display, almost freezing as they did so.

A large picture was carried out soon after I arrived, and the frozen porters held it clumsily, blocking the view of a client wrapped in a warm coat and fur cap. The bidding commenced. Slowly the Continental gentleman waved from the depths of his fur coat. The auctioneer took a bid from the wave of that arm, and the porters moved the picture for it to be more clearly seen, as they thought, from the direction of those masterly waves. The hand went on waving. The auctioneer took his bids. Over and over again the hand waved. Half a step at a time, the shivering porters shifted their huge canvas, the auctioneer's voice rising in delight at each gesture. At last that great picture was full in face to the fur coat, presenting yards and yards of green paint surrounded by the glaring gold of its gilded frame.

The Continental gentleman threw up his arms in horror and turned away. Down came the hammer, and the auctioneer, as he enquired his name, raised a congratulatory smiling voice to the Continental gentleman, who denied the bid with indignation! In the cold of that tent sparks of anger began to fly as the crowd were told, in a Continental declamation, that the picture was not worth house-room, better put it in a cattle market. The auctioneer called his audience to witness that obvious bidding. The client's friends, who had also wanted to view the picture, shouted in his defence. The auctioneer suddenly perceived how the status of that vast mass of oil and canvas was falling as with each exchange of repartee the crowd shouted its appreciation. He must have realized that his preliminary patter about the Kaiser and this picture had been wasted. No doubt he had some twinges of conscience also, for who was the under-bidder against those sweeping handwaves?

Suddenly he cried, 'Next lot, please! We run short of time!' Then, turning to the assistant clerk, as if he were the offender, 'Take his name!' he shouted. 'A bid is a bid.' But the clerk, hurrying across and making a show of pencil and notebook, took nothing but groans. As the high fur collar went up, the fur cap stalked out of the marquee.

Halfway through the sale that picture walked mysteriously back, the legs of two porters showing underneath. The auctioneer, poker-faced and humourless, brushed away one more attempt to secure a bid until just as mysteriously, like a donkey in a pantomime, the huge picture trotted out of the sale.

By quite a rising of human temperature, the incident had warmed up the marquee. The auctioneer associated one or two further items with the occasional residence of the German Kaiser in pre-World War I times. I myself rose to the occasion and bought a nice silver teapot of William IV's reign and several other smaller pieces of that early nineteenth-century period. Apart from the association, mythical or otherwise, of that plain round pot with the ill-fated German Emperor, its possession caused me to develop further my admiration for the style of post-Regency silver and to collect it where and when I could. It achieves a pause between the flamoyance of the Regency times and the drift into decoration of the Victorian. The period is scarcely supplied but unsought after as yet, and I value the few good items I have chanced upon not by frantic search nor reckless spending of money but by moving around and happening to be where opportunities are likely.

Once, I remember, Watson's of Bishops Stortford had a charity sale in aid of the Cheshire Homes. Generous folk had sent in odd items of silver, and among some of these I bought a heavy Argentinian maté cup complete with its platinum infuser stem. Bizarre and romantic, like a large flower, supported by an active parrot, it now conjures up visions of gauchos drinking on the pampas, or else wide verandas with Argentine grandees in mid afternoon sipping their maté tea.

Though I did not know at the time, to those dealers in Watson's sale-room it was only 'foreign silver' without any promise of profit, but what a delight for my eye to recognize another version in the display case at the Victoria and Albert Museum and to realize quite immodestly that mine was far the better example!

Now I often stand my two teapots side by side and gloat over the contrast: the silver that has travelled from South American cattlemen and the fine English teapot with the woodland leaves and twig upon its lid from the Kaiser's residence at the Depperhaugh in Norfolk. The pampas are far away, but I can well imagine the prim

Edwardian maids in their black and white duty dresses bringing in the tea tray on an autumn afternoon when the Depperhaugh hosted their German guest.

Someone else had bought the Kaiser's magnificent chair – I had seen a grander one made for him like a cavalry saddle at the palace in Corfu – but I had the Kaiser's teapot and had come out of that Norfolk sale in triumph!

Once I dropped in casually to Phillips' silver sale, a sale which is deadly serious and has neither room nor time for trifles. I had not been to view the lots, and any attempt to do so made me feel even more *de trop*. A large silver coffee-pot came up; lotted as Maltese, it stirred my interest. It was heavy silver but, of course, 'foreign silver'. Nevertheless, since it was antique and of a bold and massive design, it fetched £450. The shape and the effulgent style attracts me, haunts through my memory even today, though it is over twenty years since I saw it sold and suffered that pang every collector feels when a coveted artefact passes into another's hands.

The next lot that was produced was a vase in old and blackened silver, the metal thick and cast. Men in chain mail were shown fighting a great battle upon its sides, but it was impossible for me to see more, and even while I hesitated, the bidding finished at £120 and the sale had moved on. No one's name had been called as purchaser. There was that detectable hesitation in the auctioneer's voice. His eye had swept the room searching for another bid, so that I was half sure the vase was unsold. I sat through the sale and waited for the queue of buyers to pass the desk and then, seeking my opportunity, asked the clerk haphazardly enough, 'Did that black vase, lot number so-and-so, belong to the same vendor as the Maltese coffee-pot?'

He looked it up in his book, 'Yes, it did.'

'It was not sold, I believe?'

'No, I am afraid not.'

'And the reserve price?'

'£145.'

'I will give that, please!'

It took me very few seconds to write the cheque as he scribbled the delivery note. Wonder of wonders, the vase was mine!

I dared not look at my treasure before reaching home, and then I realized. The whole scene of the Fall of Troy was sculpted there, cast in heavy relief: the bannered towers, a warrior flung from the battlements, mounted cavalry charging, Hector in his chariot challenging, shields engraved with the threatening faces of heroes, bowmen and lancers in ancient chain mail, infantrymen locked in deadly struggles while all the weapons of war flew around as in that famous siege. The epic lore was continued on every space the silver vase allowed.

It seemed I had stumbled upon a masterpiece, perhaps one brought out of Greece or Asia Minor by the warring Knights of Malta when making their forays against the Muslims, perhaps found in some Crusader castle of the Middle East. Years before, I had lingered in the famous silver market of Trabzon and chatted with the Anatolian silversmiths there. The Byzantine emperors had set up their rival palaces on that hinterland, secure in the deep ravine. Who could tell from whence the artist of my vase had come? Perhaps indeed from far Tbilisi in Georgia, although there was no Georgian inscription anywhere.

And then I turned the vase over and looked at the base underneath! Unprepared for the shock, I was staggered, for the metal base was new, perhaps no more than 150 years old. The Ottoman silver marks were there and of that date, clear enough, and alas, a crude kilted figure was engraved to balance his sword and clumsy shield. As depicted, he was not even standing upon the ground, his legs carried no weight of his body as he waltzed in a townscape of palm trees before some mosque, some building that might have represented Cairo – at that time, of course, within the Ottoman Empire. This was why no one would buy that treasure! No one except such an optimist as myself ...

Only a moment or two of pondering and my delight returned. Of course, the bottom had been repaired with a new plate, and a dozen explanations could be imagined for the removal of the original. The silversmith, probably an Egyptian, had done his best with the repair. He had tried to depict a Greek or Turkish warrior in the ancient style but had overdone his unsuccess by surrounding it with a garlanded chain of flowers. His burdensome effort, coupled with the important silver marks stamped upon it, had made a troublesome task in a place that need never be seen but proved the high regard in which the treasure had once been held, evidence ignored by all those silver men in Phillips' auction. Of course, in their fashion they were right. How could they sell the Tale of Troy to their clients or talk about Trabzon, the silver market and the imperial Byzantine palaces.

So elated was I with my discovery that I ventured to take it for comment to the British Museum, going from person to person until I came to Sir Pinder Wilson, the head of the department in this connection. I had some little trouble convincing him that I was not engaged in an exercise preparatory to selling the vase but only seeking comment. Medieval silver of that kind was so little known that he could only advance the same opinion as I gave him, except that he was sure the sculptor had used a pictorial image from some old drawing of the Homeric tale – an old print, maybe. Perhaps I might come upon it one day. Perhaps I may, but in the meantime the battle is shown there clear and distinct, not in paint, neither in printer's ink, but cast in the silver of that ancient land, echoing the most enduring of epic poems, and it ranks as one of my greatest treasures.

In this latter part of the twentieth century scientific methods have been developed for examining works of art. There is the more powerful magnification by progressing through the optical microscope to the scanning electron microscope which allows identification of minute micro-organisms in the physical material in a painting, the canvas fibre or the deposits on a panel.

The most used and almost ever-ready technique is the ultra-violet lamp, under which linseed oil or varnish coating will fluoresce very pale pink, which, after oxidation and molecular degradation have set in with ageing, will vary in intensity. This will betray any restoration work – as, for example, in those four distinct varnish layers on Rembrandt's *Jacob Trip* in the National Gallery that reveal the history of the painting's restoration. Modern remedial work on bronzes or repairs to porcelain becomes visible immediately under the ultra-violet light unless some animal or vegetable glues have been used or a recent soap washing distorts the response.

For detection of some forgeries, however, the secrets revealed by X-ray photographs are instantly shown by the lead constituents of the white pigment. Increased knowledge and use of micro-chemistry enable actual identification of the artist's pigments. If a forger used paints that were unknown in his day, such as prussian blue (developed in Berlin, 1704-7) or cadmium yellow (unused before 1834), ultramarine instead of the expensive lapis lazuli, the palette anachronism is obvious to the chemist at once, and, of course, even the Trade knows how to look out for and beware of the use of viridian in a pre-1838 painting.

Anyone dealing in the art market can be temporarily thwarted by misinterpretation of skilful over-painting to an old picture. The brief viewing and the press of onlookers the day before the sale do not give a potential buyer much latitude. If a picture is in a sale-room, over-zealous enquiry and examination can be resented and frustrate a deal. Once a doubtful picture is bought, anxiety redoubles and the need for verification also. The collector himself may find confidence failing, construing lack of judgement in the quick decision of his own eyes.

So I felt when I examined a panel I had bought at a sale in Birmingham. It was unframed and had been lying under a table in that old sale-room of Islington Row. The picture was dirty but the panel appeared quite new, yet just such as supported seventeenth-century Netherlandish pictures. I had seen many such oak panels looking as new as this: sometimes restorers have cleaned them at the same time as the picture, actually planing down their reverse side; sometimes re-framers would to this also, even cutting down the panel to fit the frame. Maybe that had happened in this case, the picture being discarded while its frame was fitted to some more saleable painting. My first glance indicated that it was disreputable market-wise, a representation of the famous Van Dyck, Charles I, with horse, equerry and groom, painted for the martyr king about 1635 – the picture which 'escaped to France' and is now in the Louvre. While the panel impressed me as old oak planed smooth, the painting filled me with doubt, for it was not direct upon the panel but on something such as parchment or paper laid down upon it.

I dared not look further, for I was then known in that sale-room and any interest shown could provoke underbidders against me, so with a wry face I put down that piece of wood, even refraining from marking my catalogue till I had moved far away. The lot was knocked down to me for, as I remember, about £12. Not bothering much, I collected it with my other purchases. Another of my gambles, I reflected, and gave no attention to it for some time. When I did dust the surface, I was puzzled, for the reverse had been cleaned and smartened as if to remove deep identity marks. Though I am experienced in reading the age of these oak panels and can reckon to half centuries on them, having handled so many, I could say nothing about this. Neither could I go by the craquelure either, since the paint was not on canvas nor on wood but lay down as flat as if on parchment or some kind of leather. Yet the paint had influenced the picture's surface and could be on paper, old, thick paper laid down.

So it could be a print, yes, and that was why I had it so cheap, with probably just my old friend the auctioneer running me up against the reserve, with no underbidders at all, thinking I could well afford that £12.

I took down from my library shelves Wilenski's magnificent books *Flemish Painters* and there Volume II, plate 644, was a good photograph reproduction of the famous picture. But in mine there was an extra leaf painted bottom right against the stump of the tree, and writing which could be read as an inscription or a signature or both, not so obvious as that upon the rock in the bottom right of the Louvre picture. The explanation for the horse's open mouth is clear in my version, for the horse has dropped a piece of gilded cloth equipage which he is chewing; King Charles also has an ostrich plume trailing, and in my landscape the ship, clearly painted, is in full sail. Other small differences pointed to my picture's individual existence. Was it, however, merely a print taken from some other version, heavily over-painted in oils, even no more than a contemporary artefact? Certainly King Charles himself would have been gratified to have many such regal versions in circulation, for it was cunningly composed to flatter him. Though short of stature himself, he was depicted as taller than both the equerry and the groom, towering above the restive war-horse they are holding, as, hand on cane, sword in his royal sash, he looks serenely, loftily even, out of the picture over the heads of mere mortals who might be watching.

As I looked and made comparisons with the pictures, doubt alternated with conviction. The faces were different. The groom's beard was not so neatly trimmed nor the moustaches pointed, and the King himself not so intelligently refined but more powerful, even arrogant. Enough to justify the picture as a sketch for an alternative version. Of course, the crux to be decided was whether it had been first done on paper by pencil or silver point to determine the great picture, then perhaps finished off as a presentation version for one of the King's friends, or whether – bathos that might follow hope – it were an over-painted print!

A London auctioneer once confessed to me, 'Well, we haven't time for all this investigative stuff. The end of a safety pin will tell us, if it is on paper at least, and more besides.' But my picture was on paper! To place it in some London auction would be to say goodbye to it at little more than the face value for which I had bought it, though now surrounded with a suitable frame.

Perhaps the Courtauld Institute's laboratory could determine something of the matter in a better fashion than a safety pin. I had been a Friend of the Courtauld since they were started and would try them. I knew that the major auction houses and dealers sought their help quietly and without ostentation. Having made an appointment, I arrived with the panel unframed but carefully wrapped. I passed the minion grudgingly guarding the door and went through and across the garden to meet Mr Rees Jones. Pale, tall and thoughtful, he listened patiently, and we went from his study into the laboratory, where the panel was put through all the procedures I had learnt about, bright lights, microscopic examination, tiny dissection of a fragment of paper carefully done and earnestly explained.

The picture was not a print, nor could he find traces of a drawing beneath, but it was on paper.

'Had the paper always been on that panel or had it been stuck on after the painting?'

'There are no folds,' he answered, 'but the wood of the panel has moved as it changed with time, with the paper constant. No, it could be that the paper was applied to the wood before all the picture was done.'

'So you don't think it is a print, that paper?'

'No,' he replied. 'It is paint on paper and not a print.'

He had taken all this time, nearly half an hour. I was effervescent in gratitude.

'Would you say it is by Van Dyck?'

'Oh,' he replied, smiling, 'that is not for me to say. Others could decide that.'

'Well,' I continued, 'it would be good to determine. You see, whether done by Van Dyck himself or some pupil under his direction, I regard it, now you have proved it is not a print, as a Royal Picture.'

The professor's face changed. I read his thoughts clearly as in a book. Some casual decision of his might be spread over the pages of a tabloid newspaper under the heading: 'A royal discovery! The portrait that survived Cromwell and the Puritans.'

He was going to have none of this. His changed attitude promptly showed he would not hang his reputation on that line. As once again I thanked him, pleasant as he was, duty called him; he must return to his work, and wisely uncommitted he retreated into the security of his study.

I came away more than happy. Not an over-painted print but on old paper with a seventeenth-century oak panel! Who would require a portrait of Royalty in those succeeding days of the Commonwealth when likenesses of Oliver Cromwell were grudgingly in demand? No wonder this sketch for Van Dyck's main picture went into limbo, its frame given to something more fashionable! The finished picture in the Louvre is attributed to about 1635, and it could be that William Dobson, Van Dyck's assistant and favourite pupil, had the major part in the preparatory work for it. Certainly in Dobson's portrait of Endymion Porter (National Gallery, London) are the features of the groom with his slight beard and hirsute upper lip, while the other, younger groom turning his head away at the back of my picture is the same, with hair-style and open mouth in silhouette. Both features have the identical lower lip. My panel gives a rougher and more robust impression as against the slender sensitivity of line and refined style of that master: ostrich plumes extend from the regal hat, and the right-hand side carries more detail and is more sketchy and unfinished than the larger picture in the Louvre.

I have had the painting all these years before gradually recognizing the hand of William Dobson, directed by and working for the great Flemish master. Too easily does our own cultural history come to be ignored by reverence for an accepted establishment. Obviously there were native painters in the land from the time of the Wilton Diptych to Hilliard and Isaac Oliver, long before the foundation of the Royal Academy. They existed without the recognition a foreign style could provide, unrecognized not just today but by their native contemporaries.

William Dobson is a striking example. He was apprenticed to Robert Peake, a dealer and portrait-painter afterwards knighted by Charles I, who arranged for him to copy pictures not only after Titian but by Van Dyck himself. Such was only journeyman work, however, and when he left to paint on his own account, recognition continued to elude him until Van Dyck happened to be going along Snow Hill where he was surprised by a picture set up for sale in a dealer's shop window. Astonished by its merit, he enquired of the painter and found Dobson toiling with his work in a miserable garret. Van Dyck rescued him from such poverty and provided patronage and employment. Soon he brought him to the notice of the Court and recommended him to His Majesty's protection. On Van Dyck's death in 1641, Dobson was appointed Sergeant Painter to the King. He travelled with the Court to Oxford, where he painted the King's portrait as well as that of Prince Rupert and lived in a glow of recognition painting the nobility around the throne, a short-lived splendour for him as his fortunes fell with the melancholy destiny of his royal patron. His art was not required by the new regime and could not provide the income to settle his many debts. The prison into which he was thrown began his ruin and, though rescued by a patron's intervention, he died in 1646 at the age of only thirty-six years, an Englishman who had won the esteem of the greatest collector of the time, Charles I, and the fellowship of his sponsor, Van Dyck.

That little panel I had bought from under the tables in the Islington Row auctions must have drifted through family possessions of folk unwilling to assert any Stuart associations, drifted for a couple of hundred years or more until, without provenance, undistinguished even as a copy, stripped eventually of its period frame, its face value masquerading as a varnished print, it came to me.

Some collectors may regard my enthusiams as over-optimistic, but they are the supreme pleasures of a real collector, so it matters not at all, nor can any denigrating argument destroy my delight. Each picture takes its stand along my walls beside its neighbours, and holds its place there by its own instrinsic merit, its power to give joy and stimulate my own pleasure in acquiring knowledge, so that I shall never go to the Louvre without more enjoyment than contemplating the famous Charles I painting where it hangs in splendour within those galleries. Shall I grow tired? Will seeing the work of Van Dyck himself triumphing there shake my satisfaction? Time will tell, but I do not think so, for in that picture also, in the two grooms there, I detect the work of William Dobson, Sergeant Painter to His Martyred Majesty, just as it shines in the portrait of his own Endymion Porter!

8   Fakes, Forgeries and Deceptive Copies

Though there are continually advancing techniques to determine forgeries based on analytical examination of materials to allow for comparison of the periods of manufacture exposing metallurgical processes, while neutron activation analysis, atomic absorption spectroscopy and X-ray fluorescence spectroscopy allow for the examination of very small samples from the object which add to evidence confirming suspicions of fraud, there must be suspicion first. And this suspicion, as far as works of art are concerned, is a matter of the eye by which, acting like a computer, the brain stores and assembles its memory bank of associations, so that an individual, blessed with the gift of complete recall, can develop over long years of experience in art appreciation an automatic realization and sense of values.

Providing this memory bank is stored with images of the truest kind, it can differentiate, for example, between a painting by Willam Blake and Fuseli. Only enthusiasm and energy over an active life can cultivate this, and an individual who has the greatest enthusiasm for a particular artist is likely to be the better judge, according, of course, to the extent of his experience. The snobbish quip levelled against Ruskin that, by his criterion, the policeman at the National Gallery should be the better judge has no validity at all and only shows how stupid dogmas are.

As a young collector I was misled by the assertive theory that all genuine old paintings had a hard paint that would never respond to solvents. It was presumed that painters, like rich men, would buy the very best, using the most expensive materials to make their pictures. The test of a genuine old painting once was whether it could be destroyed by certain solvents. I remember being impressed by a 'runner' who came into Wengraf's Gallery off Bond Street carrying an old canvas. Pleasantries and discussion led into an argument

which was settled by the painting's being stood on an easel while
Wengraf literally scrubbed its face with a wad of impregnated
cotton wool. The 'runner' looked on with some anxiety as
Wengraf's face expressed the determination of a dealer not to be
duped. Then gradually a woman's face, with clear and smiling
features, appeared out of the gloom within that dark canvas.
Wengraf reached for his chequebook while the 'runner' grew taller
and smiled triumphantly.

Yet such a test so brutally applied could have ruined, and
unjustifiably so, a good painting. The assertion that ancient
painters used only good and indestructible paints does not
universally hold true, and I know now that some of the paintings I
myself have 'cleaned' and tossed away as fakes merely because of
paint quality could have been authentic works. It is a myth that
artists of old times never used inferior materials. This may have
been so in the case of the greatest masters, with their studios full of
pupils and apprentices mixing paints and laying grounds, but
always there would be unestablished poorer artists trying hard to
make a living on their own. Especially was this so in Italy. When
attending a lecture at the Royal Society of Arts on the subject of
conservatism in early Italian painters, I was surprised to hear
quoted instances of contracts by ecclesiastical authorities specifying
that only good-quality paints be used, and I was able to ask the
lecturer if cases were known of these old painters ever using inferior
paints.

'Yes,' she replied. 'Only recently at the National Gallery, when in
course of cleaning a painting of the period under discussion,
over-painting by some past restorer was removed, and surprisingly
it was found that the paint below – that is, the original paint of the
picture – had deteriorated as being of even less durable quality than
the restorer's paint!'

I stress this authoritative quotation, for all through eighteenth-
and nineteenth-century critical comment one finds that the test of
strong solvent is the touchstone for validity of a painting, and, alas,
it is one I have myself often employed, though far more cautiously
than Wengraf, for, if my purchases were faulty, I would have to get
my money back on re-sale by giving some new owner the chance to
acquire such valuable experience as the use of strong solvent might
provide. Linseed oil does indeed go rock hard with the centuries,
but only late in my collecting did I learn that not all old paintings
relied on this, though dealers did and even today still do.

Of course, though one maintains that the eye reigns supreme, there will always exist the craving for proof, real proof, of authenticity. Modern materials make it possible for the faker to simulate age and paint with varnishes and pigments which defy solvents. Provenance also can be provided. Nowhere is this illustrated more pathetically than in the quest by the collector I never cease to admire, old Arthur Kay, who devoted so much energy in attempting to prove that Raeburn painted an early portrait of Robert Burns which he had acquired. All his correspondence, all his researches into canvases and into the lives of Nasmyth and Raeburn, amount to nothing so much as his concluding remark in *Treasure Trove in Art*: Oliver & Boyd, 1939. 'The true test of most things is living with them.'

I have kept a copy of the *Daily Telegraph* for 14 May 1979, on which two faces of Sickert's *La Giuseppina* are reproduced with the caption, 'The painting on the left is a fake.' How so? I read and re-read a good half page of print and found no answer except arguments about source and provenance between the Mayfair dealer Mr Marshall Spink, Dr Wendy Baron, Miss Lilan Browse and a previous owner. The caption over the photographs declares boldly, 'Slavish imitation of brush marks and details betrays forger.' But it does not, for they are not there, not in those photographs; in fact, the picture on the left declared as a fake seems more hurried and more likely to be genuine than its companion.

How typical is this reaction! When a picture is condemned, the rejectors will seldom place their reputation on the line by precise illustration, while the owner, after failing to justify his possession by the delight it gives, falls back on previous owners, buyers and dealers to substantiate authenticity.

It happens that I have also been intrigued by Sickert and have a sketch of a flower-seller made by him. His life was far from the gray and black of his paintings. His persistent letters to the newspapers used to be amusing enough, but I had friends among the East London Group to which he sometimes gave talks and encouragement. One of them was employed by Sickert to accompany him with a camera and take photographs of 'paintable subjects' at what was at that time the reasonable wage of £1 a day. He had then reached almost the final stages in eccentricity, would make hasty drawings, leave works behind, lose others he had done quite fecklessly, give away paintings to landladies and make pictures, sketches and copies of work he had completed long before, like someone retelling an old and favoured recollection. Often he was in debt, and often he disappeared, leaving his debts behind.

Well-wishers at the Royal Academy made a collection to re-establish his domestic situation, for, tough as he was, nevertheless they feared for his health. They made the mistake of giving him the money outright, which immediately facilitated his disappearance for a longer time until some newspaper photographed him lounging on the south coast wrapped in an old seaman's coat and wearing a taxi-man's cap.

'The first and last purpose of Art,' he had written in one of his letters to the *Daily Telegraph*, 'is illustration!' There were lads in that old East London Group who knew he had found another 'first and last purpose' – namely, to raise ready cash. This, however, in his later years he would seldom stir himself to do, and I have no doubt in my own mind as to the identity of the so-called 'forger' of that illustrated picture, for who else could so well reproduce his own work or treat it so lightly?

If the public is unused to the quality of some particular artist because of the rarity of the corpus of work that can be admired, there is less likely to be a valid response when new unknown works come forward for presentation and acceptance. The most telling example of this is the tragedy of Van Meegeren. I take up the remarkable illustration in Hanz Tietze's book *Genuine and False* (pages 58-9) where a genuine Vermeer is illustrated opposite *Christ at Emmaus* done by that famous forger. How could it be that these downcast, lidded eyes, the sullen lips and open mouths, the lifeless hair, were ever taken as by Vermeer unless the critics were seduced by the 'orthodox' Vermeer colours when so few Vermeers could be actually viewed?

This test of quality by staring hard at the faces in a painting is almost infallible. I used to see those Continental émigrés who had come into the picture trade during and after World War II applying it regularly in the sale-rooms. The life-enhancing spirit a good artist can conjure into the eyes and into every line of a face is something few mere forgers attain, for every face is the same to them – just a figure to finish a picture. The message of kindness and enlightenment, the fancies of enticement or the terrible despair at the end, these are for original genius to depict, and only the largeness of soul in such genius can truly imagine. Indeed, in considering the pretensions of such forgeries it is not in the pictures that interest lies but in the purposes and emotions, the lives of the fakers who made them, sympathy perhaps for the motives of a few, scorn for others, but for many I am afraid one finds little but the boredom of trivia.

Some collectors have found it easy to make a collection of fakes. The British Museum had a fascinating exhibition as long ago as 1961, but it requires considerable courage for a curator to exhibit his own errors. In quantity their proliferation can be depressing, for, once a faker's defects are perceived, they seem to plagiarize everything he has, reappearing like the sadness in those Van Meegeren pictures, and any interest really lies in the human mystery that motivates such productions.

While the story of Van Meegeren is still fascinating and the Italian biography of the Florentine Ioni, boasting of his daring and imitative skills, never fails to make one astonished, our amazement springs especially from the false judgement and mistaken decisions that are exposed and held up to ridicule not just by news articles of journalists but by authoritative books full of that wisdom which becomes so much wiser after the event. Widespread appreciation or perhaps rather thirst for the art of deception causes a cloud to hover over great picture collections. The Amsterdam project set up in 1968 to help celebrate the 300th anniversary of Rembrandt's death sent two experts to the Wallace Collection to inspect *The Good Samaritan* in the office of the Director, Terence Hodgkinson, who told the *Sunday Times*: 'They took the picture to the window: after long examination and some muttering in Dutch, they produced the art historian's classic balancing act: "Interesting ... it seems to pose more problems that it solves".' The same newspaper reported in a following paragraph (4 December 1977): 'Since 1935 successive catalogues of Rembrandt oil paintings have been identifying wrongly-attributed pictures in what some connoisseurs think are "alarming numbers". Forty years ago, a Dutch art historian, Abraham Bredius, cut the accepted total from 750 to 620. In 1966 another scholar reduced it to 600. Three years later, Horst Gerson, professor at Groningen University, slashed the number of Rembrandt oils to 376.'

Now and again, as in the case of the doubts cast on the Rembrandts in our National Gallery, some new critic seeking notoriety will denounce respected works and try to impute the faker's hand. Every gallery tightens hold upon its standard works, promotes their identity and defends authenticity against outsiders, especially those new-found ones without lineage. Gradually doubt can spread to create the delusion that every masterpiece must perforce in this twentieth century be comfortably lodged and documented in some public gallery, else exist in an aristocratic collection known to the public and supported by powerful authorities.

An artefact that apes the past and fakes a presence to represent the authenticity of a bygone period makes an anachronism not difficult to detect, but by this very deceit it is offensive, being more insidious than a false idea expressed in printed rhetoric. The latter makes a violence which cannot be tolerated because of its solid thrusting existence. Yet, for all its subtlety, a forged painting, if it lives with a genuine collector, will impress that same violence upon the human spirit and in time be rejected.

While some Western collectors are seizing the opportunity to make collections of fakes, collecting the life stories of such pseudo-artists but finding them mere shadows compared with the life-style of the artists they mimic, Continental authorities destroy any proven forgery as sternly as the British hallmarking control will crush out false silverware. Most collectors regard the presence of a fake as a trespasser disgracing any collection, yet who would not wish to possess the statue once made and buried by Michelangelo to perfect the faking of an antique master? There is irony today also, for not many would care to have at home an arranged collection of fakes and sit comfortably knowing that the makers of several were in gaol or in peril of going there.

It is understood now that some of these fakers may be genuine artists impatient of recognition, who have mocked the merit of others, painting fakes in some kind of taunt against contemporary judgement. Van Meegeren was probably one such, and collectors now appreciate his own original paintings. I have even seen one sold at Christie's with the signed certificate of provenance to go with it, and, one 22 March, Hans Peter Bekker came from Belgium to buy for only £220 a pleasant oil of a Dutch hamlet signed by Hans Meegeren in his own name! The under-bidder was Larry Adler, the maestro of the mouth organ. If he retained the picture, by now it should show a handsome profit!

Jean-Charles Millet is remembered as a tragedy of thwarted ambition; perhaps the name he inherited gave him false hopes of immediate success. Member of a distinguished artist family, he was the grandson of François Millet, the world-famous painter of *The*

Angelus. Between the wars, in 1930, a tide of paintings by François Millet, Corot, Diaz, Degas turned into a flood. Police enquiries found one of Millet's paintings had been sold to a London buyer for 1½ million francs. They traced it back to the painter-dealer Casseau's workshop, where a sorry tale was unfolded.

Young Millet had drifted into debt, largely owing to loans made to him by Casseau, who was more pretentious than a mere painter and had a flourishing business as copyist, dealer and restorer. Now in the hands of his creditor, Millet had conspired to produce masterpieces in quantity and trickled them upon the art market through such dealers as would connive at the fraud. Millet was eventually arrested along with Casseau, and both were tried and sentenced.

Great profits had been made by this swindle but the reputation and also the value of the Millet family's work were corrupted, for the men who made the greatest profits were never specified, nor the whereabouts of the paintings; neither is it known even today how many of these fakes are posing throughout international collections as authentic works of the masters. In the days when this conspiracy flourished, money flew from eager collectors to greedy dealers, but the subsequent exposures blighted the art market. Cynical statements such as 'Corot painted 2,000 pictures in his lifetime of which 5,000 are in the United States' enabled budding critics to feel on safe ground when challenging authenticity, for it became so easy to throw suspicion on the unauthenticated works. Genuine pictures which had been bought by collectors in admiration and passed on as inheritances to descendants became suspected and difficult to sell without some ratified provenance. They fall easy prey to collectors like myself, for they wander forgotten through the auction-rooms, where reputable dealers will not take up the challenge of possessing them.

No one believed in that picture loitering on the overcrowded stand, nor that the six dancers gliding through a forest glade, a tamborine player leading them, was by Corot. Signed it was, but the mill-board panel had become concave by the damp of some garret into which it had been thrown, perhaps by disgusted owners afraid of its attribution. Though it carried the label of a famous Paris exhibition pasted on its back, no one looked closely. Dirty and neglected, as Lot 26 in the poorer early section of the Midlands sale it tempted no one and, affecting a vague disinterest, I bid nonchalantly and it became mine for £50. That was hardly ten years ago; only three years before, for a handwave of £25, in the same sale-room the signature 'COROT' and the suspicion that travels with it had given me another painting on board, of boatmen angling under a wooded hillside. The skilful painting of the wind moving leaves and silent waves should have alerted the sale-room folk but, luckily for me, they looked only at the signature, which, if undated, tells nothing in the case of Corot.

He was wont to impress his work with the uniformity of a manufactured stamp signature. Even the work of his friends sometimes came on the market bearing his name. A long list of his faked works can be seen at the Cabinet des Estampes in Paris, and he had gained the invidious reputation of being the most faked painter of all time. Not only was he careless, but he actually encouraged emulators and imitators. All sorts of reflective drawings and paintings became 'Corotized', yet the beauty of light travelling at dawn or departing across the evening, the flicker of moonlight and the breeze that will shake colour across foliage – no one had captured these as he did, and the message upon his pictures for those who can read matters more than the printed capitals of his signature.

Profligate as he became with his accomplishments, never guarding reputation, he scattered his wealth across the city where he had endured so much poverty. Most bountiful to the poor as well as to fellow artists, he deserved their esteem as 'Le père Corot'. The Gold Medal his colleagues gave him in recognition of his generosity must have pleasured him quite as much as all the succession of medals culminating in the award of the Cross of the Légion d'Honneur in 1846 and his elevation to Officer of the Order in 1867. He had scattered his talent, his reputation, as widely as his wealth, so all these years later I feel a strange elation not quite pride, nor triumph either, but more of duty fulfilled – in having rescued these two works of his from aspersion, from oblivion perhaps, and in having placed them where some of their magnanimity might fall with life-enhancing power upon myself or my friends.

It must be the excitement of determining authenticity, the search for the identity of the faker that has caused increasing public interest this half century. For a person still to be living, to be passing off his own work in garments of the masters through the galleries or sale-rooms, trickling them while existing as some living individual one might actually know if his disguise could be penetrated merely from his brushwork, creates a mystery like the lure of the chase. This side of the Channel the attitude towards fakes and forgers is milder, without that feeling of disgust, of treachery to national pride, the betrayal of the dead or denigration of the living. Perhaps the Englishman does not have such an acute sense of his own share in the national culture as they have in France or the Netherlands and so does not sense the blasphemy when standards are adulterated. Across the Channel fakes are condemned to destruction, guilty purveyors go off to prison, but in Britain retribution is not so swift, and only caution appears necessary, though the courts may decree recompense for financial loss to a duped buyer.

'The man is no use to me!' a dealer commented to friends after a sale in Kent. 'Restorer he may be, but he won't put a signature on a picture.' That remark, of course, prompted my curiosity, but the dealer became dumb to any of my enquiries and has never given me any chance to meet that virtuoso.

Looking through the *Daily Telegraph* on 24 March 1973, I came across the following advertisement: 'FAKE OIL PAINTINGS of genuine English, Dutch, Renaissance schools. £40 upwards: Xxxxxx Art Gallery.' The address etc omitted for obvious reasons. The need for copied examples of such 'schools' may have been real centuries ago but, remade with the rapacity of the like of that Kent dealer, how long before they masquerade as more than imitations?

Towards the seventies, quick, modern fakes multiplied, presenting a violent contrast to the older forgeries of the seventeenth and eighteenth centuries which might take a painter the greater part of a year to perfect. Yet these latter could be tested by those who were wise with experience. In post-World War II days I used to see dealers – exiles from middle Europe they, and skilled in separating the dross from true artefacts – who would stare into the eyes painted in a picture, examining the countenance more closely than a psychiatrist his client. They sought the life within the character, searching for the man who painted: for no copyist, no forger can continually conceal the personality of his style, the strength or the weakness of which penetrates every line, every piece of brushwork. A collector can become as cognizant of this as of the handwriting of a friend, in the eyes the test of their kindness, in fruit the reality of dimensions that recall flavour, or in a flower the rhythm of petals that conjure perfume.

These tests of the connoisseur are swept away by the so-called

Modern Art. How look for handwriting if the equivalent of a writing-machine is used? When Salvator Dali, hearing of the value of his signature, called for sheets of paper and triumphantly signed thousands of them, the art critics instanced this as charlatanry, impervious that it was no mere profit-taking but a symbolic attack on the very outlook of their modern trade. Picasso, when asked to veryify disputed pictures, would sign if they pleased him, regardless, asserting, 'I just say, yes, if I like the picture. If I don't like the picture, I say, no.' When years ago in Moscow I had lunch with Ehrenberg, his flat was lined with amazing Modern Art given to him by artist friends while he lived in Paris as a journalist. He pointed one example out to me which had several times been challenged as a fake. Tired of resisting such insinuations, he sent it off to Chagall, who returned it duly signed, and there it hung boldly enough and not a whit out of place beside paintings by Matisse and the other artist friends he had made in that city.

Chirico, on the other hand, took a dislike to everything he painted before 1948 and rejected them all, every one of them, as spurious. When the Tate Gallery, always so ultra-clever in ultra Modern Art, hung three paintings attributed to Giorgio di Chirico in 1963, the enraged artist declared them fakes and demanded they be taken down at once or he would tear them from the walls. The Tate accepted his dictum and acquiesced that they were forgeries. But why? What yardstick was used? Was there not once a schoolbook with the Chinese fable of the Emperor's new clothing?

Temptation once tugged at my own elbow. I had a rusty cast-iron gate which I had painted with anti-corrosive and then black paints, having rested it upon trestles, placing a large green panel of plywood to keep the drips off my concrete path. The work done and put to dry, I happened to glance at the variegated surface upon the blue-green ground of that panel and realized I had created a vision in the best tradition of Modern Art: any critic could declare the favourite contemporary sagacity – 'It made a statement.' Temptation tugged still harder at my elbow. It could advance as an entrant for the Summer Exhibition at the Royal Academy! For such a large painting I had already some good framing – and also a friend at that time most disillusioned with the committee's hanging arrangements. With his collusion, a satisfactory hoax could be set up.

Unfortunately, when the time arrived, he began to think more highly of his own pictures and backed out from associating himself with mine. Let the committee beware, for that panel with its dribble and streaks of black still holds itself ready as a potential entrant, its 'statement' becoming more and more in the ultra-contemporary fashion!

In the post-war years the confusion between ideals for wall pictures and designs appropriate only to rugs, carpets and floor coverings caused temptation to divert many an artist towards immediate profit. Even for students, Modern Art banished the necessity of making copies by sitting long hours in the Louvre. Colour reproductions of the most sought-after paintings were available, illustrated magazines and auction catalogues in colour abounded. Only folk like Van Gogh who threw paint straight from palette onto canvas were difficult to impersonate. Possessions acquired on the tide of rising prices gave distinction to millionaires whether on the Côte d'Azure or in Texas. Fakers arose who passed from clandestine forgery to notoriety and put their own signatures upon their wares to challenge the art trade and demand their own price. Two of them caused as much confusion as all the others put together.

David Stein was unusual. He had caught the twentieth-century philosophy that, 'There is no such thing as bad philosophy.' From the time of his 'discovery', he had sixteen months in which to resolve this truism during a prison sentence.

'My ambition,' he declared openly, 'was not to paint forgeries all my life. My ambition was to attract the attention both of the collectors and the public, and to sell my work!'

His British father had been a doctor engaged in research but, being a Jew, was persecuted in France during the war. He himself was born in Alexandria and lost his father at the age of sixteen. Married to a French woman, he had a home in Paris as well as London and moved between the two capitals. During the seventies his huge and rather bloated figure could often be seen lunching at Les Ambassadeurs, his glittering silver Rolls-Royce parked ostentatiously outside, just off Piccadilly, wherever it would be most likely to attract notice. He had a public gallery on Park Avenue and a private gallery in New York with a district branch in Palm Beach. The impression of wealth exuded from his massive figure.

There were five years of fortune-making in Europe for him, but in the eighteen months during which he flourished in the USA, he is said to have netted $865,000. Then suddenly he was indicted on ninety-seven counts, counts of counterfeiting and grand larceny. For sixteen months he went to prison in 'The Tombs', New York – cheerfully enough, for he was allowed to paint there and to philosophize on the art trade in general. The prison staff actually encouraged him to start a fraud bureau to help the authorities detect forgery! The Wright Hepburn Gallery arranged an exhibition in which every picture was sold, whereupon they hastened in their newly opened gallery on East 60th Street to arrange an exhibition of the pictures he presumably painted in prison!

Unfortunately for Stein, on his release from prison he found himself seized and facing the same charges in France, which were to cost him an additional 2½ years in prison there.

'It was a very long time,' he reminisced, 'but I adapted to it quite easily because they permitted me to paint.'

He came out of prison confident and self-assured. 'I did my best to be caught,' he declared. 'It was absolutely premeditated. I wanted to be discovered. Why does one artist acquire fame whilst another, who is just as talented, does not? When I asked myself this I understood. What I wanted to do was to get known, one way or another, and I chose a very unorthodox way to do it.'

No longer did he need subterfuge. He could not even remember how many fakes he had painted nor where they were, but considered the dealers had cheated him and enjoyed their profits while he was sacrificed as a scapegoat. Nevertheless, he made use of them to recoup his fortunes and openly painted pictures by the modern masters as before, placing his own signature boldly across them. He engaged the attention of Brigitte Bardot and painted her likeness in twenty-five portraits in the vein of Matisse. Seeing the American and the French interest for the British royal family, he painted the Queen in the manner of Picasso and talked of a project to serialize all the royal family. He was brazen enough to present an exhibition of imitation Chagalls and to lure Chagall himself to visit and comment upon them, publicizing the old painter's comment, 'Diabolical!', to increase his own reputation.

How different is the story of another outstanding adventurer in this manufacturing of pictures. In 1974 it was reported that Elmyr de Hory had been taken to Palma Prison, Majorca, having been arrested by Interpol in his cliff-top house on the neighbouring island of Ibiza to which he had just returned from London. A Texan millionaire, A. Hurtle Meadows, had found that he had paid over

$800,000 for paintings purporting to be by Matisse, Dufy and Modigliani, and these were now alleged to be by de Hory. The wealthy art-dealer Fernando Legros, who was alleged to have supplied them, had already been arrested in Brazil. Extradited to France, he then remained in a French prison.

From the flamboyant life style and wealth he had flaunted in the world's capitals, de Hory, now in his mid sixties, dropped clean out and into a prison environment surrounded by drug-pushers, drunks and every variety of criminal. A reporter described him (in *The Sunday Times* on 24 June 1974) as 'totally downtrodden, depressed and shattered', adding, 'If he could kill himself, I think he would.' To add to his misfortunes, the courts in Ibiza reversed their earlier decision that he should be granted residence there. A stateless Hungarian, he had cut a real dash in London during the previous eighteen months. At dinner parties he had seized opportunities to capture attention: at one, for instance, he sought an argument on art with Marlene Dietrich and found the event a useful anecdote. Immaculately dressed, he had the poise of an aristocratic *émigré*, a diplomat, perhaps, of the previous century. His three-week exhibition of drawings, lithographs and paintings had been a celebration of success.

A shrewd art-dealer, Angela Nevill, had sponsored his Chelsea show. 'The world is going to see me as a great artist in my own right,' he had told the press. 'For too long others have profiteered and used my works for their own ends. But I have never sold a picture without my signature. If I have deceived anyone, I would not be sitting in this charming drawing-room. I would probably be chained in a dungeon somewhere. Why am I always branded as a forger?' So he had complained, unwitting of the irony, of the hubris he had provoked for his future. All his life he had toured Europe making his pictures, but always he denied that he, former pupil of Fernand Lèger, ever copied the great Masters, asserting that he produced pictures only in their spirit, by their inspiration. Yet he could at the same time boast of the great galleries he had duped: 'It would be most embarrassing if I should name the illustrious institutions which display my work,' he would brag. 'The directors sitting in their luxurious offices prefer to keep quiet rather than own to their poor judgement. But maybe they have something better?'

De Hory had already achieved notoriety as the subject of Clifford Irving's book *Fake*, which portrayed him as 'probably the world's greatest forger', and this he had relished: 'Elmyr de Hory is a household name now,' he gloated. 'Before the scandal nobody had ever heard of me. When I lived in California, I couldn't sell a painting even for ten dollars. I used to go to the market in downtown Los Angeles to buy old bread because it was cheaper than fresh by a few cents.' Yet he did not altogether approve of Irving's book *Fake*, as if for insurance against public condemnation asserting, 'In his book he embroidered things I had said to such an extent that I didn't recognise them any more!'

As if making a similar insurance, he always maintained: 'I invent, I never copy. I've never pretended and I've never put someone else's signature on anything. No one can come to me and say I sold them a painting with a forged signature on it. No one!'

He also denied knowledge of the Texan millionaire's collection: 'They may have been my paintings but I certainly did not sign them. I never met the man.' Often he would repeat his proudest boast: 'People will remember me as the genius who could re-create the spirit of an artist's soul on canvas.'

Such a man had good friends who accepted him on his own valuation. The well-known American lawyer and literary celebrity Arnold Weissburger stood by him and resisted attempts to implicate him as the forger of the Texan's paintings. The leading criminal lawyer in Palma, Dr Rafael Perrera, demanded a statement of the charges against him. The first two applications for his extradition were rejected but meanwhile the uncertainty, the halting of prepared exhibitions in Japan and Madrid, haunted him. Though by now he had been released from prison, the third French extradition attempt hovered forebodingly over his existence. He tried to pick up the threads of an autobiography that would redress the balance of his life against the insinuations of Irving's book.

The threat of extradition to Paris became daily more ominous. The attitude of France to those who appear to adulterate the quality of her culture is well known. De Hory had hoped to secure for himself a nationality, any nationality – a passport – for, as he complained, 'Stateless, I have absolutely no protection!' But now, back in his beautiful villa, La Falaise, with his Ibiza cliff-top garden and none to console him but his West Highland terrier, he foresaw no prospect, no future, and was found dead in the cottage, having terminated his life with an overdose of barbiturates.

From his London exhibition he had repeated as his favourite text, 'The world is going to see me as an artist in my own right. For too

long others have profiteered and used my work for their own ends.'
Alas, he had only allowed the world to see him through his
shadows of other spirits, never by the light of his own. For, as the
sages say, drawing from their great store of hindsight, the world
bestows immediate recompense for cunning, but for recognition of
true merit, 'Chance and fortune befalleth them all.'

To an artist who has found toiling the slopes of Helicon
wearisome and the summit unattainable, the spurious glory of
proving himself 'as good as' the greatest masters is like a double
panacea, offering wealth on the one hand, revenge against the
slights of society on the other. As a cold society opened its
moneybags to buy a culture it neither understood nor truly enjoyed
for itself alone, no wonder many took what they reckoned was their
share.

Where there is human contact as in Europe and the West, ripples
of human thought and invention spread through contemporary
nations and blossom simultaneously, a revolution here, another
there, scientific discovery and the enterprise of invention running
through the nations like philosophies hardly explained by history,
contagious, and proceeding like the shockwaves after an
earthquake. So it was this mid-century with forgeries, the billows of
international faking finding smaller waves in Britain. De Hory and
Stein were giants at this trade, education by television and
photography quickened public appetite, and a host of smaller men
arose to satisfy the demand. Women do not appear to have become
involved, except as minions of this commerce. Some painters were
bold enough to advertise themselves as 'Master Fakers'.

A certain Warren Madill allowed himself to be photographed
faking a painting in his studio near London's Regents Park (*Sunday
Times*, 29 June 1975). He sold his work from a gallery actually
entitled 'The Fine Art Fake Shop', where, according to the
information he supplied to a *Sunday Times* journalist: 'For £100
Warren Madill will supply you with a Manet or Utrillo. Old
Masters like Rubens or Canaletto come a little more expensive at
£300. They are not the real thing, of course, but amazingly
meticulous copies ...' and then, as some indication of the lack of
real enjoyment of true art he expected his clients to possess, ' ... it
makes sense to put the originals in a bank, and have mine on the
walls.'

Such openness may have freed the copyist from the reach of the
law. Works of art of this kind, however, entangled in other hands

and passing from auction to gallery to collector, were beginning to bedevil the art trade of the day and providing fodder for such enterprising journalists as Colin Simpson and Brian Sewell. On 10 July 1983 the *Sunday Times* splashed an article – '52 fakes fooled Christie's' – across its front page, following by another a week later dragging in the names of the Tate Gallery and Sotheby's.

Three years before, on 2 March 1980, the *Sunday Telegraph* had exposed some Old Masters dealing with a front-page heading – '*Old Master Fakes Enquiry: Drawings Advice by Blunt.*' The following quotation gives its substance:

> They have been sold on the International market by Eric Hebborn who professed to be a British sculptor living near Rome ... Many of the drawings sold to the British Museum, the National Museum Washington, and leading art galleries in Europe have now been withdrawn from public display. At the time that he sold the drawings in London between the mid-Sixties and early Seventies for an estimated £50,000 Mr Hebborn was a close friend of Blunt. When in London he was a regular over-night guest at Blunt's flat at the Courtauld Institute where Blunt was Director, and would return the hospitality at his house near Rome. Professor Blunt introduced Mr Hebborn on at least one sale to the dealers while Mr Hebborn was staying with him. Mr John Herbert, spokesman for Christie's, said, 'It would be correct to say that Professor Blunt provided the expertise for these two drawings. We often refer to him for expertise, particularly for drawings by Poussin and Claude.'

On 3 March 1980, the *Daily Mail*, however, if I may pun, came out much more Bluntly with a whole page in which Saron Churcher narrated her interviews with Hebborn near Rome:

> As Edgar Alegre, his daily live-in Filippino companion, made tea, he explained that on the occasions when he used a middle-man it wasn't Blunt at all. 'It was William John Gaskill,' he maintained. (Mr Gaskin, Blunt's closest companion, is a one-time Army bandsman who is currently recovering from a mysterious 80 ft. plunge from a balcony at the homosexual self-confessed Russian agent's home.) 'It is absolutely monstrous to say that Anthony authenticated the drawings I sold,' elaborated Mr Hebborn, a heavy set man whose small blue eyes were almost hidden beneath a grim felt hat. 'I sent the photographs (of the drawings for sale) to John Gaskin, not Anthony. John was a band boy. He used to deal in Art on the side. He knew very little about it but he was an excellent salesman.'
>
> Still showing no anger, Mr Hebborn hoisted a carved oak chair in the

air for effect. 'A drawing is a drawing, is a drawing,' he said, 'like a chair is a chair. It's only when I sell it as a Chippendale when it is not that it becomes a forgery.'

What a nimble philosophy for a dealer! What a tale of subterfuge and intrigue, with its connotations of falling out of windows so reminiscent of Czechoslovakia and the Russians in whom Blunt confided! What was the quality of art expertise when such a man as he advised the leading auction houses, became Director of the Courtauld Institute and even Keeper of the Queen's Pictures, while the people who put him into those offices were never mentioned and it took a popular daily like the *Mail* to speak clearly, while the more voluminous ones trod gently and softly, overawed by his pretensions, just as some visitors to Bond Street will cringe before 'the gallery voice'?

9   Controversies in the Courtroom

In most instances of passing off works of art, the faker has been an artist at heart, and the records illustrate there have been efforts to avoid the accusation of deliberate fraud. Even as one reads the evidence, there arises the imputation that the forger artist involved is almost doing a favour to dealers and collectors in sharpening their sensibilities and to the public by urging them not to be led by the nose.

The Scots are more practical people, harder in temperament than those ripened and softened by the warmer Mediterranean shores. The High Court in Edinburgh listened to the story of Anthony Conduit with stern severity. His defence that dealers paid more attention to an artist's name and the dealer's label was not regarded as significant at all. He declared that he was motivated by a desire to ridicule the big auction houses and embarrass William Jackson, his former employer. He was proud to rejoice that his forgeries had duped the experts.

When his demand for an increase in salary at the Scottish gallery once known as Aitken Dott was refused, he had left, taking with him the records and ledgers kept by Aitken Dott & Son right back from the turn of the century. These had enabled him to put convincing titles and stock numbers upon the stolen labels which he could attach to every fake he painted. Thus he began to build up a profitable, though nefarious trade: four of his fakes had been sold for £3,420; one he attributed to S.J. Peploe fetched £2,400, and he was discovered in possession of seventeen others ready to be offered for sale with such attributions as W.G. Gillies and Joan K.H. Eardley. Even 'works' titled by living contemporary artists he dared to circulate among auction houses and dealers.

Scotland has always been proud of its native painters, and in Edinburgh the High Court Judge Lord Ross had no hesitation in declaring that the accused's scheme was a sophisticated fraud that had grave consequences for the art world. He sentenced Anthony

Conduit, aged twenty-nine, who had already admitted his guilt at the Sheriff Court, to eighteen months.

In the South of England, in Essex, there was a painter-collector whom I had seen now and again in the sale-rooms and who now found himself suddenly charged with faking paintings. As the case was for trial in Chelmsford Crown Court, I attended as a spectator. All the pictures concerned were of the East Anglian landscape I know so well. They were stood up all round the Sessions courtroom, making it look almost like a picture auction sale gallery.

The accused, Clifford Douce, aged forty-four, proprietor of a Colchester hair-dressing emporium, was in the dock. The confiscated pictures were on trial also, for, all on parade, they stared around, presenting their surfaces in frames like stern golden-wigged judges, as indeed judges they were, summing up in their own right to those who knew the language.

In the silence before the trial began, in the blank stretch of waiting emptiness where no one among those human beings stirred, I fell into a speculative dream explaining to myself my own intrinsic purposes: not surely to exhibit cleverness in writing but rather to unravel for myself that love for beautiful things, things that are waiting to inspire the spirit in admiration for the power of truth they invoke, and by no means merely to display that empty intelligence that takes a man promoting himself through competitive examination to the highest ranks in government bureaucracy or donnish hierarchy.

Here in this court room were to be ranked the judiciary, the summoned jurors, the accused, the bureaucracy, the legal devotees, the experts and the meandering public. Among these, as a collector, I watched attempts to mock at experts, their learning or lack of it, and triumphs one way or another seemed empty. Where amongst all these was that inheritance of individual decisiveness in art, that flair which has graced the British aristocracy and which should not in sentiment or tradition pass away to be the life-enhancement of foreigners whose judgement it is expected the British accept because they are Continentals?

As the trial dragged onward in circumstantial bits and pieces, the thought returned again and again. How hopeless: all these men trained in the use of words, how blind they are to the prospect art provides! Day by day the spectators dwindled to a number so few that the protagonists, all of them British, seemed many in comparison and tense, as if guarding their knowledge or concealing their lack of it. What did it matter? The criss-cross of answers to questions and questions to answer: would such not conjure knowledge, culture even, from the very floor of the court? As I sat there, I nurtured a hope that the purpose of my own writing might stress how the public must not abrogate their judgement, their pleasure in art, to the tyranny of the self-appointed experts but take up their own privilege as in the olden time to enjoy, to decide, just as these jurors would eventually, after all the presentations of facts by words in sentences, after all the questions answered, unanswered or lightly avoided.

The story began to unfold slowly and soon entangled itself in such a mass of irrevelant and circumstantial detail that the very threads, the sequence of incidents, were lost in trivia, travelling between forensic opinion and attempts to twist out fraud by cross-examination. At one point the defence counsel alleged that the prosecuting barrister was attempting to bully his client by demanding false answers from him, and professed to be so enraged that he walked out of the court protesting, leaving his senior pupil to take over. However, he returned after some twenty minutes, but whether to unthread or string together the patchy unravelling was quite unclear. One looked around for authentic 'experts', but only the aggrieved artist himself, Edward Seago, made an appearance, the rest sought anonymity, although auctioneers, critics, collectors, sale-room cataloguers and dealers, made an array of the deceived or the culprits, like schoolboys who had read the wrong answer-book.

Clifford Douce was an artist in his own right who for his hobby would attend house auctions looking for *trouvailles* among the pictures there, and these he would prepare for entry into sales in London or in selected provincial venues. London West End dealers have their own 'runners' searching these sales, and such individual entrepreneurs are never welcome unless they are prepared to step in and out of the 'ring'.

Douce attended the auction sale of the contents of Mill House, Lexden Road, Colchester, and bought a group of pictures bundled together into one lot. These he recognized as in the style of Edward Seago. As Seago lived in Norfolk, at Dutch House, Ludham, Douce assumed he had discovered a cache of this local artist's work and began selling them, sensibly not unloading them into one sale-room but spreading them in the most strategic way. Phillips had some; Wells & Dufy, Watson's, Boardman's of Sudbury and a number of others received the paintings, which went on their way from auction house to dealers and galleries.

Now, if a dealer buys a speculative painting, he does not content himself until he has some evidence, some certificate to guarantee provenance and authenticity. For this he might have to pay dearly to some noted museum expert or art critic. In the case of a living artist, the routine could not be easier: just by despatching a pleasant complimentary letter with a photograph to the residence of the artist, one would hope to obtain the painting's history.

It was not long before Edward Seago began receiving such letters. On returning home to Norfolk, he found three enquiries with photographs, each seeking an authenticity for a doubtful picture. Later Clifford Douce and his wife visited his home with two other pictures, which both proved forgeries. The pictures now attributed to him caused so much exasperation that he engaged the Norfolk private detective agency Barry Peachum & Co to investigate.

One day Mr Douce felt uneasy. There were noises at the rear of the hair-dressing saloon. Someone had crept round to the back and was trying to get into the shed. He saw another intruder there also, a fellow with a skinhead haircut. Well built and burly, Douce had no hesitation and accosted the interlopers. Staggered to hear their purpose, he averred that he himself had just been to see Mr Seago about paintings, asserting, 'I got the Jaguar out and travelled all the bloody way to Norfolk.'

Taxed with a particular picture, he exclaimed, 'This is all balls! The painting was 20″ x 30″.'

'I understand you do painting yourself?' queried Mr Peachum.

'So what does that mean? That I am a criminal? I bought a lot of twenty to twenty-five paintings from a sale at Mill House, Colchester, about two years ago, maybe longer, and only paid a few quid for them, with the Seagos along with them. All the pictures, as I understood, came from a private entry. As from time to time I have a sort-out before placing my pictures in sales, I took two to show the artist himself. I thought, "Good, bloody good Oh!"'

'Ah!' remarked Mr Peachum with a detective's insight. 'Mr Seago couldn't understand why you were not more worried.'

'Why should I?' argued Clifford Douce. 'I only stand to lose a few quid. Had I paid good money for them, I might be concerned.'

'Ah,' commented Mr Barry Peachum, 'at least you should have been more suspicious.'

To which the prompt rejoinder, 'How do you tell a fake

painting? Even artists are known for disowning pictures they do not like.'

By this time, as the procession of dealers and auctioneers going into the witness-box revealed, cash was being paid out and cash refunded, for pictures had been travelling back to their vendors or into the hands of the police. When his easy acceptance of cash profit for his re-sale was remarked on, one West End dealer declared lamely, 'I didn't think Seago was big enough to fake.' Another, a picture-cataloguer, Joaquín Medrano, challenged on the quality of his expertise, admitted he had examined one forgery but assumed it was real because he ' ...didn't expect anyone to try to forge anything but well-known paintings'.

Clifford Douce sat there in the dock, his face more and more concerned as the days went by. Always neat, with his Napoleon III pattern of beard, he might have been the standard artist type from an early poster. A red rose in full bloom, new each day, flourished in his lapel.

The police action in this case does not make good reading. The account deflects interest from art and painting and Seago and dispels for such as myself the comfortable illusion of the individual freedom we cherish. As the evidence dragged along, despite the long pauses for stenographers to catch up, it became clear that Anthony Scrivener, the barrister for the defence, was fighting for his client like a tiger. He cross-examined Detective Inspector Turner and any police involved in visiting Mr Douce's premises to seize possession of his paintings. He elicited that Douce had been detained in the police station without access to a solicitor. Although a Mr Humphries had seen him on the very stairs there and sought admission, he was at first refused access and then delayed as long as possible, the lame excuse being given that Mr Humphries was not an accredited solicitor but only a clerk to a firm of solicitors. The prosecutor, Brian Higgs, suggested that Humphries haunted police stations to procure business, enquiring, 'Would you say you are a man who follows crime, or does crime follow you?'

On the other hand, unpleasant suggestions were made that the police had attempted to cajole a confession from the accused, and the police did not dispute that they had threatened their prisoner that, unless he made the admission they wanted, his wife, Draga, might also be arrested and charged, remarking repeatedly, 'Either you or your wife? We don't want to involve her. You haven't any friends when you're in trouble.' The police listened on but did not dispute this account of their interrogation, until the judge, Duncan Macrae, interrupted to comment that, though it was not disputed by the police, it was a matter for complaint against them, rather than affecting what was at issue there and then. Any listener, however, could not fail to react as I did and realize that it would influence the humanity of the jury, for it was obvious that such a threat against his wife to a man held incommunicado came close to blackmail.

One by one the paintings were produced, with Mr Scivener attacking the information the police produced and suggesting they were confused, their knowledge both of art and of circumstance faulty.

One by one the dealers, cataloguers and auctioneers came to the witness-box for interrogation, each one looking as if he rued the day any Seago painting had crossed his threshold.

Edward Brian Seago himself took the stand. He was the painter. He had hired the detectives. Famous as a painter of Norfolk landscapes, he had exhibited in London his paintings reporting World War II in Italy and had sprung into fame in 1957 with his exhibition at St James's Palace of paintings made during the World Tour of the Duke of Edinburgh. It was known that pictures by him were in the royal collections. In quite a different location, he now simply gave his quiet, determined opinion on the pictures staring down all round the Chelmsford courtroom.

'I do not regard these as copies but as bogus pictures based on mine,' he declared. 'They are based on pictures of my paintings published in a book in 1967. I have studied landscape and skyscape for forty-five years. This person has done it for considerably less, and this is not the way I paint. It is like knowing your own handwriting,' he observed. 'It is handwriting in paint.'

Unchallenged, he left the Court of Sessions at once, walking straight out, as a celebrity should. (That very spring, on 17 February 1971, his painting of *The Gardens of the Tuileries* had auctioned in London for £1,300.) Any debate on authenticity was finalized. He had concluded it precisely enough.

The defence, however, produced another artist, William Burton, a local Colchester painter of 'award-winning pictures', mostly of Essex scenes, one of which *Essex Gold* was claimed to have sold 10,000 print copies. He stoutly defended Douce. He went to great lengths to illustrate how paintings that were produced as Clifford Douce's own were totally different in every respect from the forgeries and also from the original works by Edward Seago. To prove this he produced a spatula and demonstrated to a rather uncomprehending audience exactly how Clifford Douce's painting was done. When he had seen that odd bundle of pictures from the Mill House sale lying about, he had remarked to Mr Douce, 'They are Seago's; they might be worth a bob or two – or a pound or two!' As he said, to neither of them did the name Seago count for very much.

I noticed how Mr Douce's appearance was always as neat as ever, but the fresh red rose he wore each day shook as from time to time he started with anger, and his beard bristled with indignation. It was about the fourth day of the trial before Duncan Macrae had found a white rose for his own lapel, which seemed to spread a certain serenity around him, and this was so to appear right through the progression of the trial, while his questioning became more and more understanding and perceptive. Many of us, he was to remark, had now learned a great deal more about painting than we knew before.

Nevertheless, in such a controversial case the pendulum may swing either way amongst distractions of detail such as the heated argument which threw Duncan Macrae with the two opposing barristers into a kind of triple disagreement. For the defence submitted that under some Forgery Act, 1930, Section this and Sub-section that, a forgery is defined as a document which conveys a spoken message to those who can read. No case in their knowledge apparently existed showing that a painting was a document; therefore it could not be a forgery under that Act; therefore none of these paintings was a forgery! So there was no case to answer? I thought of my old friend A.P. Herbert, and how he would relish seeing real life stranger even than his humour in *Misleading Cases*. But as that argument went on, not a breath of humour wandered through the courtroom, only incredulity and impatience until the judge expressed both with his curt, 'I am not with you in this!'

Then a dealer rival to Clifford Douce, Ivor Weiss, came into the witness-box. I had often seen him in the provincial sale-rooms looking out for bargains, especially in old pictures. He had a gallery in Colchester and also dealt in picture-framing. He affirmed that he had been involved in the arrangements for the auction of effects from that Mill House where Clifford Douce claimed he had bought the paintings. He declared he had never seen the disputed pictures in that sale, and if he had, they would have been itemized separately in the catalogue. Questioned again on this, he declared, 'I am positive that the four forgeries were not in that sale.'

I was most surprised to hear his confidence, for there were blank lots in the catalogue and it is commonly known that bundles of unidentified items get slipped in during house clearance after cataloguing – often inserted by porters with just a chalk mark if they are only neglected pictures, for which in those days furniture auctioneers used to have no respect at all. Lots 301, 302 and 303 were instanced as last-minute lots – Lot 311 as 'M. Thorpe various futuristic paintings', and again 312 as 'various'.

Mr Weiss stated that in the sale he did not look at anything new, nor at Lots 311 and 312.

Douce declared, however that he did actually bid for these.

Ivor Weiss again declared that there were certainly not any Seago paintings in those bundles, arguing fallaciously that if they had escaped the notice of cataloguers, could they have escaped the attention of others? He admitted having seen Mr Douce at the sale.

The crux turned upon these lots. Another auctioneer's assistant, Mr Harker, admitted that Mr Douce had bought Lot 312, a quantity of oils, for £6, Lot 301 for 30 shillings and Lot 311 for £5.10s. and he produced a receipt confirming this. The witness said he remembered the name Seago mentioned, but in what connection he could not say.

Next to the witness-box came Charles Thorpe to say that his mother at Mill House was an amateur painter, but all he remembered of her painting was a copy of El Greco!

Now the rector of Stratford St Mary, the church so famous as once a subject for Constable, brought his memories to the stand. He had come to know Major and Mrs Thorpe in 1954, although by 1967 both had passed away. Mrs Thorpe, he explained, did paint pictures, and he remembered scenes in bright colours but nothing like those on the courtroom walls. The name of El Greco was taken in vain once more, but all the reverend gentleman could really remember was a row of trees.

The judge, Duncan Macrae, was adjusting the white rose in his buttonhole as Mrs Thorpe's former housekeeper came to dawdle in memories of the pictures where she worked, talking of women's heads and of a shop, but the pictures shown around these walls, these she had never seen.

A Mr David Cox, occupation artist, took the oath, and he

declared that he gave painting lessons and had given them to the late Mrs Thorpe. (What a pleasant survival from the days of Old Crome of Norwich to know there were still gentlemen artists going along in East Anglia giving painting lessons to ladies of quality!) As Mrs Thorpe got older, her style changed to 'cubist', he averred, but sternly looking at the exhibits, he said, 'It was not within her capacity to paint in this way.' He became most emphatic about his pupil: 'Certainly she was not guilty of such forgery. Certainly, certainly not! Seago's manner was slick. Mrs Thorpe would have objected to this manner and as for the hardboard they were painted on, Mrs Thorpe would have objected to this. Signatures? You don't put a signature on a painting except to authorize authority!

The bright sun was shining outside the courtroom as the days went by through the lovely June weather that was shut away from all these questions and answers, answers to questions. I began to see them all, these enclosed people, like actors on a stage all actually enjoying their parts, all except Clifford Douce, frustrated artist if ever there was one, his red rose flaming upon his lapel, his beard bristling with fury, but fighting to control his explosive indignation which had spread to his defending barrister, while the judge fingered his white rose and calmly wrote his notes even when Mr Scrivener, defending, irate and protesting in some raging breach of court etiquette, came very close to contempt.

The jury had looked on, almost prisoners they, racking their brains about forensic evidence, paints and solvents, hardboard and canvas, palette work or brushwork, like some schoolroom class doomed to eternal boredom even when they retired – but not I, for the June days are few and Essex summers green, and I found the air outside in the town square fresh where Chief Justice Sir Nicholas Tindal brooded in bronze, his robes shining in a timeless patina upon his famous statue.

Reporters, journalists of the East Anglian newspapers and photographers came back to the Shire Hall for the verdict of that jury who after four hours of deliberation had found Clifford Douce 'Not Guilty'. Now, looking none the worse for that eight-day ordeal in the dock but without his artist's jacket and the full-blossomed red rose, he was able to come out from the Shire Hall into Tindal Square and pose for photographers who helped him to fill a glass of celebratory wine, with Draga, his wife, beside him, smiling even more than he, while in the background on the other side of the square Judge Tindal, once famous for his courage in defending Queen Caroline, threw a thoughtful dark bronze shadow from his seat above.

Douce had brought out one of the paintings and was holding it up for the photographers when he had to break away suddenly and dash back to the courtroom for his hat and coat, which 'he suspected had been taken away by souvenir-hunters'.

Fame was destined for him, the fame newspapers provide on their wings of publicity, good or bad, and he could loftily say with unconscious, almost naïve irony of the Seago who had launched the detectives upon him: 'From what I have seen of him, he is a very fine artist. I can detect a subtlety in his work.'

10 St John's Hall, Woodbridge:
A Spectacular Sale-Room

One of my haunts throughout the 1970s used to be Woodbridge in Suffolk, where I could spend a pleasant morning loitering beside the River Deben and go to Mr George Arnott's sale in St John's Church Hall at twelve noon. I had been to the regular boat sales he had years ago and the whole location attracted. There was once a sale of the remainders, the literary bits and pieces, of Edward Fitzgerald, who had a boat there at one time and loved the place, far though it was from the sands of Omar Khayyám. Where George Arnott obtained pictures for these sales always seemed a mystery.

In one early sale I had bought a remarkable picture, unframed and so dirty as to portray apparently some goatherd grazing goats beside water that mirrored a factory. But with the dirt and varnish removed it proved to be a version of Pembroke Castle painted by Richard Wilson. A few pounds was all it cost, sold in one of the first half-dozen preliminary lots.

There is a ferment for collecting in East Anglia: collectors and dealers came to Woodbridge from as far as St Albans, Cambridge, Norwich and Epping. The local Suffolk collectors would be hunting for paintings by the brothers Smythe or Thomas Churchyard of Woodbridge, in which George Arnott of Arnott & Calver Estate Agents could claim to have cornered the market. Visiting dealers and 'runners' from the West End would be suspicious but tentatively hoping for greater finds.

I arrived late for one particular sale and found a seat towards the back. A small water-colour lying by the tables was held up for sale. Catching a glimpse of heavy body-colour and a glow of varnish upon the darker shades, I joined the bidding, which leapt away from me, for a known collector, Mr Robert Gathorne Hardy, had left a much higher bid. Nevertheless, a couple in front of me carried the price right up to £610. George Arnott hid neither his surprise nor his delight and cried, as he was wont to with expensive or frail items, 'Hand it to Mr Squire, please!' As it came across, I reached over to catch a glimpse, but Mr Squire's companion snatched it away and quickly covered it up. I never saw it again and have no idea where it is today, though I soon learned that it purported to be by Samuel Palmer, a sketch of *Shoreham Church by Moonlight*.

That price – £610 for a piece of unattributed paper in a frame out there in Woodbridge – had left the audience astounded and the auctioneer enthusiastic. He sought out the vendor, Miss Jane Kelly, who often brought paintings and sketches along, and suggested that if she had any more like that in her collection they would do well in his sale. There was a market for them. There surely was!

Well in time for the next sale, Miss Kelly brought a cardboard box which was passed over the counter at Arnott & Calver's offices. The principal feature of its contents duly appeared in the sale catalogue as *Sepham Barn*, not only fully listed as by Samuel Palmer but illustrated on a whole page to itself!

The Woodbridge catalogue had a distinctive red border design of linked flowers which I had often caught sight of upon the counters and office racks of West End galleries, and now that ephemeral little brochure travelled and brought into Suffolk Richard Kingzett from Agnew's, John Baskett of Baskett & Day and David Posnett from the Leger Galleries, amongst others of that ilk.

The porter held the picture up with both hands. George Arnott commanded him to show it better. 'Turn it round to them!' he ordered expectantly. He was not prepared for the response. At £2,000 he lost his cool and reverted to counting in hundreds. The assembly corrected him. He adjusted his figures and began again at £2,000. It made no difference, on went the bidding. Whilst everyone twisted necks to catch glimpses of the bidders, up and up the figures went for this second remarkable piece of paper till bids stopped at £9,400. John Baskett, the well-known dealer in water-colours, had dropped out.

There was a real handclap of appreciation. That quiet Suffolk audience was astounded and applauded and applauded again.

Mr Arnott, trembling with pleasure and excitement, wrote down the price, for he knew his auction-room would now be in the national press. Suddenly he looked up. 'Who was that bidding?' he asked.

No one came forward, not a hand showed, not a movement anywhere. The successful bidder had vanished.

'Where is he? That tall gentleman at the back? Where is he?'

One of the porters, old Johnson, a wily, cynical fellow who it was said had been at school with George Arnott and favoured him by helping at these auctions, developed a cynical grin.

'He's gone,' he declared. 'Run for the station. You won't see him no more!'

The assertion provoked panic on the platform and another 'Where is he?'

'Gone!' repeated old Johnson. 'Gone for the train!'

'Fetch him back somebody!' cried George Arnott. 'I must have his name!'

After a scatter from the back of the hall and a long breathless pause, a tall, thin figure with a sharp nose looked round the door.

'We must have your name, sir! You can't go away without that.'

Delight at his re-appearance mingled with obvious anxiety about his credentials. The atmosphere of dramatic suspicion infected the person concerned; the name he gave could not be heard. The auctioneer was now smiling a forced, uncertain pleasure. 'Please repeat,' he pleaded. 'I have to write it down.'

Once again the name was given, inaudible now because of the buzz of undisciplined conversation everywhere until it was picked up by some burly farming lads and shouted out, Suffolk-style: 'Leger Galleries!'

'Ah! Get the particulars!' Arnott commanded his assistant clerk and, fussing impatiently to recover his auctioneering sang-froid, as the lad hurried down with notebook and pencil, 'We must get on! Next lot, please.'

That water-colour and its price certainly brought Arnott & Calver's sale into the news. Critics and admirers of Samuel Palmer came forward to publicize their interest. The day after the sale a matter-of-fact account was published in *The Times* with an accompanying photograph of the picture.

David Gould, who had not been at the sale, immediately wrote a letter which *The Times* published in which he pointed out that the picture was no more than a pastiche from already known paintings of Samuel Palmer. He added the comment which was to prove so illustrative of the many such paintings shortly to emerge: 'To my eye it lacks the idiosyncrasy which infused Palmer's eye with an indomitable poetry.' He prophesied that so few examples of Palmer's work existed ' ... that spurious ones will supplement an insufficient supply'.

David Posnett was furious, and the whole of his firm became devoted to faith in the painting he had acquired, even to the extent of illustrating it on the cover of their next catalogue.

The lady who had visited George Arnott with her cardboard box was stirred into action. Alas for her, she and her accomplice were ignoring that tried motto of the Medici so glorious in Florence – 'Do not attract attention'! She arrived at Leger's and sold them three more Shoreham drawings, and also provided a family tree to justify a provenance so realistic that it lasted into the future so far as to be reproduced in a sale at Phillips Son & Neale on 15 December 1975, and illustrated in colour on the front page of their catalogue, which publicized the following specific provenance. (And let this be some warning to those who depend on documentation rather than aesthetics!)

SAMUEL PALMER, R.W.S.

P.46 At Shoreham, Kent: Moonlight, a View of the Village with the Church on the right, a Barn with Carts to the centre, in the foreground a Pond and a Shepherd by his fold, *signed, sepia heightened with white oil paint, inscribed indistinctly on reverse, bears label with the inscription:*'At Shoreham – drawn by Mr. Palmer – Thos. Farr, Esq.', 30cm. x 25.5cm.

Provenance: The Rev. John Farr of Gillingham, Norfolk.
Thomas Farr, Esq. who emigrated to Ceylon, circa 1868.
May Elizabeth, daughter of the above, who married a tea-planter, W.H. Douglas Kelly (1874-1967)
Major W.H.D. Douglas Kelly (1903-)
Jane Kelly, a gift of the above, her father, 1970.

LITERATURE: James Sellars, Samuel Palmer

But all this did not make a sale, for, according to *The Times* of 16 July 1976, the picture was bought in at £5,000.

By this time wandering water-colours of 'Samuel Palmer' had surfaced, glorified or denounced in letters and articles, committees of enquiry and museum testings. Jane Kelly was also about her pilgrimage, visiting potential buyers, though unwitting that dealers or shopkeepers such as the Faustus Gallery hardly ever make a purchase without delaying to solicit the known experts first. All the pictures she offered to the Faustus Gallery were rejected. Pictures began to be catalogued by Sotheby's as 'by a follower of Palmer', one unsold at £15, another getting no more than a bid of £12. Experts began to turn over leaves in the popular monographs on the painter, and one or two found these new wandering drawings to be mere pastiches, composite patchwork from photographs of paintings from the very books they themselves had written!

How simple it is now to look at photographs and detect this, forgetting that, unless a picture has to stand in an 'identity parade' with its genuine fellows, it may never be arrested even by the sincerest collector's eye!

I have myself acquired two little signed paintings by Samuel Palmer, each bought for no extravagant price a faker would demand, and long before there was any excitement about this artist: one, a little sketch of the Adriatic beside a church from his honeymoon period and the other more typical, *Moonlight over the Darenth valley*, with initials in signature scraped in the muddy road before the river bridge. Neither was attributed in their catalogues, nor were they titled, but they slept on in their sales until my own miserable bids of £2 or £3 only.

As the story continued to confuse confusion, suspected pictures began to appear even in the popular art books about Samuel Palmer. Mrs Geraldine Norman compiled a detailed list of this borrowing and faking, with the remark, 'Somewhere there is a spirited painter at work.' Alas, that painter had chosen the safest path for a forger to take – to use the work of a little-known but admired artist and to 'improve' on him.

All four of the drawings sold to Leger came to be illustrated in James Sellar's book *Samuel Palmer* (1973) and *The Horse Chestnut Tree*, which had been purchased from Leger's by Mr Colin Tennant, was catalogued by Sotheby's as genuine and in June 1973 sold for £15,000, remarked upon as the record price for a Palmer water-colour. (Sotheby's, of course, refunded this when the independent inquiry established that it was a fake. It had apparently been purchased by Mr Ramus Needler, a chocolate-manufacturer.)

In *The Times*, 11 August 1976, Geraldine Norman wrote: ' A book published by Carlos Peacock in 1968 entitled *Samuel Palmer: Shoreham and After* contains some two dozen illustrations whose attribution to Palmer the scholars dispute' – this although the book contained only twenty-four black-and-white illustrations and eleven colour plates!

The large photographs of Samuel Palmer's drawings, real and unreal, that appeared in *The Times* provoked an interest in the artist which had previously been felt only by enthusiasts. But money had been changing hands. The passion of collectors became damped by caution. The art market was thrown into confusion. Egg was on the faces of famous auction-rooms and galleries.

No doubt David Posnett considered that the more paintings they had in the style they had approved, the more the evidence to confirm their view, evidence so easy to unravel with hindsight, for certainly Jane Kelly's pictures were the work of one painter. Posnett at Leger's was looking for documentary proof by provenance.

Others, however as true admirers of Palmer, were looking for the poetry and spirit of the visionary that had delighted them. Finding it absent, to them these pictures became purposeless and doubtful. As tests began to be made and official inquiries started to probe, quite a number of imitation paintings after Samuel Palmer surfaced, giving rise to suspicions that others reposed slumbering away undiscovered, awaiting a distant but lucrative resurrection.

Egg might be on the faces of the dealers and auctioneers. It was their trade to know, so if they lost money, well, theirs was a business where money ought to be lost by ignorance. For the public, however, who needed to build up a cognizance, who relied for guidance towards a discriminating appreciation of art, to be led to worship fakes was a different matter; and, worse, the mud that was besmirching the reputation of a delicate artist by the widespread existence of faulty pastiches corrupted appreciation of the uniqueness of his talent and, if accepted, destroyed his posthumous merit, adulterating his life's achievement in the eyes of an untrained but would-be appreciative public. If some pseudo-literati went on producing Restoration dramas or odes by Keats, exposure would be swift enough. How then did Samuel Palmer's art not quickly rise to expose the meretricious unless he had been deliberately selected by the forger as 'little-known'? His rare and highly priced corpus of work was sparse and not widely available for comparison. The forger was trading on the sensitive reputation of a rare spirit, in befouling which his deed was cruel and wicked.

Something of this guilt must have penetrated into the conscience of the faker, Tom Keating, for in *The Times* of 20 August 1976 he made a qualified confession, so qualified that it by no means merits absolution. There was no acknowledgement of his 'transgressions with his sins ever before him' but a pretence of being a benefactor of the art world at large.

'I flooded the market,' he wrote, 'with the "work" of Palmer and many others, not for gain (I hope I am no materialist) but simply as a protest against merchants who make capital out of those I am proud to call my brother artists, both living and dead.' Under his oil-paintings, so he declared, 'I have written my own name or the word "fake" or even a rude remark if I felt the work would reach the target I was aiming for.'

No one came forward to point out these mysterious inserted codes that indicated his avowed purpose, and he did not return any money from sales, excusing himself lamely with 'The innocent suffer with the guilty in war.'

So for a time he lived happily, travelling on his motor-cycle and spending in Madeira until Nemesis overtook him.

From my seat in the public gallery at the Old Bailey, I watched him there below in the dock, arraigned on a serious criminal charge. He sat there, sleepy and unconcerned, scribbling with a pencil and doodling, beside others he had implicated. The gallery dealer from Constable's Dedham village, accused of purveying some of the fakes, sat there worried and tense, while Keating himself appeared unperturbed as the trial dragged on interminably with its pauses and long-drawn-out weight of slow evidence.

My own thoughts wandered away to that distant valley of the Darenth by Shoreham. Long ago the Romans had selected it for relaxation. Now the haste of journalists, masters of the news, had no time at all. In this chase of action to make a story, none felt nostalgia for that valley or associated Palmer with the whimsical poetry of its mysterious woods by Dunstall Priory, where Lord Dunsany, premier baron of Old Ireland, had conjured humour earlier this century, or thought back to the days of Izaak Walton walking by the Darenth to stalk the great chalk-stream trout, when the Roman tesselated pavements were as covered and unknown as the villa.

Today's newsmen had something quicker to capture the interest of the masses than would the delight of a few eccentrics. Here was the tale of an artist – perhaps not 'failed' but rejected – shaking his fist in revenge at the dealers and those art critics or academics who had spurned him as unknown and 'undiscovered'. Here was an artist brave enough to turn the tables on their judgement, daring enough to take huge profits from hated dealers, a Robin Hood among painters! They had a human story in Tom Keating, a story that needed no connoisseurs of art, one that could be read by a public always ready to side with the persecuted and defend them in trouble.

The stage was set and the player was ready, albeit as yet consigned to the dock at the Old Bailey.

The high prices paid at Christie's for genuine paintings by Samuel Palmer on 8 June 1976 – £18,000 for *The Bellman*, £11,000 for *The Eastern Gate*, £10,000 for *The Lonely Tower*, which, with three others, made a total of £67,000 – caught the public's imagination. No wonder the accused had specialized in this painter!

Another painter, almost naîve and little-known except in Canada, Krieghoff, could only be bought by large sums of money. The bearded figure down there in the dock had boasted he had painted 2,000 examples. Was it all fantasy? There were no specific exhibits I could see hung around the walls of the Old Bailey. There must have been plenty available, since *The Times* of 29 September 1976, reporting Keating's first visit to Scotland Yard, stated that about thirty paintings had been handed in by the Redfern Gallery for a check!

In the body of the court old black-gowned figures moved and voices halted for the stenographers, stultifying the afternoon and driving me out into the fresher air, where scarcely a London journal could emerge without some item of sympathetic news: 'Prickly and bohemian and established at one stage with a young lady at Kew, he appears to be the Typical Artist Incarnate,' declared the *Evening Standard* on 8 August, remarking on 'the widespread amusement at the sight of dealers trying to pick themselves up'.

Tom Keating had served as a stoker in the Navy and on being demobbed had availed himself of the educational opportunities offered to ex-servicemen, hoping to acquire a diploma that would provide him with a living, possibly in some teaching sphere. But that was not to be, for while his painterly technique earned praise, his student report deplored 'lack of original composition'. Nevertheless, he had bravely clung to the life in art he had chosen and accepted whatever restoration and freelance work came to hand. Little wonder people could regard him as a genius, presuming that, fostered in a more furthering environment, he could have reached the heights.

The slow progress of that trial, the enormity of Authority there, the menace of Law Enforcement, all had been bringing tensions to bear upon that bearded occupant of the dock. His idle pencilling became slower, his face deepening in colour; his head seemed heavier and he slumped as the time dragged on. Suddenly it was announced that he was in no condition of health to continue standing trial. The hearing was abandoned. Those who might yet have to give evidence and expose their mistakes and lack of discernment breathed with relief. There was no money to be got out of the defendant by process of law, and he wandered away to his old haunts, not as a criminal but as a celebrity. The letter-writers who had pontificated in the correspondence columns of the newspapers dried up.

Geraldine Norman, however, the journalist who had specialized in this topic through the pages of *The Times* from the beginning, announced that she was compiling a list of Tom Keating's works and would be writing a book about him. She appealed to owners of any paintings thought to be by him to allow her to see them so that they could be listed and indeed authenticated by Tom Keating himself, for he would be collaborating in the book.

It was my practice at the Woodbridge sales, especially after I became known, to buy worthless bits and pieces for a few pounds each. In this way, apart from some minor profit, I deterred rival bidders who either came to think me unknowledgeable or else burned their fingers when I dropped out of the bidding. Sometimes I would re-present any worthless pictures and bid them up to get a small return, thus, I do confess, contenting myself by punishing any individuals who might be bidding only to trade upon my knowledge. Once George Arnott sniffed as he got the confession out of me, 'Shouldn't have thought that necessary in your case,' he grumbled. 'Who would think you had any knowledge, not down here?'

So I had found myself in the possession of two waterside drawings, both with 'Guardi' written upon them unobtrusively but seductive to anyone looking over-anxiously.

Returning one afternoon from the Woodbridge sale-room where the name Keating was anathema and totally banned, I decided to turn aside and see his studio in the cottage at Dedham. It might be quieter now. Perchance I might come across the celebrity who had become so elusive and gone to ground, although, as I drove down the deserted drive there, I remembered the report in the *Evening Gazette* of 20 August 1976: 'Mr Keating was still missing from his rented cottage at Lower Park Dedham. But the owner, Mr Michael de Muscote, has demanded that he come home and explain himself.

"It's about time he showed up and told us what's going on," he said. "In the past two weeks, since the controversy over the imitation paintings broke, hordes of photographers, reporters, and film camera men have trooped through the grounds" ' And in another interview with the press: ' "This is not the sort of thing we want to be mixed up in," said company director Mr de Muscote.'

I parked my car outside. The little two-storey house was empty, its windows without curtains, the grass-grown garden deserted. Inside, scanty bits of furniture did not conceal old discarded garments, woollen socks cast upon the floor, but nothing, absolutely nothing told of an artist. There was not a canvas, stretcher or panel, no colourman's packages, neither palette nor easel, not even spilt paint on the floor or the walls and, as I walked around, neither poultry nor chickens to chat of life in the country.

Then at the back I came upon the pond! There were ducks paddling upon it, four or five of them in a scenic style with the cottage for background! They were the ducks I knew in my two pictures, surely these same Suffolk ducks but transported by pencil to Venice, paddling on a canal with the glorious name of Guardi scribbled above them. Without a doubt they were Keating ducks, and this was their pond! They only needed his name in the bottom right-hand corner. What fun! I would write to Geraldine Norman and get this trifling detail settled. Certainly Keating's works were 'collector's items' and might more than earn their keep. So in due course I responded to that appeal and delivered both drawings to the offices of *The Times*.

It was some weeks before a telephone message came and I called to collect them at Geraldine Norman's flat in Baker Street, appropriately enough not so far from the fabled residence of the renowned detective.

'No,' she broke the news gently as to one in for great disappointment. 'He doesn't acknowledge them. He knows nothing about them.'

'But I left them for him to sign!'

'He won't do that if he says he didn't paint them.'

'Well, then, I know his signature. I can easily sign for him.'

'Don't you dare!' she forbade. 'He has seen the pictures and he won't have them as his. If you do that, there will be no end of trouble. You'll see!'

I think she realized I was merely being provocative, for she began trying to impress me with the importance of Keating, with his ability as a genuine painter of merit who had the capacity of a genius. The walls of her study were hung with paintings and drawings, mostly water-colours, from ceiling to floor, some acquired, some presented to her in consequence of her being a newspaper art critic. Two she pointed out to me as evidence of her thesis on Keating. They were small water-colours done by him with infinite care and extraordinary, unnecessary detail, fussy without purpose but decorative and meticulous. I was surprised, for nothing I had seen or for that matter was ever in the future to see by Keating came near them, and they represented clear evidence of the forger who, with no dynamic style of his own, can force his mode of expression like the genie into the bottle, shaping to any style.

I did not sign those two drawings. They still repose within a dusty folder in one of my back rooms, but my expectations eventually came to pass. The value of Keating's pictures surged: even my local galleries, Brandlers in Brentwood, began complaining that a daring forger of Keating's painting was at work!

Geraldine Norman and her husband, Frank Norman, together completed their book *The Fake's Progress*, a biography of Keating which had an accompanying catalogue volume of 166 *Illustrations to the Fake's Progress*. The narrative details the faker's claim to have executed about 2,000 paintings in imitation of the popular high-priced artists. Nothing recherché was there, no admiration for any forgotten artists, no love for uncanny, eccentric things out of the popular ken nor away from the wealthy purses – a point both authors and the reviewers missed. The faker's choice of artists might have been made by a popular tabloid on the one hand or an auctioneer's price list on the other, yet through each there is a blurred and fluffy style easy to recognize even from the mass of photographs.

Why then were those dealers not fooled? The question arises to face similar explanations. Single examples were encountered in the heat of the auction where rival buyers wrestled with optimism, temptation and the auctioneer's reserve prices. Removed to the cool of a dealer's gallery, each picture placed on the line not only the purse but the reputation and the dignity of the dealer. 'Speculators may be encouraged to learn a bit about Art!' The warning once given in an *Evening Standard* leader fell and continued to fall on idle ears.

Glamour attaches to all publicity these days, and the faker, juggling with great names and great prices, had it all. Prophecies were made about the investment value of such pictures. Christie's South Kensington began to negotiate for a Tom Keating sale. Television producers planned a series of celebratory painting instructional talks by this affable, friendly and plausible exponent of art, in which, like a mirror, he reflected the popular impressions. A special evening was arranged to exhibit and sell all available Tom Keating pictures at South Kensington.

I bought the expensive, illustrated catalogue and found the sale-room so crowded that there was standing-room only for such as myself. Television cameras and journalists were present in force, but reputable dealers (The Trade) were not in evidence. The buying public, optimistic individuals, were really there, no doubt about that, with, as they thought, fame and fortune before them. Had not the Cecil Higgins Art Gallery at Bedford made such a fuss to compel Scotland Yard to return their *Barn at Shoreham* which had been seized as evidence? Those gallery officials said there was much more interest and they thought the picture was more valuable now than when they believed it to be a genuine Samuel Palmer!

South Kensington sale-rooms had presented a considerable *oeuvre* for one artist, covering the walls and facilities of the picture gallery. There were 135 pictures altogether, some quite large ones, and one or two 'Krieghoffs' that had not yet been passed off. Keating had gone to Canada and, with Jane Kelly, professed to have toured collections and galleries in an attempt to point out his fakes of their national artist, but alas for him Jane Kelly had by now met and married a Canadian and become Mrs Maurice.

Assembled together, his brushwork and furry style seemed to carry his bearded portrait across every picture, and the impact of all these brought together betrayed the reality of his work, whether his pictures or his fakes, a fussy, friendly and indeterminate personality in a style that had never reached maturity but can yet be recognized.

It was reported that none of the known 'Trade' was bidding at all. The television cameras swept the sale-room from rostrum to the corridors, and I found myself full length in their line of focus and on the News later. It did not matter to me, but when the News showed the record on the screens, West End gallery folk must have been glad to have been absent. The bidding was astonishing. Estimated prices had ranged from £50 to £1,800 but Keating's imitative Constable fetched £5,500 and his 'After Renoir' copy of *La Grenouillère* £1,800, his '*After Keating*' self-portrait made £460, while even his palette fetched £180.

The painter sat behind a railing on the left of the rostrum, and as the prices rose his face grew redder, his beard more white. One could almost see the beat of his heart and his tension of breathing.

'This is bad,' I remarked to his girl-friend, gleefully watching. 'He is under strain, as everyone can see!'

'Ah, but it's a nice strain,' was her comment.

After the sale, as clients were gathering to pay, there were congratulatory speeches by Christie's staff, and the public crowded to get their catalogues signed by the celebrity. He had just heard the actual total of £75,000 for that sale, and his new girl-friend and secretary, Jacqui Warhurst, seemed even more abashed at the result than he. Various questions were invited. I ventured to comment that some of his pictures were signed, but not all, asking, 'If one brought pictures along, would you sign them?'

'Oh yes, I would,' he replied on a real high peak of pleasure. 'Bring them in, and I'll sign them.'

But Bill Brooks, Christie's auction-room manager, had recognized me and, protective and paternal, came forward, his brows darkening, to whisper sternly in Keating's ear. The latter looked round to find his questioner, his smile temporarily lost. 'Oh yes, indeed. That's if I painted them,' he corrected, 'or else you've got another thing coming.'

As I moved along the queue my catalogue was duly graced with his signature; large and clear and characterless, it could be the easiest of all to copy, but who would copy it? To the place where he had now arrived, others might seek admission under such a lucrative cloak, and they did! In the coming years my local gallery was not alone in protesting there were wandering 'fakes of genuine Keatings'!

That sale took place on 12 December 1983. The diagnosis of Keating's health which Sam Silkin, the then Attorney General, had accepted during the Old Bailey trial and my own impression of his condition were confirmed. His meteoric rise from the shadows of a prison sentence to wealth and fame set him working harder than ever. Television producers urged him on. Christie's held out prospects of another ex-studio sale, and in the *East Anglian Times* of 24 February 1984 Dedham friends like old Herbert Flatman and his wife could spread his boasts about how certain pictures in the National Gallery had actually been painted by the redoubtable Tom Keating. The more the National Gallery's Director and his press officer, Miss Sarah Brown, might deny such nonsense, the more provincial folk and their newspapers spread it.

On 12 February 1984 Keating's heart condition worsened and he died in a Colchester hospital, at the age of sixty-six. The *Observer Magazine* published his significant last words on almost the same day; 'If I had been a proper faker, you would never have heard of me. I would have been a millionaire living in luxury!'

Indeed, such was the state of connoisseurship then that one can only surmise that, but for the ghost of Samuel Palmer hovering over George Arnott's sale at Woodbridge, he might have!

My first publisher, Reginald Caton of *The Fortune Press*, used to be mournfully delighted when one of his poets died. Whether the relatives rallied to help establish his work, whether the public now read his obituary and sought to read him was all the same: each offered a prospect of profit. Off he would go in black jacket and black Homburg hat to collect from relatives of such as Lord Alfred Douglas, or Dylan Thomas reliques or unfinished MSS.

So we find the press immediately questioning David Collins, the picture director of Christie's South Kensington, remembering and querying those high values.

'They are bound to go up now,' David Collins replied. 'When any artist dies, the flow dries up and they are worth more.'

There were 205 works left in Keating's studio, and Christie's moved to promote these for sale. To encourage local buyers, they were first exhibited at The Minories, Colchester, and then brought to be sold in South Kensington on 10 September 1984. Here and there a voice attempted to discourage the enthusiasm of would-be collectors. In *The Sunday Times* of the previous day, Sarah Jane Checkland had written: 'The many portraits of doe-eyed young women with come-hither expressions would look more at home on the walls of Woolworths than at Christie's South Kensington ... In between are dozens of garish tributes to artists whose styles he used to adopt, portraits of Constable, Gauguin, Monet and his family.'

A caution disregarded! Once again little notice was taken of Christie's conservative estimates. Away went the bidding to a sale total of £276,000, with every picture sold, that Monet painting of his *Family in the Houseboat* (signed and dated 1983) making £16,000 against the estimate of £700 to £1,200! Once again Bond Street was absent and foreign buyers non-existent. Though the art world might sniff and the dealers stay away, the public had crowded to buy. They did not have to worry about provenance or authenticity! A picture by Tom Keating – what a talking-point for any visitors! What a spectacle at any house party!

And as for value, only Time, that humourless old plodder with his heavy and lugubrious sharp scythe – only Time will tell, though many like myself will prefer not to gamble in this regard.

'What made the Keating sale so unique,' David Collins had said in the *Daily Mail* on 10 February 1984, 'is that the public were buying, not the Art Dealers. Keating was more than just an artist. He was a character who caught the public's imagination. They pushed the market up at his Sale.'

11   Motives: Desire for Verification

When, some twenty years ago, the history of my collection was published, many letters began to come from people wanting some assessment of their works of art, and when it was published in the United States, even more followed, enclosing photographs of paintings. From the United States estimates of value were not requested so much as attributions and written statements certifying authenticity. No one can be adamant about such a matter merely from photographs, and actually in these doubtful cases only suggestions can be made. There is no touchstone by which a painter's style can be immediately and impersonally tested. In the course of years an artist's brushwork and his use of materials may change, just as one's own handwriting does. Life-style alters, and expression of it also; even choice of subject may vary with patrons' requirements and the fashion of the market.

Always, however, the demand persists for factual evidence, documentary details of provenance or physical proof with the picture itself. This is particularly the case when values are demanded, and in this quest pictures are presented before auctioneers. I once read an angry letter from Stafford in the *Art & Antiques Weekly* of 13 June 1970: 'I am often astonished by the immaturity and lack of knowledge of trainees who stand behind the counter in the principal London auction rooms and pour forth words of wisdom with the air of an experienced expert. As for valuations given by London auction rooms these are beyond my comprehension. A painting for which I had paid £550 (which my wife disliked) was taken back to the same place where it was purchased and I was shocked when a long haired youth expressed his view that the picture justified a reserve of only £80.'

Of course, the lesson here is that one cannot usually recover one's money in the same auction-room without several years having passed, and gone are the days of Sir Alec Martin of Christie's and Mrs Gronau, Sotheby's, two noble experts who never considered it demeaning to appear behind their counters. Today the volume of business has extended so much that dominating experts are too pre-occupied for counter interviewing. 'Trainees' at some premises pay a large fee for such education there. A man who buys a picture these days without a genuine desire and admiration for it (and the letter quoted remarks his wife did not like it) may be in much the same case as another who assembles a library but cannot read.

Those who have not taken the trouble to acquire a collector's eye will continue to demand evidence, not so much from the radiance of the picture itself as from its provenance, its history and associations and its material composition. Catalogue lists with details of prices and former owners and exhibitions can sometimes stifle doubt, but for important works X-ray photographs can show a specialist the infrastructures while the ultra-violet lamp, now obtainable in more convenient, almost pocket, size, will show differences and ages of varnish to reveal over-painting. To read and understand this needs experience and will often tell only what an experienced collector determines with a glance or two before his purchase. In the case of modern paintings, the lamp is mostly quite useless.

Unless you are well known to the auctioneers, you may find it unwelcome to pick up pictures, turn them about to see the light falling sideways and inspect their backs. (I well remember the horror expressed by Christie's porters at the great Lonsdale House sale – Christie's were undergoing post-war repair building then and King Street was empty. They looked up from their tea and noticed me lifting the heavily framed Rembrandts and holding them up to let the light show on the brushwork. Not a picture there but was worth millions of pounds!)

Paintings on panel betray the way linseed oil has dried, clearly indicating the painter's style and methods and defying the faker. By constant buying and handling, one becomes able to estimate the age of a panel according to its wood structure growth lines – oak, beech, lime, poplar or mahogany – and I myself can date the ground support of an old painting to within fifty years in this way.

All ex-Christie's pictures have letters and numbers as reference marks stencilled in black, and I once thought to compile a useful date list of these. Alas, such stencil marks can represent paintings handed in by batches, sometimes of half a dozen at a time, perhaps then rejected as 'not going through a sale'. One picture I had was 'A boar hunt, style of Snyders', whose reverse side was entirely covered by these Christie's stencil marks. I presented it at the King Street counter only to be told it was unsuitable for a sale, for it was only an old copy which had been travelling in and out of those doors for years, getting stencilled and re-stencilled.

At one sale I attended in Nottingham I can recollect a small painting, quite obviously only a copy, being held up while, as the bids raced upwards, the auctioneer continued to murmur lusciously, 'Been through Christie's this! You are getting something here! Been through Christie's, this has!'

Despite any factual evidences there may be, a picture can best be judged by the spirit of the artist which his hand and eye have expressed to you and the quality of delight provided. The merit of a bird's song is not provided by its plumage nor the genius of a book by its gilded binding, and to train yourself to enjoy a particular artist you have to see all you can of his painting. If you do so and you are confronted by an unknown work by him, you will know whether it is in tune, otherwise you will pass it by. Not unadvisably did Sickert take down his own sketches from his lodging-house walls which he plastered with reproductions from the time of Degas! Reproductions of the Masters in colour and faithful photographs of drawings are accessible even through ordinary bookstalls, while the great photograph collections at the Courtauld Institute and the copious examples of the British Museum Print Room have extended areas which once had closed boundaries.

Nor is it enough for a collector to be satisfied with books or photographic examples from the currently reported auction price lists. To develop and train his eye he must possess pictures for his own. Only by living with them over the years in association with other fine works will he receive, beyond the delight that is in the gift of art, the satisfaction of Truth in association with Beauty.

One can learn more by contemplation of lives such as that of Berenson, that great connoisseur whom it has become fashionable in recent years to denigrate. In a land of fakers, in his villa I Tati on the slopes above Florence, where forgers like Ioni could thrive, he was sometimes haunted by thought of the adulterations which the unscrupulous might perpetrate undetected, and he wrote, in a letter to *The Times* as long ago as 1903, advice on this subject blending with warning, as concisely as has ever been done:

It may pertinently be asked how the collector is to escape the forger? Escape absolutely he never can. Even the expert buys his experience at the cost of his purse and his vanity. He can only hope to avoid being too grossly deceived if, having a definite passion as well as a talent for the subject, he devotes himself seriously to training his eye to distinguish quality. Let him not imagine that a practical acquaintance with last year's forgeries will prevent his falling victim to this year's crop. Moreover, let him not pay the slightest attention to supposed pedigree or provenance, not to the various papers and documents and alleged traditions that purport to guarantee the genuineness of a work of art, for these are much more easily forged than the work of art itself, nor is there anything to prevent a picture being painted or a marble carved to correspond with a description in a perfectly authentic document.

For myself, being a scribe, my vanity has been constantly protected by the notable tenet of Samuel Johnson, 'No man is ever written down but by himself', and my purse safeguarded by the advice of a skilful artist I once met, Mr Flatter: when in the late forties I bought a picture by asking him to divide it from a bundle he had just bought at Bonhams' auction, he, assessing my *naïveté* and looking me squarely in the eye, advised, 'Never give too much money,' repeating, as if he foresaw my enthusiasm on the road to ruin, 'No, never, never give too much money for a picture.' So the moment an auction purchase or a seeming bargain leapt in price towards disaster, I would drop it. From a variety of small outlays, I could retrieve capital by restoration and re-sale, profiting by the lesson each mistake might teach me.

Underlying Berenson's letter is the message, so clear to those of experience, that understanding art is for the true connoisseur rather than for the financier seeking wealth from his security vaults. Superficial values have little to do with it. Most letters people write to me are concerned with this theme of value; all the oft-quoted newspaper reports and magazine articles seem to be prompted by such great concern.

One letter I particularly remember arrived after a television appearance. It came out of Ireland with all the celebrated verbal charm of that land as it rhapsodized on and on about an old picture of the Magdalene the owner wished to bring to my attention. She quoted the various individuals to whom she had applied for some convincing help, all of them indefinitely noncommittal, from Sotheby's to the Irish National Gallery, including 'the late Dr McGreevy, who had declared the picture had been restored and badly some two or three times'.

'This picture is not to be sneezed at!' (she quoted him as proclaiming). 'If you do not value it, give it to someone who does.'

He went a good distance away from it and then said, 'Can you imagine what that picture looked like when it was newly painted?'

I remembered his words that day when I was going downstairs as a shaft of light suddenly fell on the picture and I suddenly realised how glorious what had seemed an old 'flat' painting really was. So real did it become that I found myself speaking to her, 'Magdalene, if Titian really painted you, surely you can do something about yourself?' When I read your book it seemed to me she had taken my challenge! What about taking over this poor deprived painting and doing your best for it? Then sell it and pay yourself well out of it!! Here is a very old picture in great need of attention whose owner is too poor to give her a new lease of life.

On and on went the appeal through its eight full pages, typical of how such a possession can arouse high expectations – expectations, yes, but only financial ones! Years have gone by. I never could spare the time to go and see it; besides I have a firm rule never to buy or trade with a private person and am not tempted, although I wonder, does the sunlight still fall upon its face where it hangs downstairs in the semi-basement that was used for only a few months in summer? Age and religiosity, so reverenced in Ireland, will surely have protected it, and as cultural appreciation widens, the merit of an old copy may come to recognition even of this subject, the most painted of all.

'What's the use?' Haining, auctioneer at the old Robinson & Foster's, once said to me. 'Copies! When a subject is done, that's the end of it. You go to the Louvre and see hundreds of would-be artists, all making copies there. And at the National Gallery on Student Days, there they are! All making copies!' I have been there, of course, and watched the copyists but never have I noticed one that could hold a prospect of being confused or mistaken for the original, nor in embryo state actually showing the promise of genius.

Among the most interesting of paintings are those of the artist at work in his studio. I think of Ostade particularly. Not only does one notice the apprentice boys mixing paint and grinding colours; sometimes a leading pupil can be seen either preparing a panel or actively copying one of the Master's works. In all those pre-photographic centuries the fame of an artist depended on what he allowed out of his studio. Even replicas had to be up to standard and made so whenever necessary by the hand of the Master. The signature itself was unnecessary. The artist's particular accomplishment, his style, was what was sought, and the patrons and connoisseurs of older days recognized this without regard to the writing of the artist's name thereon. Only in more recent centuries has the signature appeared to define or perhaps defy the individuality of the picture.

Among the more productive of the Old Masters, how much may be the work of a pupil can become a matter for debate to the critics. The potentates of earlier times would send out portraits and copies of their portraits, for loyal subjects up to the times of the Stuarts would require them, not greatly regarding whether they were painted by pupils or by Kneller or by Lely themselves, for it was a 'likeness' they treasured. Today, however, the entire brushwork of the Master rather than his few final touches determine value to a collector and has to be distinguished and sought after.

Consideration of the studio routines of the Old Masters has to be understood as an explanation of how there are varying versions and even almost identical replicas spread throughout the greatest collections – examples of Leonardo's *The Virgin of the Rocks* in both the National Gallery and the Louvre, for instance, a duplication which causes the authorities in each collection to wrestle for sole authenticity for their particular painting. On page 33 of Liana Bottolon's *Life and Times of Leonardo* (Hamlyn, 1968) are shown reproductions of six imitations and interpretations of the *Mona Lisa*, some beginning even before Leonardo had finished the painting!

For another example, I have before me (from the *Art & Antiques Weekly* of 2 February 1971, a splendid colour reproduction of a Raphael painting. It carries the caption: 'The National Gallery staggered the Art World last July with its discovery that their version of Raphael's portrait of Pope Julius III was the original and the version in the Uffizi Gallery, Florence, which had been accepted by art historians as the original for over 200 years, was a copy. The Gallery made its claim after extensive cleaning and X-ray studies had revealed under-painting which could only have been the work of the original artist, and an old inventory number which corresponded with that in the records of the Borghese collection which was known to have contained the original in the 17th century.'

Anyone who has been intrigued by those interesting paintings of artists at work in their studios must realize that many pictures were on the go at the same time and that it was not Rubens alone who ran a picture 'factory'. Linseed oil takes time to harden. Paints vary in their drying capacity. Whilst waiting, the artist did not shut up shop and let pupils and apprentices run off through the town. Of course, in cases like these all the versions are 'genuine', but which embodies the first conception can be problematic.

In this century colour printing has progressed so much that excellent reproductions of the world's great pictures are well known and accessible, of course, to copyists. Some forty years ago I can remember beautiful copies at Bonhams' auction galleries of portraits after Ingres: one on panel of *Madame Moitessier* was particularly good but, though catalogued as *Portrait of a Lady*, was not thought by the auction clientele to be anything except a beautiful and decorative copy, nor did the sale price indicate anything else, so that painting vanished and now, I speculate, decorates somewhere in semi-anonymity.

But in to the possession of the London art gallery Hazlitt, Gooden & Fox, whose chairman was Lord Goodman, came another picture to be sold as Ingres, perhaps his most famous – *Le Bain Turc* (*The Turkish Bath*), one which, reproduced in books and magazines after the painting in the Louvre, is known everywhere. A distinguished American art collector, Mrs Catharine Curran, of Chester Square, Belgravia, saw the drawing and bought it in 1970 for $18,000.

It turned out to be only a photographic copy!

The Hazlitt Gallery, though admitting their error in selling the work as genuine and by the famous French artist Jean-Auguste Dominique Ingres, 1780-1867, refused to refund the purchase price. How much they gave for it and where and when they bought it Mrs Curran was not immediately told, for they maintained that the 1980 Limitation Act relieved them of liability, since more than six years had elapsed. The picture had hung in her drawing-room and, had she not had it valued for insurance purposes, might be there today.

Mr Justice Webster ruled in the High Court in 1982 that the gallery must repay not only the purchase price of $18,000 but the interest this money could have made, amounting to an additional $23,400, and also costs of the three-day hearing, estimated at some £10,000 or more. On 28 May 1982 *The Daily Telegraph* reported: 'Mrs Curran left court with her money back and the dealers left court with the framed copy. A gallery spokesman said: "We have not decided yet where we will hang it."'

In these days the camera has made the *oeuvres* of such painters as

Ingres available in small pocket editions, so that so gross a mistake seems incredible. A magnifying-glass, the tiny scratch of a pin would have told enough. In pre-camera days the grand houses would employ local artists to make copies of their possessions, royalties and aristocrats would have copies made of their personal portraits for presentation, and the artefact was valued *per se* rather than for its authenticity of attribution, whose correctness the modern connoisseur treasures and defends with all the expertise he has acquired.

So, for example, out of an old bundle of portraits long ago bought at Bonhams, I chose to keep one of Hannah Harmer, a member of the Paget family, painted with all her age of eighty-five years in the antique costume of her time. The artist delighted in depicting a beautiful posy of two Old English moss roses fastening the lace and wrappings of her shawl. A local painter of Bristol, he was said to have attracted high praise from Hogarth, but so little has survived of his work that, except for the signature 'Jn Simmons pt 1763', there would be little on which an attribution could be based. Now I rejoice in this find, as both a good example of an early journeyman portrait painter and a delightful piece of eighteenth-century flower painting by which the artist has rescued the subject from the melancholy of age and old lace.

Memories of brushwork, the clarity of eye which recognizes and defines individuality of style, the strength of an artist's line or the delicacy of a shadow, such things, when summoned from memory over years of experience by the gift of complete recall, make it possible to judge quality and to provide a reliable attribution. Even recollection of items from a painter's studio furniture and especially of his human associates is useful in identification, once the difference between the assurance of the master's hand and the effort of a pupil have come to be perceived.

In seventeenth-century Spain it often happened that peasants and studio servants were employed as models in the paintings, and these studies were used again by pupils in their own compositions. In *Los Borachos* (*The Drinkers*), once bought by Philip IV of Spain from Velasquez and now in the Prado, Bacchus crowns the soldier with vine leaves. The other figures around often re-appear in contemporary paintings, sometimes separately, sometimes, as in *The Two Topers*, taken from the mid-centre background, and again together, full in the centre of the picture in *The Game Larder*. Many similar examples exist and, I remember, were noted in *Country Life* on 31 May 1956.

Of recent years there have trickled into the smaller picture auctions quite a number of Spanish and Italian works which consist of a fragment apparently cut from some larger painting or a sketch for the same. Upon old canvas or a well-seasoned panel, they can delude at first glance, until the memory measures them up against the real picture, from which they may be a pastiche, albeit contemporary and student-exercising.

R.H. Wilenski, in his magnificent two-volume *Flemish Painters*, takes quite a stand against stylistic criticism. He does not accept any attribution as being definite to show the hand of a particular master unless corroborated by a signature or by a document. Such an approach, if pursued, rules out vast areas from appreciation as well as research, and could cause hesitating museums and collectors to cold-shoulder them. As for me, I can have none of this, for the basis of my collecting is the eye and not the chequebook. So many of my acquisitions have been bought because falsely attributed, mistakenly identified or with meretricious signatures imposed. To rely entirely on provenance and certification would not only take the sport out of collecting but send a collector straight down the wrong road, for, as Berenson often pointed out, history, provenance and documentation can be much more easily manufactured than an important work of art, ancient paper is easy to get, as Tom Keating found, and Christie's stencil marks are only what they are. Nevertheless, as works of art come and go through the sale-rooms, opportunities for collectors to attach life-stories to their treasures increase their power as connoisseurs and enable them to silence those disrespectful cynics who seem to be always waiting in the wings to scoff, making news regardless, from Rembrandt to Graham Sutherland.

Some years ago Sotheby's began to release on microfilm their catalogues dating back to 1733, a massive work involving thousands of them, all located in the British Museum and bound in 2,000 volumes. 'To say the least,' Dr A.N.L. Munby, editor in chief of the project and librarian of King's College, Cambridge, declared, 'the catalogues are over-used. One needs a truck to transport them because they are so very difficult to handle and the wear and tear on the originals really is intolerable. No one collector would want the 10,000 catalogues, but 20 or 30 libraries really should have them.'

As the project proceeds, for dealers, galleries and museum curators another source of 'provenance' opens that will add to the definition of Christie's stencil numbers, for many of Sotheby's catalogues are well illustrated. The time may come when every important picture will be sold with its autobiography, and the day of the speculative collector like myself be done. Television *Road Shows*, mass-produced illustrated art books, the proliferation of auction sales, the growing hunger for cultural identities in the Newer Worlds will take prices out of reality, and the collector become as much a museum walker as in a Communist country.

I was once invited to lunch with Ilya Ehrenburg in Moscow and there, all around his flat, hung some of the finest examples of this century's French painting given him by his artist friends when he was a young journalist in Paris.

'How is it you can hold and enjoy this collection privately?' I enquired.

'Ah,' replied that cunning old man as he put a sliced lemon into the vodka, 'I have left it all to the nation, every painting, everything is in my will for the people. It is for them to choose.'

Why compare realities? In Russia. In Britain. He might will it. Our nation takes it, will or no!

Taste is no god-given reality but evanescent and fleeting that in a nation changes in passions without laws that endure or loves that lead, as if senses inflame with spirit or flag with *ennui*, that hurry forward with appetite or are easily glutted and halt for ever, it seems, till a new token arises and points to some forgotten joy and the nation acclaims, hastening to measure indeterminable form by what it calls value.

So in a lifetime the individual person changes, deaf to yesterday, ignoring the delights of his elders as if someone ignorant of 'lines of beauty' has shouted 'Make it new!', and this is all he can hear for a definition of art, and this only provides some psychostasy of purpose easy to release into Modern Art. Yet the rise and fall of a nation's interest is only reflected within its individual spirits, resist as one or two may.

In an unselective sale near Birmingham, I bought haphazardly a pack of prints, among them quite a large oil on card, 20″ x 30″, unframed and signed Helen Allingham, a name that at the time meant nothing to me. I did not know of her as the sister of the poet William Allingham but I liked the picture, every leaf of each tree beautifully delineated, rather too many of them perhaps, a milkmaid crossing from the farmyard to the cowshed – flowers and summertime – and birds enjoying it all. It was Victorian! Had I not turned my back on those pretty things to seek messages from the great, the good, the powerful? For all that, I liked the picture. Nevertheless, I had 360 pictures in my collection, and this was not in sympathy with any. Every leaf painted! Oh no, such realism carried no message. I sold it in some East Anglian sale and got £30 instead of the £10 I expected, and was quite satisfied.

Since then taste has changed and prices for Helen Allingham's pictures – for water-colours, it is true – have risen, being estimated as ranging from £5,000 to £8,000 and more. Tranquil farmyards with pigeon-cotes, rose-gardened cottages far from the madding crowd have caught the public imagination, and mine as well. That delicate picture would have made a good contrast on my walls to the bolder work of Thomas Cooper, and its appeal grows stronger because of its absence. Yes, I did slip here, and badly!

Rising art prices, fluctuating decisions forecasting values, difficulties in determination of authenticity, the temporary acceptance of fakes: all have bewildered the public's sense of probity and sometimes stunned it with the extravagent accent on particular prices.

A telephone call came to me one morning from a London newspaper: 'We have a discussion going on in the office. Can you lend us a work of art from your collection to make a test of current valuations? Something worth at least four figures? Please, if you can, bring it up today.'

'A painting?'

'Doesn't matter, but something good. Four figures at least. We'll pay expenses. Take it as a challenge!'

So later that morning I was arriving at the *Daily Mail* offices, not at all sure whether what I had chosen would be acceptable. It was to be a test, so whoever was to decide must be an expert impervious to superficial appearances. I had gone down my garden, taken the lid off a beehive and retrieved an old jersey riddled with moth holes and reeking of pollen and beeswax from the frames below. Its woolly softness would protect my treasure from abrasions and casual knocks in transit. Into this I fitted one of my two panels depicting *The Legend of St Ursula*, in an old carved frame, the distempered surface flaking with paint and whitewash just as when long ago it had been snatched from some worthy religious building.

'How much?' came the anxious query from Richard Lay, the *Daily Mail* journalist.

'£5,000 to £8,000,' I declared.

'If you say so,' he assented approvingly.

The *Mail* photographer took evidential photographs and off we went.

The *Legend of St Ursula*, one of the saddest of those medieval tales of the Crusades, tells how the saint gathered 11,000 virgins with a view to converting the infidels but at Cologne was frustrated by a jealous and vengeful queen. The two panels in my collection depict the tragic incident of her boat being drawn ashore from the Rhine towards the king and queen and then her final execution, naked but still wearing her saintly crown. Both panels had been hanging for years on the door of Louis Meier's shop in Cecil Court to keep folk from peering within. The National Gallery was only a stone's throw away but no one had bothered to notice their merit. Louis Meier himself had been persuaded they were 'museum squeezes' and told me so, but I had seen this could not be and bought them for £12. They were very old, either decayed alabaster upon baked clay mounts or else under the old paint and distemper entirely sculpted and fired in clay.

As we set out and were passing the High Court, I reflected that for the last three days the judges there had been trying a serious case over a statue which a Mr Lavington had relegated to his coalshed. He had been in poor health and living on Social Security, so had been granted Legal Aid to pursue the matter, something usually denied to the English middle classes. It had been alleged that, after the statue had been ignored in his coalshed for many years, he had taken it to Spink & Son, the well-known London art-dealers close by Christie's. The firm had offered him £1,200 for it, which apparently he had been glad to get. Then he had been shocked to learn that Spink's had sold it to a German museum for £20,900, and now he sought to claim £10,000 damages, alleging that he had been given a reckless or misleading valuation by Spink's.

At this trial Mr Justice Stocker came to say there had been no valuation, and Spinks had not known until an expert examined it just how valuable the statue was. He ordered Mr Lavington to pay costs up to the time he was granted Legal Aid. Mr Lavington was reported as storming out of court with his wife and daughter, crying, 'I don't know if I am going to appeal or not!'

I stress this anecdote. The lesson I have tended to emphasize and often one rightly given to collectors is the old '*Caveat emptor*' (Let the buyer beware') but unless like me you are a miser, a mere hoarder, you need to reverse that caution into 'Let the seller beware!' Pseudo experts are about, academic experts differ in opinions, even the folk so respected at television *Road Shows* are often only auction-room officials and must surreptitiously consult sale-room records.

I drove on with the *Daily Mail* journalist and parked my car opposite Christie's in King Street. I did not want to go up those venerable steps. I was often there in those days so that not only folk at the counter but even the doorman would know me, and whoever came forward might be reserved and suspicious. It was agreed I should stay in the car, where I waited interminably until my companion emerged, hugging that old jersey and smiling. The expert had examined it and said: 'It is fifteenth-century, made in Nottingham, out of alabaster, I think. Quite a few were made, but we could certainly put it in a sale. My estimate is about £800.'

Making the excuse that his friend was involved, the journalist resisted the invitation to leave it to go into a sale. Spinks important galleries were just opposite. Neither did I want to go there, having once dealt with them for coins, so the wrapping was pulled back and through their great door went the journalist and the jersey to learn.

'It looks like one of those Nottingham jobs. Probably not alabaster, but plaster of some sort. We do not really deal in this sort of thing, but it is probably worth between £1,000 and £2,000.'

It was suggested that either it should be left with them or, if a decision must be made at once and it was not a matter of selling, it be taken to the Victoria and Albert Museum. The antique-dealers Barling of Mount Street would help. They could be told to expect a visit.

Mount Street could be taken in on our way to Sotheby's, so we called there, only to find expressions of interest and insistent requests that the sculpture be left 'just for a few days, and for a test'. I saw the manager's face harden as we politely refused. Were we really wanting to sell it? He took it to a place under a stronger light at the rear of the shop and came back with the verdict. 'No. It is plaster. A lot of museums took casts from originals. Worth a few pounds only!'

On we drove to Sotheby's, where I declined to carry that old moth-eaten jersey up to the counter but went in and stood by nonchalantly while my companion laid it down in front of the engaging but inscrutable Mary Macarthy, who arranged for an expert to come forward.

'What is this? Why have you brought this here?'

Disdainfully he picked at the ragged holes in the jersey, and his gallery voice commented, 'Looks a bit moth-eaten, the sort of thing better taken to a second-hand shop.' He took out a key and without permission chipped at the back, breaking off a piece of paint.

'There!' he declared. 'it is a plaster cast from an original. We would not be interested in selling. It is probably worth between £10 and £20. If it were alabaster, it would be worth several thousand pounds!'

Now for the experts! On to the Victoria & Albert Museum, down the corridors, up the stairs and through the sculpture gallery to ring the bell at the end door, where a girl assistant brought forward her colleague. The sculpture panel was laid bare and flat upon a table. He stared, rubbed his chin and fetched another colleague.

'We never give valuations,' she warned, as they turned St Ursula over and over.

'These things are difficult,' commented the curator. 'Alabaster changes according to life and environment. Maybe it is on an earthenware base.'

They asked permission to scratch and took chippings from the back, wondering whether it could be a plaster cast, and then came the decision, 'Well, I think it is St Margaret, and to be sure, you could send a photograph to sculpture expert Mr Francis Cheetham at Norwich Castle Museum.' His name and address were written down for me, but far away he was and in deepest Norfolk, and of course this was not the purpose of the exercise.

Next, at the Chelsea Antiques Supermarket, the most promising stall was visited. Here the dealer looked hard and wisely, turned St Ursula irreverently round and round and finally shook his head. 'I don't know,' he said, 'Not my sort of stuff, really.'

Further along the King's Road, still in Chelsea, at the Joanna Booth Antique Shop, the proprietor peered carefully, making the comment so often used in the trade: 'It looks too good to be true. It is not made of wood – what a pity, so it must be a cast. You might get £40 in a small London sale-room.'

Actually I got a chuckle, for the *Daily Mail* told the story next day with photographs. Of course, I have the two St Ursula panels today and enjoy the mystery they evoke, the proof they offer also of the adage I commend as so applicable to antiques: 'Let the seller beware!' The last laugh is mine still, for the *Daily Mail* rewarded my effort with remuneration many times more than I had paid for them in the first place.

After a discreet lapse of time, in 1979 actually, the *Observer* appropriated the *Mail*'s idea and sent Michael Wigan and Paul Larkmar round four London auction-rooms to test 'expert' opinion. Perhaps the newspaper could not find a collector bold enough to lend at such risk a major work as I had, for their ten test artefacts were very much down-market: a walking-stick, Indian brass deity, tin box, clay pot and so on – objects suitable for the lower-class mantelpiece really, easily identifiable or to be denied with immediate headshake and dismally raising no estimated valuation more than £40 to £60, except for one piece of calculable silver which Sotheby's estimated at £200 and Bonhams and Phillips at between £80 and £100. The other items were accounted mostly trivia in the £15 to £30 range, hardly an exercise to illustrate 'blunders' or portray academic knowledge, and one that any collector can apply. Should he do so, acting on the well-known but doubtful theory that the only way to test art values surely is in sales against a reserve, he must bear in mind that when it is bought in he will have to pay auctioneer's commission, offering-charges etc. Not only so, but its presence in the sale-room and its price will be marked and noticed by the most active dealers and collectors, and it will hardly be possible to offer it successfully again for some years!

Of course, the opposite process is now recognized as a disastrous fraud, but one by which those who buy on provenance alone are snared. That is when some stooge, preferably of notable name and lineage (and they have been available), is used to enter a work of art for sale with a high reserve and against this the accomplice dealer bids to acquire an auction receipt and so-called provenance. This, after a respectable interval, he can flourish before potential customers. Today London's principal auction-rooms are well aware of this and would be chary of accepting too ambitious a reserve, notwithstanding a presence in *Burke's Peerage*. They arrogate to themselves an authority over their cataloguing and procedures, which is, of course, only as good as their own expertise.

12   Provenance

A flaunting and exaggeration of mysterious expertise can be misleading and damaging to a picture's value, not that such a collector as myself should grumble, for my own collection has been made because of the cracks in this overlay of aesthetic discrimination. Sir Alec Martin used to be blamed most for contriving the belief that the merit of a picture depended on where it was bought and where sold and by whom. Indeed, he managed to suggest – and successfully – that unless a picture passed through Christie's auction-rooms it had somehow lost caste.

During the nineteenth century an expert had to be bold enough to outface owners and to put his name and reputation to any decision. In 1875, for example, Bernard Berenson openly denied ninety per cent of the attributions in the Venetian Exhibition at the New Gallery. The story of the Marshall Collection, however, is more recent and authoritative, though anonymous, as far as advisers and 'experts' are concerned.

Mr and Mrs Fielding Marshall from Chicago used to own a house in Brompton Square in London and from the end of World War II had built up a magnificent collection of Old Masters. Mr Marshall, a banker and his wife assembled a volume of researched information around each of their 125 selected pictures. From the representative photographs supplied, Sotheby's eagerly accepted the chance to hold the sale. Photographs and the record of the long years of collecting were embodied in an illustrated catalogue for whose printing the Marshalls undertook to pay a four-figure sum.

They did not object to the guarded proviso Sotheby's published in the introduction, taking the following as a customary formality: ' ... that the facts recorded in the catalogue, and the opinions expressed therein are the responsibility of the compilers and that the attributions suggested here are not necessarily those which will appear in subsequent auction catalogues'. Obviously neither Mr nor Mrs Marshall realized that this gave Sotheby's the right to hold and even present attributions different from their own. On 23 March 1974 *The Sunday Times* reported: 'Only when the crates arrived from Charlottesville did Sotheby's experts begin to sing ... or rather to object. A member of Sotheby's staff later conceded: "The dismay was considerable. The scene resembled the opening of both Pandora's and Joanna Southcott's boxes".'

Mr and Mrs Marshall were not going to have such a transitory light of transatlantic expertise fall withering upon the pictures they had collected, admired and researched for a great part of their lives together. Instant illustrations of differing opinion only inflamed them. Mrs Marshall's favourite treasure, by Lucas Cranach, as she opined, was to Sotheby's 'only a mere fragment of a German picture'.

There was no cooling-off period.

Mrs Marshall left the stage in dudgeon and, as soon as the Guercino was described as 'impossible', out went Mr Marshall likewise. At the nearest telephone box he contacted Bonhams and offered them the sale. Bonhams accepted and paid for the new catalogue.

I went to this sale and received the fresh catalogue printed on fine, thick paper and was given the Sotheby's volume as well. In the new issue the offending claim to alter attributions made by Sotheby's had been removed, but nevertheless Bonhams safeguarded themselves with the printed addenda on the introductory notice ' ... that while privileged to have been instructed, they themselves are unable to accept any responsibility for, and must disclaim liability in respect of all such statements, descriptions or attributions'.

Both these disclaimers from their rival sources are clear indications of the modern trend in which auctioneers puff themselves into pretending the prestige of being worldwide experts but back off into being only 'agents for the vendor'.

Mr and Mrs Marshall were present in person at the viewing, and I had the privilege of a chat with them to try to ascertain their motives in selling this collection that had been the pleasure of their prime. In their quiet confidence I understood the impetus demanding recognition for their work and justification for their attributions. I felt they had hitched their own prestige to them in a tremendous effort, 'seeking the bubble reputation' – something not wise to do in this our century unless in fun. They had a magnificent collection which spoke for itself. They maintained bravely that they

Flowers on a ledge
Balthasar van der Ast, 1590–1656

A river landscape with bridge, village and boat with fisherman
Rembrandt Harmenszoon van Rijn, 1606–69

The forge of Vulcan
Sebastiano Bagolino, 1560–1604

Dancers in a forest glade (detail)
Camille Jean Baptiste Corot, 1796–1875

Urban canal scene
Camille Pissarro, 1830–1903

Portrait of a girl (black chalk, heightened with colour)
Moïse Kisling, 1891–1953

Portrait of a Swedish pipe-smoker
Adolf Ulrick Wertmuller, 1751–1811

Courting
Adelaide Claxton, *ob.* 1860

Dame Laura Knight discussing equestrian bronzes at the exhibition

The author displaying some exhibition treasures

would re-imburse any purchase that could be proved the reverse of its catalogue description and quietly asserted that, unlike 'the book-bound experts', they could back their judgement with cash.

I felt sad as I went round that well-lit gallery at Bonhams. There was a quiet impassiveness there which made one wonder about the wisdom of battling in these high chimerical fields of attribution. For instance, Lot 109, *The Toilet of Venus* (Il Guercino), which actually was to make £7,800, was clearly not by the same hand as Lot 36, *The Vision of St Jerome* (Il Guercino), which was to fetch £1,000. What of that? It was a powerful impressive painting nevertheless.

On the sale day I was ushered into a front seat and wondered at the respect and deference of the porters, the pleasant smiles of others also, until I realized after the sale that I had been sitting on a ticket inscribed in large letters 'DUKE OF ST ALBANS'!

Good prices were realized: Julius Weitzner paid £14,500 for a Siennese Nativity panel estimated at from £15,000 to £25,000 and an anonymous buyer £15,000 for a tempera on canvas by Hieronymus Bosch, which had been estimated at from £10,000 to £30,000. These, like the others, were middling in the estimates, and the sale total was reported as £291,130 as against the anticipated 'worth almost £750,000'. This amount made for Bonhams their highest total for a single sale up to that date, 28 March 1974. Many said it proved that, 'It is by no means *where* the pictures are sold that decides whether they are genuine, for that should be the function of an expert market.'

Easy to say this, but once doubt and suspicion are thrown about, the 'expert market' becomes thin on the ground and chequebooks fold up. It is not where a picture is sold, but how. The Marshalls had bought their pictures, had paid good prices for them and were amenable to research. Though they could profit by the accelerative values of art in this half century, I still find it hard to understand how they could bear to let them go. I myself have an assembly of outcast artefacts picked up by the wayside, from back rooms of shops, the often unascribed rubbish of country auction-rooms, but I cannot divorce myself from them and would not had I bought them under grander heraldic titles. The Marshalls had apprised me of their children's maturity and their need to seek smaller accommodation. They were astonished when I mocked the matter of insurance expenses and boasted of my own rejection of these. I wonder how they are living now, without a collection or assembling another, but I give them credit, applause indeed, as connoisseurs in their own right for having the courage to stand against the dictatorial authority of the tradesman 'experts' in the auction-rooms.

One of the happiest of auction sales I used to look forward to attending was the one I have mentioned before, that of Arnott & Calver in the little Suffolk town of Woodbridge. From the time of Constable, from all the activity of the Norwich School, an enthusiastic group of collectors, connoisseurs and so-styled 'Suffolk School' painters had settled there. Dealers had sniffed them out and all met together, as unsociable as could be here, those from Bond Street even to the Norfolk Broads. Himself a connoisseur and learned in local topography, the auctioneer George Arnott had studied the Suffolk painters, especially the Smythe brothers and John Moore. He ferreted around the families of Woodbridge and Ipswich and knew those having relatives who had bought pictures from the painters during their life. Always he watched his chance to tempt local owners into his auctions, making picture-hunting more of a hobby than a trade. Norfolk and Suffolk are peppered with art-dealers who always had clients waiting and would be agog to acquire pictures for a sure market, and George Arnott, churchwarden of Woodbridge church, knew the families who had them. One could only attend the picture sales to learn and admire.

The Woodbridge family of painters, the Churchyards, were George Arnott's special interest. He could be said to have salvaged, almost to have re-created, the reputation of the local amateur Thomas Churchyard. From Arnott's connection with the relatives and the store of remaining work he drew out of the old studios, he had become the world authority on this minor master. Thomas Churchyard had trod so carefully in the steps of Constable, yet remained individually marked by the ideal beauty of this particular valley of the River Deben, with the liquid green of its watery landscape, and by the spontaneity and directness of observation displayed in the little drawings and colour studies he made.

Born in 1798, twenty-two years later than Constable, Thomas Churchyard was himself a noted collector of the East Anglian artists, most of whom had the misfortune to be overshadowed in reputation by the stature of Constable. He had seven daughters and three sons and brought them up, as many as could, to be artists in his own style. He would write their names on the backs of his pictures to be willed to them after his death, but such is that pervading legacy of the Deben valley and so definite the Churchyard style that it is not easy to be sure which merits the attribution, father or offspring.

Never was there at the Woodbridge auctions a sale without a Churchyard until George Arnott began to threaten and forecast the end of the supply. I must have bought one of the last lots – a small parcel of water-colour studies for which I took care to obtain a signed certificate of provenance from the auctioneer after the sale. So sure had I been of the continuity of supply that I had refrained from buying examples, and this lot proved to be the last of that Woodbridge remainder.

Churchyard, a country solicitor, was known as one of the 'Wits of Woodbridge'. Edward Fitzgerald, along with George Crabbe, was another such 'Wit' in a strong literary tradition. Fitzgerald had lived and kept his boat there and had left memories. As a keen sailor, George Arnott, surely himself a worthy 'Wit of Woodbridge', associated himself with this and welcomed the task, in the preface to one picture sale, of auctioneering all the Fitzgerald literary remains left in Woodbridge.

Such literary associations, coupled with a social prominence as churchwarden, gave him a certain confidence, not to say arrogance, as I well remember when I first met him, not at any picture sale but when he was taking a boat auction on the Woodbridge quayside. I was contemplating a lot consisting of ramshackle bits and pieces of boating gear and had just made the successful bid which he acknowledged with the reprimand, 'Don't look so miserable, sir!'

He really amused himself in St John's Church Hall as from the stage there he conjured bids, plucking them from his audience or from the very walls. Remarks such as, 'What's your name, sir?' 'Sharp!' 'Oh, yes. I hope you are!' – or, 'Oh, it is the lady! Madam, it's the new hat you're wearing!' – or again, 'You are looking so much younger today! I didn't know you were bidding!' – and then the real triumph: 'Are you disputing, sir? Let's have a dispute! They always make more money after a dispute' – and sometimes: 'If I don't see you, let me know. We'll put it up again!'

He actually carried this too far sometimes by running up the bidder past the reserve, past the bidder's bid, and then, when his own dud bid was not followed, falling back and taking it posthumously, so to speak, thus: '£30, 32, 34 – 34. 'Tis yours at 32!' against some innocent who had been run up from perhaps £20 and might have gone on unsuspecting to any figure.

To the inexperienced visitor, who did not understand that George Arnott was following in true line the 'Wits of Woodbridge', this was exasperation itself. I saw one well-known dealer at his first time there shout, 'Sharp practice here!' and walk straight out of the sale-room.

Arnott's supercilious and slightly mocking tone conveyed itself to the porters, old Woodbridge schoolfellows of his, who adopted it in very matey fashion, making a backchat across the audience which sometimes offended their master's dignity. Once or twice this rebounded to my advantage, as when, 'Munnings! Who wants a Munnings?' he bantered. Someone laughed, for his tone implied that only a fool would expect to buy such a picture there. Old Johnson the porter coughed and his crony muttered something. No one bid except myself for, as it turned out, Lord Cranbrook had left a reserve of £40, expecting to get it, this fine signed painting of a girl at a horse show. My bid of £42 exceeded his, and the picture was mine!

Months after the sale I was to learn that Arnott had visited a lonely old Suffolk bachelor farmer when selling some property and, as was customary, besought him for any pictures that might go into one of his sales. He brought out this picture, boasting that Munnings had given it to him to settle some farming obligation. George Arnott did not believe him but entered the picture in his next sale and sold it with appropriate caution. Events had made him suspicious, especially of paintings which were not made by the hands he could recognize – the Smythe family, Robert Burrows, John Moore and those sparkling summer landscapes of rainy Woodbridge by Thomas Churchyard.

The delicacy of all these might be overshadowed by the reputation of Constable, but in George Arnott's sales the locality of Churchyard subjects was pinpointed and their admiration indicated by prices higher than ever London sale-rooms could make for them. No painting attributed to Constable obtained such respect; indeed, as befitted a 'Wit of Woodbridge', George Arnott was wont to present any random Constable attribution with some levity. Sometimes this would happen unconsciously, as when he sold a sheaf of fine water-colours under the Constable title for prices of £300 to £600 and then, fearing prices might flag, commented enthusiastically on the last item. 'Now, this we really think *might* be a Constable.'

He was concerned only with safeguarding the interests of his vendors, the local people who had given him pictures to sell. These outsiders from London who knew the values so well, ah, they could pay those values!

Intruders sometimes did get into his sales, pictures bought by local folk in the big cities or even by West End dealers, and they tended to get short shrift. I remember one picture purporting to be by Vermeer, done on an old panel after the famous *Milkmaid* in the Rijksmuseum. The 'buyer', a Mr Smith, retrieved it from the porter after the auctioneer had knocked it down for £240. Several folk, myself included, heard Mr Smith energetically explaining how genuine it was, how many Continental galleries and museums had authenticated it. No one came forward to buy it from him or even to make an offer, although certain repetitive phrases in praise of the picture, coupled with expectant pauses, might have prompted such a move. Asked my opinion, I felt bound to say it was a nineteenth-century copy of the Amsterdam painting and next day found myself quoted in the national press beside a photograph of that painting. This caused me some concern. As soon as I next saw George Arnott, I felt bound to explain that I was not merely airing my views but was approached and deliberately questioned.

'Oh, that's all right,' he remarked with a smile. 'Percy Smith did not buy that picture! It was his all the time! I saw what was going on. There were actually people in the hall who had brought books illustrated with the Rijksmuseum Vermeer. I let it go and took the price up to £240, when I thought, "Enough is enough!" Then I knocked it down to him. They can't fool me, you know! This was my sixtieth picture sale.'

So it was Mr Smith's picture after all!

I have often come across dealers hurrying to get an after-sales bargain and buy from a successful bidder, having refrained from a competing bid that might lift the price and being unaware of the real situation.

East Anglia! It was no accident that Gainsborough, Constable and old John Crome had their roots there, as if skies, soil, climate, all exert the same power which inspired the Dutch and Flemish across the neighbouring sea. There was also, and is today, a firm tradition of picture-buying that fosters art as much as environmental influences. Collective picture sales can be found from Watsons at Bishops Stortford to Norwich. Norwich itself has long nursed an enthusiasm for its nineteenth-century artists which has spread over into other fields of collecting to furnish a network of galleries and dealers right across the region. G.A. Key at Aylsham has exploited – or rather serviced – this, expanding so much as to build extended galleries in the style of aircraft hangars. One can relish the genuine Norfolk accent here from auctioneer and porter to clients, echoes living on from ancient Saxon days like the local pride also stronger here than anywhere else.

D.J. Lines, the auction-room manager whose expertise springs from farming requirements, understands the Norwich painters and their work for whom he has a detailed admiration that needs neither Gombrich nor Berenson.

I have had so much pleasure from the smaller fields of collecting in such local sale-rooms where there can linger the possibility of coming upon some rare master work, of finding something that has strayed from an old traveller's estate, from the butler or the housekeeper, some picture that could be acquired with a small purse here, the like of which one might search the whole continent to find – and search fruitlessly.

Today the provincial sale-rooms are certainly not neglected by the West End art trade, and there they are shoulder to shoulder with less reputable Bond Street 'runners' who are quite prepared to wind into or out of an auction 'ring' or to conspire to make an even more complicated bidding agreement. These days, having become an octogenarian, George Arnott has retired, and his sales at St John's Church Hall have ceased. More's the pity, humour never vanishes without regret, but his regular parade of pictures provided education and uplift for that little valley, besides projecting appreciation of the local Suffolk painters into a wider world, procuring and selling pictures like Thomas Smythe's *The Woolpit Horse Fair* (26½" x 41"). The Woodbridge Gallery of Simon Carter still safeguards the Smythe tradition and often has such pictures. I sometimes conjure back to memory the beautiful painting of *Horses at a trough outside a cottage* (19½" x 29") for which Simon Carter paid £5,000. George Arnott had received it into his sale as a painting for which the owner's grandfather had paid £3 directly to the artist Thomas Smythe himself!

13　Honorary Art Curator: A Political See-Saw

Years ago a poet friend, William Kean Seymour, a former treasurer of PEN and a panjandrum at the Poetry Society, stressed the convenience of belonging to the National Liberal Club. The Author's Club met there then, the publisher Stanley Unwin had belonged, Dylan Thomas used to come and it was so convenient and central. From time to time I was privileged to run across Henry Williamson there also and find him more loquaciuous than at PEN. I soon found myself on the club's Library and Arts Committee, a Gladstone Trustee and there and then on the main committee. After my former book *Collector's Luck*, was published in 1968, I was persuaded to step into the job of Honorary Art Curator. All sorts of things happened as a result of that book which caused folk to fantasize about my presumptions of wealth and, before I realized, to shoulder me into posts of Hon. Treasurer here and there.

Someone at the Liberal Club had decided that the old political prints and drawings were outdated and that bare walls were better. Many interesting drawings – nothing superb, some faintly humorous and historical – had been tumbled into an empty room, while those left in the corridors needed to be insulated with corks against condensation. Everything needed to be listed and valued. I am afraid I shouldered David Collins of Christies South Kensington with the brunt of this discarded accumulation from the past century, which he did sell, but accused me of 'dumping a real load of old rubbish' upon his establishment.

A huge painting of an Earl Carrington was propped up in the lower hall, a grand, conventional oil, Victorian, larger than life, robes and all. Some dealer had seen it and offered £10 for the frame, on which the gold would have given him a nice profit. I saw to it that the Carrington family had the first offer. When it was found they did not require it, the great picture was offered to the

Australian state of which he had been Governor. Australia accepted it with alacrity for my suggested price of £500, and off went the Earl, carriage paid all the way, to grace his one-time residence 'down under'.

Historical stained glass windows had been presented to the club from Liberal premises in Blackpool. Stacked in corridors, these would soon disintegrate but I procured large period wooden frames, left-overs from a smaller auction house, and sawed them down to take the stained glass panels so they could be fitted before the stairway window where even today Liberal worthies of the old century can be seen staring down.

Someone on the committee, mindful of the publicity I had had as a finder and retriever of lost works, kept suggesting I should find lost Old Masters somewhere. There were none, of course, but discarded and forgotten down among the debris and rubbish were two splendid water-colours, architectural drawings which a little research proved to be by Alfred Waterhouse, exhibited in the Royal Academy Exhibition (No. 1,803) in 1885, the year Waterhouse was elected RA, and the other, also of the National Liberal Club, in 1886 (No. 1,639). Both these must have made quite a stir when exhibited, for Waterhouse was the architect of the grand new building for the club, and Liberals were a power in the land. Now, however, only one was intact, needing nothing but the respect a frame would provide: the other – alas, the more attractive of the pair – had been thrown into a recess on the flat roof outside, where pigeons had soiled it and rats eaten the top edges. On card as it was, I mounted it with adhesives upon a marine plywood panel and, with the aid of a skilful artist friend, restored the damaged patches until the water-colour was fully restored and both works were put into locations where their former splendour could be admired, and admired they were, for the club used them for Christmas card illustrations.

All unknowing, the club possessed the finest collection of English nineteenth-century party political portraits in oils, but they had stopped abruptly in the wake of the Lloyd George /Asquith disputes and successive quarrels marking the demise of Liberal dynamism. This hiatus seemed a mistake, and the more I sat in the lounge or in meetings looking at the old portraits, the absence of current Liberal worthies on the walls signified decline. I determined to remedy this: £500 was in hand from the Australian High Commission; any balance needed to engage a first-rate painter I could myself promise to raise by subscription. Jeremy Thorpe was the then Liberal Leader and it should be his portrait, to be painted by an RA who could agree to place it as one of his six allowed in the Royal Academy Exhibition, after which it should adorn the walls of the club along with Winston Churchill, Lloyd George, Asquith etc. Others in true political tradition would follow.

Everyone agreed to this, although no one paid much attention till I had found an artist and obtained his agreement. I had carefully scrutinized paintings exhibited at the RA Summer Exhibition and decided that John Ward was the best – in fact, the obvious – choice. I had admired his painting of the *Dilettanti* in St James's, Piccadilly. He had the flair for catching a likeness which came easily into a fine portrait without reversing that order, ideal requirements for a historical painter, the union of truth with imagination.

In a pleasant telephone conversation or two, the matter was settled, but I had reckoned without Mrs Thorpe, Jeremy Thorpe's mother, who approached me with her customary energy at a social function. 'This is more important than you realize,' she declared. 'This should be left to me! I will have a word with Tom Monnington about this!'

In vain did I hint the matter was settled. I reeled under her authoritative conversation, which mentioned Peter Greenham and spoke of her friend Tom Monnington, neither of whom was really known to me at that time. Explaining that the matter was actually settled, I left her talking to someone about a wedding party given to Jeremy Thorpe at the Royal Academy. Shortly after, a letter arrived from Jeremy Thorpe emphasizing his mother's suggestion, though not mentioning her, but I could not give way and suggested that chopping and changing, especially where money was involved, could cause committees to go cold, after which he assented.

Club committees are stolid and slow to accept innovations. I had obtained permission, I suspected, because no one expected a newcomer like myself, without political affiliations, to pull it off. Alarm bells began to ring. 'Have a quiet word with the chairman. It is his pigeon, this. You don't quite know the ground you are on.' Leonard Smith, now Sir Leonard, the club chairman, was adding nothing more, however, beyond his bland smile, and I finalized the necessary arrangement.

Then the storm broke. Jeremy Thorpe became unpleasant news, especially in the tabloids and the more salacious Sunday newspapers.

All my efforts to obtain historical continuity of Liberal portraiture went to ground on a matter which was never raised again. I received only a most gracious letter from John Ward acknowledging the situation.

Not long after, I took a rather abrupt telephone call at my home from Scotland Yard. Could they come down to see me at my home about a matter concerning the National Liberal Club art collection?

Would they tell me the reason?

'No, no. It was just a talk to collect information.'

The thought of Scotland Yard taking it upon themselves to intrude into my private domain filled me with irritation!

'Why come here? I shall be in London this very morning, so I will call and see you there.'

There was hesitation at this. They did not want to put me to trouble.

'No trouble to me. Much more to you to travel out, and I shall be in the West End this morning.'

Punctually to the time arranged, I arrived at the floor mentioned within that tall new building now known as 'New Scotland Yard' and waited in a room opposite another where there was some coming and going. After half an hour cooling my heels, I was asked in to where four or five officers, none in uniform, sat behind a table. I took the seat arranged before them and waited while the leader began. Some member of the National Liberal Club had written to complain about pictures being moved round, and he could not find one he had seen for years. What could I say to that?

Of course, the answer was, 'Nothing!' and 'What is this picture?'

They did not know; they shuffled papers and repeated, 'What can you say to this complaint?'

But they were officials doing their duty and I did them the courtesy of explaining the progress of tidying up, as Honorary Art Curator. The officer on the left picked up a pen and paper and asked if I would make a statement.

'Certainly not!' I replied. 'I am a literary man and my statements are valuable.'

They seemed surprised, non-plussed, in fact, to learn this, and the leader pressed a button. Immediately the person who had shown me the way in entered. Very foxy-faced he was, rather rufus in complexion, with prominent, expectant eyes and a smile.

'Good!' he murmured. 'I'll take the statement now.'

'There is no statement!' said the leader with a knowing grimace.

'No statement? What? No statement?' and when I rose to go, *sotte voce*, more severely, 'You've not got a statement!'

Going down those stairs, for I did not choose to take the lift, enjoying rather the experience, I could not but imagine I had been on the brink of some allegation, some interrogation which these folk thought, by a long wait, their assertive presence and with a few sharp questions, they could pursue.

Thus ruminating, hands in pockets, I took a pleasant stroll through Soho towards my favourite haunt, the bookshops in Charing Cross Road. Suddenly before a newspaper billboard I came to a dead stop. There, glaring at me, as large as the full billboard, I read, 'NATIONAL LIBERAL CLUB. ART CURATOR GOES TO SCOTLAND YARD.'

I could hardly believe my eyes! But there it was, without a doubt. The press must have been told as soon as I had decided to go!

I turned and with no uncertain steps made straight for the National Liberal Club. Everyone denied telling the press of my visit. They had a letter of complaint from some member but knew no more, no more at all. I was puzzled that the matter had not been referred to me, but if what was said were true, the police themselves had told the press in advance of my visit, hoping perhaps to cause scandal and flush out any hidden trouble. It was such nonsense that it could hardly be made into news and no one from Fleet Street ever rang me to hear of my wrath. At the club Leonard Smith's genial smile managed to calm me down, but I had to go on insisting that all pictures stayed in established locations since, if staff changed them round, it suggested a lack of security.

Soon after, a Canadian entrepreneur sporting the profession of millionaire took up his stand in the club, promising salvation to its desperate finances. Before he was ousted, he had tried to sell the club a flat copy of a House of Commons Speaker, in oils, and to this I strongly objected, having already drawn up a valuation of paintings etc in case they all had to be sold.

As I sat in the General Meeting, it made me sad to contemplate the dispersal of all these noble portraits and souvenirs of the past, for it seemed they could all be dispersed and nothing survive from that splendid pageant. Not even present meanderers could replace them. Already in the rented committee room I had noticed an ugly Liberal election poster pasted over the beautiful Annigoni print of the Queen.

The chairman's report in that meeting fell on my deaf ears.

Another panjandrum was taking over the club. While the speeches drooled on, I saw as in a dream the old veteran of Fleet Street who taught in my literary institute. Neat, dark-suited, always with a bowler hat, he came once a week to hold those Dagenham lads and lasses spellbound in his 'Art of Writing' class. Fearless of my authority, he had bearded me in my principal's study.

Raising his hand and his voice at the same time, 'You are like Sisyphus!' he declared. 'Always pushing the great stone up the mountain. You'll wear yourself out! And it will come down on you, mark my words! You'll never hold it up, no more than Sisyphus could.'

How true of my style, and of his, journalist of the old time as he was – he would neither change nor adapt, happy in his very boldness. His words came upon me now, as I dreamed of the past and the conventional voices droned on. I had jested, rushing into problems or shrugging them off when he lectured me in person with his energetic and forceful vocality. But now he seemed to speak out of the past, and I now believed. Sisyphus was I!

At the most convenient moment I resigned from that thankless, onerous responsibility that could make me some kind of Aunt Sally. I felt I ought to buy a bowler hat and have it handy not just as a warning but as a grateful reminder of the advice of my old journalist friend.

And as for the portrait, in the Latin of the old Law maxim: '*De non apparentibus et de non existentibus eadem est ratio* – 'The reasoning is the same about what does not appear to exist and what does not exist.'

Time sweeps memory away and the seed I had sown about portraits has sprouted these years later, for I learn that Ken Jackson, who painted Thorpe's predecessor, Jo Grimond, has painted Jeremy Thorpe also, and the portrait, not without some groans which Peterborough, *Daily Telegraph*, seems to have heard, has been unveiled at a March 1989 ceremony to enhance a clubroom named after Lloyd George! Alas for Jeremy Thorpe, he is rumoured now to suffer from Parkinson's disease and to be rarely seen in his old haunts. Needless to say, I am thankful no one presumed to worry me about the project or its financing.

14 'London's the Place!'

'London's the place for a collector. Yes, London's the place!' The oft-repeated tenet of Archibald Russell, the Lancaster Herald, used to echo through the early days of my collecting adventures. Strange his advice seemed at first, but times change: other people, other nations began to think so. Such news paragraphs as the following I quote from the *Daily Telegraph* were enough to inflame any collector:

REPORT CLEARS £500 RUBENS SALE TO U.S.
The sale to the United States for £500 of the Rubens painting, 'Daniel in the Lion's Den', which was later sold for £178,500, did not contravene the Export Control Regulations, said a report published yesterday ... The painting was sold to an American dealer, Mr Julius Weitzner, for £500 in 1963, because it was not recognised at the time as the work of Rubens. He also failed to recognise it.

He sold it for an undisclosed sum, believed to be considerably more than £500, to Knoedlers, the New York art dealers, who eventually sold it to the National Gallery of Art in Washington for £178,500 ... The picture, painted in 1615, was presented by Sir Dudley Carleton, British Ambassador at The Hague, to Charles I about 1639.

How so? I reflect. Have I not a fine panel, early seventeenth century, *Daniel in the Lion's Den*? But I know there existed a painter, a Daniel who never came to judgement, who lived by painting the *Lion's Den* much in the style of Rubens and who has made a reputation as 'The Viennese Animal Painter'. He undoubtedly painted my *Daniel with the Lions*, so I cease to expect from my picture such newsy swift travels and the financial ascendancy of powerful promotion.

'London's the place!' Not only buyers but vendors thought so too, and the stream of pictures coming into London sale-rooms had since increased to such an extent that the principal ones, all four of them, had to subdivide and multiply – Christie's into South

Kensington, Sotheby's into Belgravia and Conduit Street, Bonhams to Chelsea, Phillips to Marylebone, while some even spread their tentacles further in the provinces to the north, to Chester or to Pulborough, Ipswich and so on.

Every time I went into certain London sale-rooms, I would give a substantial tip to the porter who knew me best, for I was not merely collecting artefacts: I was collecting knowledge, and sometimes there was more of that in the possession of the porter than the auctioneer. All in a few years, maturing at the same time, the wise old stalwarts seemed to disappear, retiring as if the rush of new business overwhelmed, and today their status has vanished before the energy of younger men.

Here in parenthesis I will give advice to collectors unfledged in the smaller sale-rooms. Should it not be possible to attend the auction, always leave bids with the auctioneer, who will value you not merely as a client but as a potential promoter of his sale-room. Distrustful dealers, nurturing secrecy, avoid the auctioneer and sometimes choose to give bids to some porter to venture on their behalf. It can happen and, *mea culpa*, the less said the better, I have known of regular cases where the vendor checks with the porter before the sale and either bids against the porter's top bid or creeps into the office to raise the reserve left with the auctioneer. Of course, thus the buyer pays the very highest he had intended, the vendor gets delight, and the porter high remuneration from both buyer and seller!

In London, perhaps because opportunites are so great, money passes with lightning speed, so that humour is left behind and the fabled eloquence so traditional of the old-time auctioneer is non-existent. It is recounted that a West Country auctioneer, anxious to learn, took a speculative property to Christie's and stayed on to watch a pictures sale. Puzzled, then disgusted by the lack of drama, the mere calling out of numbers and prices, the senior of the two partners remarked, 'We've learned nothing here, and they've done nothing, neither. It's a big risk, a very big risk! They let the pictures sell themselves.'

Theatre, of course, conjured into a country sale, is the sport of a provincial auctioneer. One October afternoon 'A portrait group of the Churchill family, painted by Joseph M. Wright' had come into the Norfolk sale-room of G.A. Key as Lot 132. The bidding began to flag after the first £200.

'Come along!' urged Mr Key. 'Somebody told me it might make £2,500.'

Like a tired horse, the company limped along up to £250, when Key's rolling Norfolk voice declared, 'Sorry, I can't quite take that! Fill it up! Somebody do better, please! Fill it up!' No one did. 'There you are then! You'll lose it. You'll lose it! Not sold!'

Servicing a wide Midlands area, Ernest Biddle's auction would thrive by presenting the realist paintings known to Birmingham art-lovers. A painting by a member of the Hunt family or one of the Clares, lifted up amidst the welter of miscellaneous painters, would cause a breathless hush and the toll of thousands of pounds in a glory of painted chickens or farmyard colour that mocked the academic theories of modern art with the rustle of banknotes. Among the huge welter of pictures Mr Biddle would assemble each month, sometimes 600 or 700 in a sale, one or two paintings of great merit could lift their heads unrecognized in an assortment of bargains.

Ernest Biddle would sometimes extol the hole gaping in an Old Master canvas: 'That hole in this picture doubles the price. A real find! Never been restored nor over-painted. From an old house!' Then, as he closed the bidding, having held that lot up interminably, 'Sold! Done! Sharp! Finished!'

In London any drama is supplied by the high prices and the display of excellence. Bare interest is hardly dramatic and springs from the personalities involved that grow larger in the depths of one's memory.

I remember Leonard Bonham's struggle when the family's ancient hold on the Knightsbridge premises expired. It was bewildering to see all the picture lots arranged on the top floor of a Chelsea warehouse while the new premises in Montpelier Square were being purpose-built, planned for the smooth conduct of auction sales, but the courage and energy of Leonard Bonham, not then a young man, brought the venture to success. His new premises and the bold, enterprising style of his presentation made the first serious attack on the cliché that no picture had merit unless sold in either Christie's or Sotheby's, an assertion that Phillips had been trying to reject for so long. Indeed, it was the less authoritative atmosphere of these two firms, Bonhams and Phillips, which set the trend of ordinary folk to come buying at auction and to brave the intimidating suggestion that dealers had superior advantages there.

To move a big firm with a family history of 180 years from an old set of premises into new, custom-built architecture without stop or jolt was a daring feat. I used to sit quite regularly in the third row of the picture sales and could notice the strain as the proprietor conducted auctions, but he brought the whole to a thriving conclusion in the enterprise which Nicholas Bonham, the seventh generation, taking up after his father had spent sixty years at the rostrum, continues today. These smaller rivalling London auctions exist on their own merit, like the old Icelandic '*Han truthi a mat sinok megin*' ('His trust was his own might), whereas some other firms attempt to gain advantage by suggestion of ancient aristocratic privilege.

I notice particularly the recent tendency, now the older companies have gone public, to flourish titles of proud lineage among directors on prospectuses, possibly dredging for support from noble art accumulations. Overseas folk may be impressed – at least, Americans want to join the board-rooms, but British connoisseurs and hard-headed London dealers are less likely to be so. It is known that British aristocrats making the Grand Tour from the eighteenth century onwards relied as much on professional advice as their own knowledge, and the advisers of their descendants are rather more likely to do so today.

In December 1962 the *Connoisseur* published extracts from the trade books of John Coleman Isaac, a typical antique-dealer who after 1815 travelled the Continent in order to import treasures on commissions from the wealthy, holding exhibitions of his choicest antiques in his London galleries, sending his goods direct to customers by road, canal, sea or rail. The roll of his clients lists the most famous collectors of the day, among them Rothschild & Co, Meyrick and Pugin, the Earl of Shrewsbury, Lord Lowther, Lord Harrington, the Earl of Cadogan, the Bishop of Exeter, the Earl of Dunraven and many others of that ilk. It was he rather than they who selected the treasures with a calculating eye. Telling of one of his last journeys, Isaac writes: 'Business contacts with Venetians are not easy, for they think of nothing but Women and singing the whole night.' He found the Continental antique-traders 'full of guile' and the agents he employed 'as false as possible'.

As Britain's wealth increased during the eighteenth and nineteenth centuries, there must have been many such supplying the grand houses, and in most cases their clients bought on such advice rather than on their own knowledge. Nevertheless the sale-room catalogues today proudly vaunt names and titles as if they themselves convey merit upon each picture offered.

Many, like myself, used to associate Mr Ridley Leadbetter more than anyone with Christie's. The keeper of the counter, his energetic, earnest expression of sincerity and his smile conveyed, as much as the rose he wore, a welcome greeting. Nothing about him advanced the impression he knew a great deal about art. He knew nothing, he said, nothing; he thought nothing. How wise he was! Only once did he make a pronouncement to me, when in the inspection room, before summoning one of the experts, he stared hard at my picture.

'It is the money I am interested in, not the picture,' I remarked apologetically.

With great decision he made his one comment: 'You could not be more right!', hurrying off to telephone some department.

He had been at the front counter from 1946 till his retiring party on 1 August 1975 and had seen directors and even the chairman start at his counter, yet I doubt if in all that time a word or step was ever out of place, certainly not about art – about gardening, now, he was brilliant at that, and the raising of roses!

The reception counter at Sotheby's is downstairs, and one has to wander down there to find it. Everything gives the impression of being more welcoming and less authoritative. Mary Bethune at the picture counter could take a great deal of credit for this. Her sympathetic manner always seemed to soften the severe expertise from the days of Carmen Gronau and Philip Pouncey. Never venturing an opinion, she always appeared to radiate sympathy even to those who presented obvious and hackneyed copies. The goodwill of the picture side of Sotheby's owes as much to her own tact as to the friendly, receptive nature of the building, which takes one from room to room in a pleasant eighteenth-century style.

The reputation of London as a world art centre became most dominant after the last war. The properties from great collections took precedence, and other galleries like 'Belgravia' shouldered some of the strain from the old premises, specializing in Victorian paintings, or at Conduit Street in what were termed 'fast sales', while the main rooms produced ever more splendid catalogues. I take down the magnificent set of five illustrated volumes of the Robert von Hirsch Collection from my shelves. They are priced at £85. As I go leisurely through the pages that depict all the treasures once gathered here in June 1978, but now dispersed worldwide, it is as if a great gallery is conjured up. But not the atmosphere, not the tension, the breathless admiration of the actual sale! That was for the sale-rooms, for the company present who alone can keep the memory in their minds or in their bank accounts.

Christie's took over the old Brompton Road auction-rooms of Debenham & Coe's, a really old-world auction with special facilities for pawnbrokers to sell their unredeemed pledges by signal to the auctioneer from their lofty, private gallery. All that was changed to assume a more up-market image; the building was refurbished. Whole auction sales of pictures that had been admitted to the main King Street sale-rooms were made into a sale there but transferred here *en bloc*.

During those early transfer times, I was alert enough to devote my attention to the Brompton Road sales and picked up here in this new 'Christie's South Kensington' wonderful bargains – things that had slipped as they ran the gauntlet of doubt without any defence of research, often pictures hardly visible under old varnish, or pictures expelled from one sale-room or failed, unsold in another, lined up like applicants at a Labour Exchange, to become worn, covered with holes of drawn nails or obliterated sale marks, to be designated 'Trade Pictures', objects shunned by the Trade and collectors alike, waiting to be bought by the inexperienced.

In these days one could sympathize with experts called to the counter of a London gallery to face again the old acquaintance, some picture long ago sold or bought in at those very sale-rooms, but which has been to Birmingham or to Norwich, to the West Country, again rejected in London and then, after sale at Phillips, once again presented by some optimist confident it would be the grace of the sale, unwitting that it carried not a police record but certainly a Trade one! Folk who tend to sneer at the lofty 'gallery voices' of the picture experts might consider how often they have to convince unknown visitors that 'All that glitters is not gold'!

The reception counter at Christie's South Kensington is long, the variety of pictures and artefacts so changeable and from so many sources that the patient searcher must linger carefully and bide his time to dredge something up, perhaps on some Jewish holiday when specialist clients might be absent and the bidding low. Such patience is something I hardly manage to muster, since it conflicts with one's optimistic intolerance of boredom. In the old days, when Coe was auctioneering, he would gallop through a pictures sale knocking everything down as if it were worthless – indeed, leading most to think that so it was.

Christie's have changed all that, and now everything gets a chance from the rostrum whether deserved or not. David Collins and his team have adapted into a newer environment that could give respect to the properties and encouragement to the buyers. The occasion of such a take-over of the old sale-rooms astonished the ever-watchful Trade, especially when they perceived it was imitated elsewhere and proved that more enduring success lay 'at the bottom end of the market', for the turnover that was £1 million in 1975 was reported in the *Art Trade Gazette* on 12 November 1983, as having grown to an estimated £20 million in 1983.

15   Auction Battles Against Legality

When scanning the contents of antique-emporiums, whether in the display window or in the back rooms, there would be perhaps one item that attracted me, but on my asking the price from the proprietor he would as often as not say, 'Make me an offer' and then, taking my response as some sort of valuation, reply, 'I'm sorry! As I remember now, I have another customer that this is really promised to. If he does not turn up, you can have it. Let me know in a fortnight's time. He is bound to come in before then.' I would understand that it was either a new entry to his stock and he intended to hold it back for a reliable valuation, or the price was to be bandied about between other dealers.

And this is the trouble that a collector may have, for the price of a desirable acquisition can go to and fro like a shuttle-cock. So for many years, apart from my adamant rule never, never to buy from any private person, I have made my acquisitions in public auctions. A little courage is needed, perhaps akin to Scott's mercenary 'Courage, Camarade! Le Diable est mort!' Gossip about 'dealers' frightens the public, who are completely unaware that auctioneers will greet a newcomer to a sale even more warmly than an old, free-spending private client. And as for anyone with a small and static income, it has become increasingly difficult to make an important collection from visits to old-fashioned antique-shops.

More than a warm welcome from the auctioneer, the tyro does not need, however, for, in what has been described as 'the most devious pursuit known to man', dreadful pitfalls can await the unwary, the most controversial being that highlighted in recent years over the Duccio Case of 1968 and the exposure of the alleged Auction Ring to settle its purchase. Some of the story has been unravelled now the players have mostly retired from the field. Even after the Auctions Bidding Agreements Act, 1927, there had been no prosecution for this kind of conspiracy. All the participants needed to do was to take their shares, keep their heads down and escape notice.

Now the world was to know and Fleet Street fill its pages, a wonder to collectors, investors and financiers worldwide from the drama arising from a little Italian panel painting that had hung in the drawing-room alcove of Aldwick Court, Somerset, and was fated to blossom gloriously in London's National Gallery as by Duccio (*Duccio de Buoninsegna*), measuring 14½″ x 9¼″.

Tom R. Bridson had expired at the age of eighty-nine in 1967. His father, Henry Bridson, had been an avid traveller-collector, and after his death at ninety-two years of age, the son had inherited and left everything disposed much as his father was wont, untouched throughout the years.

This treasure-house of antiques was entrusted to Bruton Knowles & Co and, according to the gossip of Mrs Queenie Steers, the housekeeper, Mr Arthur Negus, of popular television fame, took charge of the cataloguing. She asserted that two experts from London came down to advise on the pictures, but who they were became a mystery. It was known that the auction was conducted by Mr Cecil Bruton, but as soon as publicity began to run wild, that firm and all connected with it went dumb. The entire sale of all the treasures totalled only £80,000. The critical picture was catalogued as 'Siennese School – 15th Century'.

Now, floating around all such sales are interested parties with great knowledge but little money. Before my attitudes were known, West End dealers would sometimes drop me the whisper: 'We will pay for information, you know, whether we use it or not.'

And there was an active expert specializing in Italian thirteenth-and fourteenth-century pictures, a Mr Malcolm Waddington, who recognized the merit of this Madonna and Child, even where it was hanging on the drawing-room wall in lonely isolation, and he reported this to the financial backer and expert dealer Julius Weitzner, as he says arranging to go into partnership for its purchase, ' …since he would be going abroad on the day of the actual sale.'

Mrs Queenie Steers, the housekeeper, noticed him standing on a valuable Chippendale armchair and peering closely at this one picture. She grumbled at such misuse of the chair she had guarded during her forty-two years at the house and offered, if he were all that interested, to fetch the step-ladder. Of course, the sight of the well-known Julius Weitzner helped onto a ladder by the housekeeper was a spectacle he had not come all the way to Somerset to provoke. On the back of that panel was an inscription stating it was by Duccio. He had seen enough. He moved on and subsequently, on that first day of the three-day sale, he bought the painting, this small picture measuring only 16¼" x 11¼" together with its frame, for a bid of £2,700 against little opposition. The main dealers were abstaining, pointedly abstaining.

Now it happened that Mr Ivan Nicholson, the accountant at Leggat Bros, the West End art-dealers, had left while the sale was in progress and was lunching at the Paradise Motel, Cowslip Green, only two miles away, beside the A38. (He was afterwards induced to talk to the press, and the following account appeared in the *Sunday Times* on 27 October 1968.) As he was sipping coffee there, at about 1.15, he saw Julius Weitzner enter to ask for a private room ' … so that I and my friends can have a little meeting'. Nicholson recognized them by name and occupation, but when the newspaper checked, some affirmed and some denied. How much was shared, how long the 'ring' lasted, whether it were a 'ring' or not, was never published, for no one came out of that room singing!

It was known that the Cleveland Museum, Ohio, had sent a representative to London instructed to pay over the National Gallery's offer of £140,000, should an export license be granted. Julius Weitzner preferred the bird in hand and sold the picture to the British National Gallery for £140,000.

People have blamed the dealers for this. I, however, utterly condemn the National Gallery for it. Its staff sit at desks or walk their floors, they draw salaries, but when it comes to a purchase, to avoid a mistake, to escape any risk, they pay vastly enhanced prices to some dealer (or, if I may supersede the tarnished appellation 'ring', to some consortium) who had probably been advised by their own experts or by advice equally accessible to them. Only once have I ever noticed a gallery official soiling his fingers by examining a painting in the sale-room, and that was some fifty years ago on a winter's day at Robinson & Foster's, when Francis (later Sir Francis) Watson took it upon himself to examine carefully two very large early Flemish panels that had somehow lost their way there.

'It proves cheaper and more reliable to use dealers on commission,' is the usual National Gallery explanation. So it does, indeed, if one is not as good, or as wily, as the dealer. There are few benefactors today who will wander like old Arthur Kay, always seeking a 'find' with which to enrich a chosen gallery.

The Director of the National Gallery, Mr Martin Davies, when asked by a journalist about the *Duccio with Four Angels* whether there was any disagreement as to its attribution to Duccio, replied, 'I have not heard so.' Pressed by the same journalist, who expected some wisdom on the level of Berenson or Gombrich, at least, and sought to be reassured on the gallery's own reasons for believing that the painting was actually by Duccio himself, he could only say that the painting was 'very closely' in Duccio's style and that it was 'much too good' to be by anyone else: 'The attribution follows,' he added!

Though submerged in all the publicity, there is no doubt that the Minister, Tony Crosland, and his Board of Trade staff came off very badly indeed under the criticism of the Ombudsman, Sir Edmund Compton, who was following the complaint of the London art-dealers. The dilatory negligence of solicitors had allowed so much time to elapse as to preclude action through the courts, due to expiry of limited time. The verbosity of Members of Parliament, shocked and concerned with the case, seems today ineffectual and ridiculous, although, as Sir John Vaughan Morgan MP replied when I wrote to him: 'The law is very weak and incidentally it is very difficult to draft one that would put a stop to these practices.'

Bruton Knowles, the auctioneers involved, came out upon the defensive and revealed through their solicitor, David Napley, that their expert, a Mr Clifford Duits – 'a recognized authority' – had seen the painting and in his view it was not a Duccio! On 16 July 1890 it had fetched £3.10s. when bought by a Mr Hassaw at Christie's, although there and then it was actually listed as by Duccio. (This was obvious and could have been checked by the Christie's stencils on the back of the picture!)

Alas for those who lack generosity as they crowd around the cornmill, ignoring the Old Testament proverb: 'Thou shalt not muzzle the ox that treadeth out the grain.'

Malcolm Waddington heard of the sale when he returned to Britain and, considering himself a partner, went to Julius Weitzner to receive payment, but Weitzner shook his head, producing a list of names and explaining that he was only a member of that group and only entitled to the same as they – several hundred pounds. Furious, Waddington refused to take any of this share-out. He took legal advice. Self-righteously he wrote to those listed and denied that he was the member of any ring, all of which drifted into the knowledge of the Society of London Art Dealers and also of the Board of Trade and set the publicity afire.

But the National Gallery had the picture, possibly cheaper than if in straight competition with the Cleveland Museum; the dealers had their share; Mr Weitzner had the profit and more publicity than a film star.

Photographers would rush to Christie's, seeking not a snap of the painting by the rostrum but the unobtrusive, bespectacled, grey-haired man half hidden by his overcoat in the fourth row.

'I bought nothing today, as you see!' he would tell them as they followed him down the street. They sought out his wife, hoping to catch her making some gaffe, but, 'I cannot understand why people keep asking if my husband is still going to auctions. Of course he is! He rarely misses one of the big sales!'

Julius Weitzner died, aged ninety, in January 1986. Originally a violinist from Vienna, he had come to London from New York. He had thrived on publicity since those days of 1968. Questions in the House of Commons designed to chase him for tax only elicited that his company, as registered and operating as Weitzner Inc from New York, was entitled to do so tax-free.

'All this,' he had declared, 'has been a very good advertisement for me. Everyone gets worried except me! I get a kick out of it. My conscience is clear.'

Many years ago I was sitting next to him at the time when Bonhams' new premises were opening. I was chatting affably, pleasantly ignorant of his gigantic status. Suddenly I realized he was bidding for the same picture as I.

'You like this picture?' he whispered.

'I do,' I replied rather aggressively.

'You have it then,' he smiled, deliberately refraining from following my bid. 'It is yours.' And then, with a magnanimous smile as he looked round and no one followed him, 'A peaceful picture.'

There and then *In the Stream* by Thomas Sidney Cooper RA, was mine for only £10, bestowed more by the smile of my companion than by the gavel of Leonard Bonham. A good turn, so, as the Mafia might say, I owe him – and feel my pen shivering a little. In that sale-room in 1963 he had paid £500 for *Daniel in the Lions' Den*, an unrecognized Rubens belonging to an ignorant investment group. Off to New York this picture travelled as fast as could be and was sold via the New York dealers to the National Gallery of Art in Washington for £178,000.

In 1971, pleasantly sitting in Christie's he nodded a bid of £1,680,000 for Titian's *Death of Actaeon* and in no time at all had sold it to Paul Getty for £1,763,000. He was a humourist at heart, was old Weitzner, and contributed £1,000 to the National Gallery's appeal to save the work for Britain.

His success bred jealousy. After the Duccio excitement the Board of Trade actually sent a letter to Sotheby's and Christie's (reproduced in the *Sunday Times* on 27 October 1968) saying that the Department had been told that 'something akin to a Ring is being operated in London Art Auctions' and that they had heard it was virtually impossible for any Italian dealer to purchase pictures in the London market without Mr Weitzner's blessing. The jealousy activating such hearsay that prompted this naîve effort by the Board of Trade was palpable. No wonder neither auction house responded, beyond little more than a shrug of the shoulders.

Julius Weitzner was aware of his friends and moved in an aura of respect, always ready to take a dogmatic stand in his own defence. He said of the Duccio allegations: 'I categorically deny that I am at the head of a dealers' Ring. There has been a lot of misinformation and misinterpretation. I have made a great many discoveries of works of art.' Jack Baer of the Hazlitt Gallery, ascribing to him the ability 'to make the fur start to fly', told how ' ... he did once turn to me in the middle of an auction and say "Stop bidding, boy!" – but he's done that to lots of people.' A favour done can enslave more than a threat. I glance at my picture of watering cattle, the reverse inscribed by Cooper 'One of my finest works', and my pen dries up in gratitude.

Weak as the law might be in the matter of auction rings and bidding conspiracies, continual references in the press to lack of enforcement or to any action at all made the activities of certain groups appear too blatant for such defiance to be tolerated. Everyone knew that no convictions of offenders had been obtained under the current Acts (the Auctions (Bidding Agreements) Acts of 1927 and 1969), and this flouting of the law was apparent everywhere. For instance, when arriving late at Windibank's sale, I would usually see a large group of dealers assembled outside, holding their own separate knock-out, a selected auction of valuable furniture, while the regular sale of miscellaneous and minor items continued within. As they stood on the tarmac, the expression of greed on their faces was a great deal more intense than anything Percy Windibank's hammer could arouse.

I recall also Franklin Silverstone auctioneering at Phillips when a large and splendid Venetian picture commanded attention. All the important dealers and their hangers-on were arguing outside, obviously jockeying for precedence or maintaining rights to bid in the Ring. Silverstone had porters close the sale-room doors. This gave temporary peace until they re-entered, some twenty of them. Once inside, further commotion broke out, driving Silverstone to hold up his auctioning and threaten, 'Any more of this noise and I shall withdraw from the sale the picture you've all come here about!' This dire threat silenced them until the item came up. Only one of that group bid, and the picture was sold to him, while the others watched in silence, alert and aggressively staring. Then, keeping together offensively, like a pack of hungry hounds, they left, following their leader with a muddled shuffle of feet.

Silverstone's impassive face did not betray the sneer in his voice as he remarked to the depleted company, 'Now perhaps we can get on with the real sale!'

Any agreed activities of London dealers are usually more subtle than this and leave only suspicion behind, but in the provincial sale-rooms it is quite different. Auctioneers well know that the Ring operates and even today blooms like a fruit-tree awaiting harvest and then vanishes away, but they can protect values more these days, so many are the directories, current auction price lists, and popular art books well laced with photographs to make knowledge accessible. Yet every auctioneer does need to sell; his business depends on it. In Essex and Kent I have seen a scowling group of non-bidders attack the merit of the lots, some scoffing at selected lots and then making a concerted exit leaving a crony to bid alone in feigned disgust. This intimidates local private bidders more than is realized.

Newspaper publicity has made it known that an 'Auction Ring' is a fraud that could divert an inheritance, cheating a widow and her children to spread it through the pockets of idle dealers. This has hardened attitudes, especially in Wales − oh yes, folk take inheritance and family welfare very seriously in Wales. The Chapel keeps an eye on such things.

Captain Peter Francis of the Curiosity Sale-Room in Carmarthen detested the whole system. 'There can be no benefit to the buying public, because if an outsider shows interest they will simply outbid him', he declared. 'Dealers can put front men into the sale, and sit in a London hotel eating lobster and drinking champagne and having purchases telephoned to them.' He warned his clients as long ago as 1977 that people who were taking part in a Ring would be banned. As such were not local Welsh people, he had national feeling on his side. He lodged energetic complaints to the Police Authority and specified one particular sale. The stories came out fully in the *Western Mail* (July 1981).

The dealers concerned came out of the auction sale into their usual room at the Ivy Beach Hotel, Carmarthen, where Detective Chief Inspector Evans, disguised as an electrician, had made a hole in the ceiling to set up a video camera. Video – and tape-recordings were made to show the dealers carrying sale catalogues into the cocktail bar, where against a background of piped music and the clink of glasses the secondary knock-out auction was taking place.

At the final moment the Police Inspector burst into that cocktail lounge underneath, proclaiming, 'Right! Gentlemen, stay where you are! We are police officers and have seen you carry out a knock-out. The game is up and you've been caught with your pants down! It's a knock-out all right!'

When arrested, most confessed. Keith Finch from Harrow, for example, admitted that all had mutually agreed not to bid against each other in the sale but 'to bring up as a topic' their purchases afterwards in the hotel. He, for example, had wanted to buy a bookcase, but at £380 it went beyond him in the sale-room; however, the winning bid in the hotel bar knock-out was £710, so he received £30, i.e. his share of the difference between the two prices. Another stranger, Fabio Giacomezzi, also from far away, from Southall in Middlesex, bought something in the sale but had to pay £70 in the Ring at the hotel to buy it back – 'I must be mad!' he protested.

Into Swansea Crown Court they all eventually came, and there they saw themselves on a video which lasted a whole hour and in which, as the prosecuting QC described, they were ' ... plainly putting their hands in their pockets and handing over cash, thereby holding a knock-out'.

Nine were fined £500 each plus costs between £800 and £1,500 and banned from auctions for six months, while another three were discharged on bail pending discussions with the Attorney General. This, in June 1981, was the first time anyone had been convicted under the Auctions (Bidding Agreements) Acts of 1927 and 1969.

The cost of the police investigations reached £500,000, the video equipment being made available by the Home Office. For the forty-four previous years an Act of Parliament had lain idle on the statute book!*

One would have thought the lesson plain. Perhaps the pickings were so good that the warning had to be ignored. However, in the same police authority, under the same Detective Chief Inspector Don Evans, about a year later, on 8 September 1982, there came to be a sale at Lovesgrove House, a thirteen-bedroomed mansion near Aberystwyth, where a company of 300 people, mostly locals, came to watch. After the sale a stream of about a dozen heavily laden cars and a van or two came along the road south of Llangorwen. They passed the caravan site and went down beyond Cwm Woods to the Clarach beach, three miles north of the town. Secrecy was the object. They dared not stay bare-faced at the car-park but strode across the sands where neither tape nor video in overhead ceilings could trap them. Casual tourists were shocked to see so many different vehicles so crammed with antiques. Clarach beach being surely three miles north of the town! The Police Station was telephoned.

By some fated coincidence the same Chief Inspector Don Evans was on his way home from duty when he saw that procession of cars with their roof-racks loaded. He needed no alerting to realize what was going on and responded to the challenge at once. Eight police officers were quickly gathered to come round Constitution Hill, where they had a clear view of the proceedings in the cove below. The dealers, most unsuitably attired for Clarach beach, were grouped around their leader, giving or taking bids and making definite payments of cash. When the transactions seemed almost complete, after keeping vigil for close on an hour, the police rushed that lonely beach. The dealers, as they shuffled away their rolls of notes, had nowhere to hide incriminating marked catalogues. All seventeen were carted off to Aberystwyth police station to be questioned. When searched, each dealer had up to £1,000 cash in his possession. Names were checked against those listed as the twelve barred in the Carmarthen case but none of those individuals was present. Sixteen were charged with offences under the Acts and were sent for trial to Swansea Crown Court, where they pleaded guilty as charged and were fined £500 each with costs of £300;

* *Western Mail*, July 1981

others pleading not guilty had their cases ordered to rest on the file. No London men had conspired to tread those Welsh sands this second time; most came from Shropshire, Hereford and the Welsh Marches, nominally at least, and there were no women on the list.

Offences of this kind still exist, although the two cases had shown that conduct of such conspiracies could no longer be so flagrant. Where they eventualize, they come together like clouds and vanish in the sunshine of secret mutual profit, noticed only by the auctioneer and the regular auction-goer. But the light of publicity hovers, and as far as Westminster City Council is concerned, the major London auctions have had to be licensed as from 1 January 1986 and are subject to City Council scrutiny.

16   Values: Aesthetic and Controversial

I would like to think I have not failed to acknowledge the merit of British auctions or the wisdom of the little groups of people controlling the sale-rooms. It is so easy to extol the past and decry the present. Sir Alec Martin, for example, became renowned for his tireless work for the National Art Collections Fund which enhanced all he did. Peter Nahum more recently has shepherded the spectacular awakening of interest in Victorian painting. Christopher Weston is active today as a guide to public appreciation, but I think particularly of him lifting his voice against the public rush to take precious artefacts to the smelters when, due to inflation, beautiful gold or silver objects became valued as bullion and could be changed for money printed in figures on paper, weight per ounce, an exchange to which even savages would not agree for their household gods!

In my hearing a Yorkshireman once declared of a French painting, 'There be a weight of valuable oil paint on that. No wonder it's pricy!'

Love of art is more than a matter of values. The popular press seizes with glee upon art-market price fluctuation and particularly mistakes made by the sale-room expert. The public who shrink from the effort of training their own discrimination demand some guarantee in attributions – the authenticity that is the open-sesame to delight for a collector. Of course, the principal auctioneers are responsible for this; they have to answer the demand, and by extolling their own expertise they give the impression of a guarantee, which, if the conditions of sale and auction legal history are considered, only tenuously exists at best. Any purchaser who has rashly bid will find he is dependent upon the goodwill of the auction house. A battle through the courts on any art subject gives delight and variety to the legal profession, so refreshing compared

191

with prizing away the jig-saws of a City fraud, and the costs have a way of accelerating as any aesthetic dispute dawdles on.

When the abstract Impressionist painter Mark Rothko committed suicide in 1970, he left 798 paintings. After the turmoil of the deceased's estate disposal, the New York Attorney General argued ' ... that the executors had violated Rothko's wishes by hastily putting the paintings into commercial hands for indiscriminate sale'. Like the fabulous dragon's teeth, the law firms sowed their legal fees, which came to £4½ million, including fines of more than £1,900,000 against the head of Marlborough Galleries, Frank Lloyd. Other firms collected well over £1 million during the case.

Christie's and Sotheby's have seen their subsidiary rooms develop and grow up, while other firms also have spread out tentacles to attract the business flowing into Britain towards the ever-increasing interest of the general public. I can remember the time when only dealers would be bidding in the main rooms and when the public were identifiable as folk unsure of themselves and generally ill at ease. This deliberate policy to welcome the public and provide encouragement and advice has been resented. I recall David Bathurst of Christie's being attacked for his progressive policy, and I quote from a dealer's letter published in the *Arts Trade Gazette* on 20 February 1985:

> David Bathurst's intensive marketing plans in this direction together with the aggressive methods practised by the major auction rooms over the last few years in attracting goods for sale will only make life more difficult for us, push the hammer prices even higher and reduce the number of active dealers even further to the detriment of everyone.
>
> Without the keen support of the art and antique trade the auction houses would suffer and Christie's has up to now been well aware of this.

A precisely similar attitude was taken generally by dealers with regard to the Ring. The quite natural impulse of shopkeepers is to keep customers away from the wholesale establishments, which is what auctions basically are. The absence of the public, particularly the informed public, from the sale-rooms, disastrous as it may be for the vendors, has enabled entrepreneurs like myself to run amok and make a startling collection. By the plethora of art books, illustrations, auction records and monographs, anyone with the flair can become a connoisseur these days – but so few keep what they buy; greed of cash in hand overwhelms them, then one or two false moves and their capital is gone!

Some time ago I was intrigued to read an advertisement for a book entitled *Smarty! The lid off the auction trade*! The advertisement continued: 'Get your libel suit in before the money runs out.'

Vanity, certainly indiscretion, tempted the author, John H. Collins, writing under the pseudonym 'Alec Simpson', to breach his anonymity, so that the dealers who recognized him united to expel him from their Association (LAPADA). In the course of a broadcast in the *John Dunn Show*, he actually advised how the public could bid against the dealers at auction! He did not feel it was morally wrong to be a member of a Ring, because, 'It's up to the auctioneer to protect the vendor's interests, not the purchaser.' This and other such remarks riled his fellow dealers ' … as clearly in conflict with the Association's aims'. Indeed, his book advertisement gave a blanket accusation: 'If you have been in the Trade more than ten minutes, you are probably pictured somewhere in this new book!'

Of course, once the collector enters the sale-room, surveys the wares, makes his bid and follows it through against dealers, experts and others to a purchase, he has declared himself an authority and he cannot retract. Neither the law nor the auction house will let him. He has raised the price of that picture, which, if offered in any subsequent sale, might not be likely to fetch as much for years.

In the early 1970s Mr Louis Weber, a Dutchman, attended Sotheby's where he was acting for a syndicate (magic word, revealing little but concealing much). He was the only bidder for a self-portrait of Rembrandt which was solemnly knocked down to him for £90,000. Imagine his chagrin when, the day after he made his bid, a newspaper article caused him to change his basic belief and suspect that he had bought a fake!

Although many experts declared that the painting, unsigned and undated, was authentic, it was revealed that there was one specialist who thought there were 'many strange features about it'. It had once been owned by the stepson of Napoleon and later by a Russian Grand Duke. For 140 years its authenticity had not been challenged. So here was a case come to the High Court where an experienced foreign dealer, backed by a team of dealers also no doubt experienced, had the judgement of his own eye tumbled by a newspaper article! Sotheby's, as agents for the vendor, kept out of the action which was brought by the owners, the Dutch Hoos Family Trust.

Lord Denning, Master of the Rolls, sitting with Lords Justices Orr and Browne, gave judgement that Louis Weber had no defence against the claim for payment. (*Daily Telegraph*, 5 October 1974.) Lord Denning did say, rather devastatingly, that he had been told by counsel that, if the art world had considered the painting genuine, it would have fetched about £500,000; Sotheby's, however, ' ... had acted with care and honestly and fairly'.

In reality there is scant protection for the dabbler in the tricky sphere of art auctions. In the various Trade Descriptions Acts protection seems to vanish since the sale-room small-print clauses, which might seem to renege on the auctioneer's responsibility for what is offered, actually cannot be annulled because auctions are left out of the Act by the argument that such transactions do not make a binding contract between buyer and seller! So before seeking contentment in the devious and costly path of proving that 'The law is an ass', it is better to seek the quiet and confidential goodwill of the auction firm.

Phillips auction-rooms always have more of the ordinary public strolling through them. So close to Oxford Street, they are approachable and easy to enter. Certainly they get some surprises, as when a gunman appeared and, using his gun like a magic wand to conjure up money, brandished it until the disappointment on his face became more intense than the alarm on the countenances of the viewers. He had thought there was money in art! In the summer of 1987 a demented individual, coloured, tall and about thirty years of age, walked straight into the picture room where the paintings had actually been valued at £800,000. He looked like a workman, for he was carrying a spade. Astonished as the viewers were, they were still more aghast when he began pouring the contents of his two petrol cans over the paintings. The paintings director, Brian Koetser, snatched away the box of matches as the intruder was about to strike them. Mr John Matthews, who had once played rugby for Stowe, stopped his viewing and grabbed him, as he described, 'fighting like crazy'. In the pandemonium the intruder broke free and dragged them into the corridor, to begin smashing the porcelain vases, six of them there valued at £2,000. Of course, no time was lost before he was handcuffed and led away 'to help the police with their enquiries'. The seascape by Magnasco so unexpectedly 'tested' by petrol was later sold for £5,600.

On another extreme but less exciting occasion, I was standing by in the picture room when a tall, blue-suited fellow with a haughty voice accompanied by a well-dressed young woman put out his tongue to soak his hand, which he wiped across a charming poultry yard painted by Edgar Hunt. I had been thinking of bidding for that picture and re-selling at a profit in Birmingham. The horrible smear he made annoyed me more than his lofty pretence of expertise. He had destroyed the painting's appeal and I felt impelled to say so, upon which he stared and did it again, causing me to let such a volley of abuse upon him as brought out porters and everyone from the back rooms. He and his partner vanished with the speed of light, leaving me in the middle of the echoes with folk unsympathetic to my explanation staring as if I had been the sole cause of that unwanted hullabaloo!

The picture had lost its interest for me, and I forwent the opportunity of purchasing it, alas! Any chickens painted by Hunt or fruit by Clare are such as do actually cause the mouths of Birmingham folk to water in reality, and the ink never dries on the cheques therefrom.

Those Birmingham sales that began in the converted monumental chapel in Enfield Way and expanded into the complex of auction rooms at Ladywood have done great things for art-appreciation in Birmingham. Under the cognomen Biddle & Webb, Ernest Biddle had made it his profitable hobby, besides ordinary chattel auctioneering, to seek out and promote Birmingham art and history. A devoted and patriotic following could always be found at the picture sales ready to bid thousands of pounds for Birmingham celebrities. The beautiful still lifes of Oliver Clare and the farmyard scenes of the Hunt family of painters were searched for and promoted. Edgar Hunt had died in obscurity in 1953, having rarely received more than £30 for any one painting, and Oliver Clare was forced to hawk his work for shillings. Ernest Biddle would search out their works from forgotten corners of Birmingham, and rarely did any sale he conducted happen without good examples appearing. Of course, as he searched, other rarities came to light, and before his sale-room became so known for treasure trove, I had bought my own share.

In an early prospectus (*Buying and Selling at Auction*), he gives an instance so typical of hoarded artefacts in such a big city:

Several years ago we had instructions to meet a solicitor at a certain Birmingham property to make arrangements for its clearance.

Imagine our horror when we discovered that it was one of only twelve houses left in a slum clearance area. Of the twelve houses left, six were covered with corrugated sheeting. The solicitor found that he had almost to force the door open, and as he did so he realised that the hallway was completely blocked in a three feet depth of old clothes and rubbish. 'I am not going in there,' he said. 'I will leave you to do the best you can.'

It was the most incredible sight. Nothing had been thrown away for over fifty years. The whole house was virtually knee deep in old paper and clothes. We have seen hundreds of cluttered houses, but this one was quite a record ... As we began to deal with this house, we discovered one antiquity after another, and we realised that among the rubbish there was an absolute treasure trove, covered completely with years of dust.

We discovered that the owner had died at seventy-eight, and had never been married. His father had been a merchant seaman and had had an obsession for bringing back pieces from Japan, China and other parts of the East.

As we were clearing the last of the contents, the old lady next door told us that her neighbour had been a great eccentric who had never ever allowed anyone over his doorstep. 'His clothes were so poor and tatty,' she said. 'He always seemed so cold that I used to give him a bowl of soup during the winter, because I felt so sorry for him.'

The confidential nature of our business didn't allow us to tell that poor kind old lady that there was over £80,000 in that particular estate.

Not all provincial auctions are as reliable as their advertisements and catalogues would indicate. Long ago I felt the need of capital for, in the exultation of the receipts from my book *Collector's Luck*, I had over-bought and so resolved to sell some undistinguished items in an East Anglian sale-room, thinking to dispose of them without attracting attention. Quite by chance, I saw the advertisement for this particular sale in an East Anglian newspaper and was chagrined to read, under the location and date of the sale: 'By direction of Mrs Stowers Johnson, Major Garry, the personal representatives of Reginal Barber, Esq., and the County Courts. APPROX. 500 LOTS OF PICTURES, ANTIQUE AND SPORTING WEAPONS, ETC., ETC ...'

What a breach of anonymity! I resolved to swallow my fury until after the sale, which I attended in a very critical vein. There were my pictures before a roomful of bric-à-brac. Surprise, surprise, for that sale leapt on and the prices also. All my pictures were sold to buyers from Bond Street and the West End. Famous names were called out, dealers whose identities were shouted ostentatiously, bidding far over my reserved buying-in prices. Green, Leger,

Agnew, Colnaghi, the names flew around the rostrum like cherubic blessings.

Happily bewildered at such a success, I went off to dawdle over a pleasant lunch, lingering to make sure the sale was over and done.

The auctioneer was in his office, not at all anxious to see me. 'Not one of your pictures was sold!' he said huffily.

'But those prices?'

'Oh, I was taking them up. You have to draw them on round here. Somebody could have come in, come in any time.'

He was annoyed at my protest. 'I was only trying to help,' he declared. 'Mutual benefit, you know. One picture taken up would have done you a good profit.' And then, catching the look in my eye, 'Better bring in better pictures next time!' and he vanished.

17 The Euphoria of Possession

'London's the place!' The words of that renowned collector Archibald Russell, Lancaster Herald, once more come back to me out of the long ago as I recall the comments of J.A. Floyd, chairman of Christie's in August 1983, when he observed that 'Some thirty per cent of the firm's goods sold in London come from abroad'. (*Arts Trade Gazette*, 6 August 1983.) No doubt these, and those at Sotheby's also, came from established families and collectors. To make room for works of the greatest accredited grandeur no doubt many other British-owned works of art were pushed into 'run-of-the-mill' sales in the subsidiary auction-rooms, and it is in these very minor auction-rooms that many of my most interesting pictures have been found – not all at once, nor even in a year or two, but over long searches and seasons of forty or fifty years. I confess, however, that I do go to such sales far from recklessly, knowing they have been carefully scrutinized by the firm's experts.

As soon as I see signs in a private house sale that it does not consist of *entire* contents but of 'additional' items, I am most cautious, fearing to buy even for immediate re-sale, for I realize the possibility that, should I purchase what proves a disappointment and go to present it for sale at Sotheby's counter, I might be told, 'Ah, yes, I remember this from some weeks ago. It has often been coming here and is hardly an old friend now!'

I once gave a lecture in the Cotswolds and lunched at the house of the octogonarian lady of the manor who showed me her own collection. Every picture was defined with London auction-house labels indicating which sale it should go into upon her demise. Shades of Mazarin contemplating his treasures with 'Must I then leave all these?' had no terrors for this brave celebrity, but as I looked at the labels, indicating careful research and documentation, I understood how collectors hoping to come upon discoveries there were likely to find their optimism dampened at any 'contents sale' in such a house.

Certain auctioneers are wont to augment sales by including other pieces, often at huge reserves, and this infuriates dealers, who declare that most sales containing such intruders are 'rigged'. 'Trade' pictures can be easily detected: the brass furniture hangers have usually been removed, the frame corners and back become worn with much travel round the sale-rooms, and even in a 'collective' sale they do not always fit in. Some old-fashioned and purist auctioneers refuse to accept such 'Trade' items, especially if clumsy attempts have been made to 'clean and restore' them.

When I went to the great sale at Mentmore, I was put off by the Rothschild family confession that they had extracted items they wanted and replaced them with works of art from their other houses. So I viewed everything with a jaundiced eye, wondering how much had been kept back, how much had been taken by London sale-rooms and how much, over-examined and over-scrutinized by Continental experts, had been inserted. The great painting *The Storming of the Bastille* by Zoffany attracted me most, and I passed by the real excitement, a triumph which fell to David Carritt when he purchased *The Toilet of Venus* by Charles-André (Carle) van Loo for £8,000 and publicized it as a rare work by Fragonard, *The Story of Cupid and Psyche*, selling it to the National Gallery for a figure said to be £250,000. Of course, there was a provenance accessible to learned researchers, probably lost in the hustle of history and of battling auctions, for this very picture had been exhibited in Paris in 1754!

I have never paid as high as four figures for any work in my collection and, romantic as I am, I go round such sales as Mentmore rather to enjoy the dismal poetry surrounding the breaking apart of such a collection, the departure of neglected items welcomed in return for handfuls of money, but departing to happier if smaller locations.

The servants quarters below the Mentmore splendour here were barren and neglected: rats had gnawed their own special exits and entrances, a dead rodent lay unobserved, staining the flooring, while despised paintings still hung on the dismal walls of the servants' quarters. The lighting was downstairs and dim.

I found a path from the servants' rooms. It led across to the old church and had been trodden, but quite definitely not by the Rothschilds. The church was plain, old but completely devoid of art or decoration, even of any joyful element whatever. The thought of those poor folk coming there to pray to 'better themselves', sitting in those cold, barren pews away from all that splendour, treasures from the palaces of Europe they had to clean every day, came upon me like a cloud.

I felt the patter of rain as I passed the hurry and bustle around the marquee and took my way to the car-park, for I knew I did not require the unappreciated leavings of the Rothschilds.

'Prices will be high,' I remarked to another collector I had often seen in London. He nodded. 'They will be outrageous,' I pressed him for comment.

'Yes, they may be,' he agreed, 'but one day you will not think so. You will see.'

How right he was! Small, weathered pieces of carved stone, fragments of shapen alabaster, even broken friezes such as those once lying in the snow by Syon Lodge could never be bought today, not at those prices. Many, many collectors would like them now, but frightened, annoyed perhaps, at those prices, I had bought nothing and only now really savour the lesson. If as a private collector one chooses something, regardless of rival bids, regardless of dealers or competitive trade prices, one should buy. If a collector is buying to keep, he can outbid the 'Trade', who are restrained by the immediacy of profit motive.

Such, of course, is advice for only the mature collector. The beginner should never give high prices. He should make friends not only with art monographs, dictionaries and price reviews but with some living picture-restorer and by purchase of worthless pictures learn how to be his own restorer. A small edition of the ultra-violet lamp is available nowadays and will reveal the history of old varnishes and retouches. He may be lucky enough to learn that, if he buys what no one else wants, care, research and promotion may turn an object into something everyone wants.

As one's collection increases and improves, it can become a college of reference, the better the collection, the harder for a new entrant to hold a place within. If I accept a newcomer into my collection, it not merely has to be a representative of some art movement or painter but must give me a feeling of astonishment that it could ever be made! I am no mathematician and do not possess any qualities which lead me to admire 'abstract art', which appears to be a way of indicating thought better expressed in music or words – though, even then, some music! some words! There is so much 'consensus' these days that we fear the arrogance of a taste which disagrees with our own. If one spends one's time in the great collections, the galleries where the inspired creations of the world's geniuses preside to impart their sublime messages, one acquires an involuntary turning away from the crude or the merely plain whose criterion is not sincerity but calculated in temporary material value, a kind of psychology lesson expressed in money.

The major galleries with their huge triumphant canvases can sometimes intimidate as much as inspire, so there is often more warmth in the donor collections to be experienced in the Courtauld Gallery or Dulwich or indeed the Wallace Collection, where the taste of one collector is more easily shared. These seem to distribute a more approachable sympathy and refer me back to my own collection, where, since first I cleaned them, the small proportion of stand-oil I long ago added to the picture varnishes has gone on rejuvenating the old colours through so many years. The true and newer light of day comes upon them stronger every year. (Electric light upon a picture I abhor, as creating an artificial stance under which the painter never worked.)

In this century almost all the great personal collections have become available for us to enjoy in large 'coffee-table' books. Each edition seems to gather up a magnificence accessible to all, and the glory of modern times is their colour reproductions which illuminate the magnanimity, the wealth and the taste of the great collectors. What the motives of these divergent personalities really are is more speculative than their pictures, a search for social status in display of the Midas touch, for intellectual recognition, for mere knowledge or for sheer delight and personal interest. For myself, apart from never having had the benefit of the Midas touch, I have passed through these phases. Gone are the days when I would seek to let my pictures go out of my house for promotion in some exhibition, but I can still admit to a feeling of triumph when I bought, security as I hoarded, and now of comfort and delight as I keep and contemplate, for I know my *objets d'art*; they collected me and fastened themselves upon my existence, and we content each other.

Though I have tried to write avoiding detailed accounts of triumphant finds, I cannot conceal that each gives me pleasure. In the published volumes of the great collections is to be found a standard of consistent excellence, in mine not altogether so because purchased 'on a shoe-string', but I do find a stable source of delight, the variety and astonishment of diverse experience regardless of material value. When one has such a collection, it is like a superior university qualification, not just admitting to boring conferences and tedious academic discussions but a stepping-stone to a wider knowledge, a touchstone to life-enhancement.

So I have found the very volume of a collection deepens experience and betters discriminatory judgement. No doubt one must puzzle others in the sale-rooms, for items selected have to be potentially worthy, not just by catalogue or price estimates, nor even by contemporary fashion. They must have a particular empathy to the collector's individuality, able to take a stand triumphantly among all the accredited fellows already admitted to the collection. As the collection improves, new entrants have to endure more searching scrutiny and comparison with the establishment, a more definitive test than when alongside other lots at the auction view. Inevitably sometimes the price at the sale may rise and the coveted object escape one, but the standard of each auction will gradually tend to fall below the assembled power of one's own collection, and desirable objects become fewer but more tempting.

Only an optimistic collector can really succeed, one who never says, as many do, 'I have got all I want', but continually searches, whose eye itself demands further education and craves for the triumph of retrieving another beautiful work of art from philistine unbelievers 'for a song'.

So, despite the passing years, I still go wandering, travelling through junk shops, through house-clearance auctions, through stalls and markets, such as those in Portobello Road, where old belongings get tumbled and lie waiting, mourning for departed proprietors or cultivating a precocious glitter to find newer spirits, more jolly owners. Not purposely like a pilgrim, I go loitering, always expecting some strange happening, seeking some talisman to change a brighter future, some discovery that will offer itself in happiness invulnerable, a philosopher's stone that needs to be found.

Yet there is no talisman, no *vade mecum*, for the collector, only the cultivation of complete recall for his picture memory, in a repetition of pleasure that gives recognition the assurance of a computer to bring back past associations into the stronger light of the present. What of Luck? Ah, yes, Luck! the art of being in the right place at the appropriate time, as when I went down into that cellar of Bonhams' old rooms, opposite the Knightsbridge barracks, and bought Turner's *Sunset at Sea* with its inscription 'From the collection of Elkanan Bicknell, Herne House, Herne Hill' – a picture which led me to meet Arthur Lucas at the National Gallery and to see behind the scenes there and to appreciate his wonderful restoration work.

Elkanan Bicknell! The Luck of coincidence, the wisdom of association! For I recently acquired the *Memorials of Christie's* by W. Roberts (George Bell & Sons, two volumes, 1897). The removal of the old varnish from across the *Sunset at Sea* has brought the painting back into a radiance as good for me as it was for Elkanan Bicknell, and although his fame has faded with the dispersal of his treasured collection, his stature rises from the printed pages of those heavy volumes not only as a giant among collectors but as one of the greatest patrons of British art. Writing in 1863, the *Athenaeum* claimed him with Vernon, Wells and Sheepshanks as one of the four principal collectors of modern art, ' ... men who, unimpelled by the motive of investment for profit, collected for the pleasure and instruction they derived from contemplation and love for the art exhibited in the painter's works'.

After Elkanan Bicknell's death on 27 November 1861, out of his house on Herne Hill (where my picture had once hung) the paintings had been brought to Christie's and the *Star* of that day reported:

> There took place on Saturday an event in London, such, as we venture to think, could scarcely in the same time and under the same conditions, have happened in any other city in the world. It was not a great national event – a royal reception, or a popular demonstration. It was not anything attacking or symbolizing institutions or sentiments peculiarly British. It had nothing to do with our glorious constitution, our Lords, our Commons, our free press, our meteor flag, our climate, our racecourse, or our bitter beer. It was just something which might have happened anywhere else, and yet which we venture to affirm could not be paralleled out of London. It was merely a sale of pictures. The collection of paintings thus sold had been gathered together by a private Englishman, a man of comparatively obscure position, a man engaged at one time in mere trade; a man not even pretending to resemble a Genoese or Florentine merchant prince, but simply and absolutely a Londoner of the middle class, actively occupied in business. This Englishman, now no more, had brought together a picture gallery which would have done no discredit to a Lorenzo the Magnificent, although his name is still hardly known to the general public of the very city in which he lived. He had been the patron of some of the greatest of modern artists, and had formed a collection which would have brought tourists from all parts of the world to the dingiest and most decaying of

Italian towns. Offered for sale in an auction room on Saturday to that select section of the London public who both care about and can pay for pictures ... the collection realised a sum of money wanting only a few hundreds of sixty thousand pounds. The artists whose works were thus purchased, were for the most part, too, our own. It was no mere competition of fashionable pretenders, feeling themselves secure to praise and purchase so long as your 'Raphaels, Correggios and stuff' were in question. English money was spent upon English art.

Many years have gone by since I came up from the old galleries in Knightsbridge and rested my *Sunset at Sea* against the wall and the snowflakes, to see it in the steady light of a winter's day. The foggy varnish upon the painting did not deter me, and I was to become overjoyed when Arthur Lucas gave it the elixir of rejuvenation. Much as I have learned through hopes and disappointments, the boredom of inaction and the excitement of travel, nothing seems so spectacular as those great nineteenth-century collectors, the great amateurs of the age, and especially Elkanan Bicknell, 'a man engaged at one time in mere trade'. The purchase of that picture from his majestic collection, coming into my hands by sheer luck in my first auction sale, has influenced my adventures, becoming for me as the fabled philosopher's stone which has led me happily along his collecting path, and it seems, if I parted from it, I should lose my way and come to grief.

Appendix: Acquisitions since 1968

All items shown in the exhibition catalogue of 1968 remain still in the Author's collection but are not listed below.

British School
16th Century
Elijah ascending in the chariot and tossing his cloak to Elisha, on panel, 21" x 49½"
17th Century
Riverside baptism scene with Elijah's chariot on panel, 9" x 11½"
John Milton, contemporary portrait, inscribed, on panel, 8" x 6"
Naïve
The arrest of Guy Fawkes in the cellars, on panel, 4" x 6½"
A message from the Muse, on panel, 9" x 6½"
William Dobson, 1611-46
Charles I beside his horse with grooms, on paper laid down, 23" x 18" (related to the famous picture by his master, Van Dyck, in the Louvre)
William Wissing 1656-87
Amorini garlanding monuments, on panel, 41" x 51"
18th Century
William Blake (attributed)
Nativity scene: the Virgin and Child with Joseph in an Oriental stable, on canvas, 16½" x 15¾"
John Cleveley II, 1747-86
Gibraltar Harbour, pencil drawing, 14" x 20" initialled J.C. bottom right.
Henry Fuseli, 1741-1825
Portrait of a lady on panel, oval, 8" x 5¼"
The Ghost in *Hamlet*, on canvas, 16½" x 21"
Gavin Hamilton, 1723-98
The Music Party, red chalk drawing, 10¼" x 12½"

Moses Griffith, 1747-1819
Beaumaris Straits looking towards Bangor, on canvas, 8½" x 13"
William Hogarth, 1697-1764
Reading the news by candle-light, on panel, 7" x 5½"
Portrait of a gentleman wearing a wig and white stock, on copper,
5" x 4", signed with initials 2" up left.
Kneller, 1646-1723
Portrait of a philosopher, on panel, 10½"
Philip de Loutherbourg RA, 1740-1812
A warship anchored in a storm with pinnace sailing away,
indistinctly signed, 9¼" x 12¾"
George Morland, 1763-1804
The Reading Lesson, on panel, 12" x 9½"
The Sempstress, on panel, 7½" x 6"
A mounted drover with his dog passing a forlorn white horse in a
stable, signed, 18¼" x 23½"
Sir Joshua Reynolds PRA, 1723-92
A portrait of Dr Samuel Johnson, 30" x 25" (one of several such
studies, Reynolds being recorded as enjoying the lexicographer's
conversation so much that he prolonged his studies for this purpose)
Sir James Thornhill, 1675-1734
The Ascension, on canvas, 33" x 22"
Francis Wheatley RA, 1747-1801
The Unwilling Apprentice, on panel, 9" x 7¾", signed F.W. bottom
left.
Richard Wilson RA, 1714-82
Pembroke Castle, with herdsman and goats in foreground, 14" x
20½"
Italian river valley with figures beside a pine tree, oil on card, 15" x
12" (relates to the oil on canvas, 26" x 19½" *The Vale of Narni*,
Brinsley Ford, 'exhibited London and Cardiff only' as shown in the
Tate Gallery Exhibition Catalogue, no. 79, 1982.)
Italian estuary with buildings and peasants resting below a tree, on
canvas, 18½" x 20" (Another version exhibited at Tate Gallery
Exhibition, No. 10, 1982, as 'River and Farmhouse, 1951, painted
in Italy', 16¼" x 20¼", Victoria & Albert Museum)
English School
St Michael and the Dragon, on panel, 12" x 8"
English School
The Demon Barber, on canvas laid down on panel, 30" x 26",
related to a popular print of the time

East Anglian
Thomas Churchyard, 1798-1868
Six water-colour sketches (ex collection Elizabeth Churchyard)
John Constable RA, 1776-1837
The Cottage in the Cornfield, on panel, 9¼" x 7¾", (ref. detailed story in text)
Sir Richard Steele's Cottage, Hampstead, on canvas, 12¼" x 16½" (There was another picture exhibited at the Royal Academy, No. 147, 8¼" x 11¼", and there is also a mezzotint.)
A bridge on the River Stour with barges being rowed, on panel, 8" x 12"
John Snell Cotman, 1782-1842
Hay barges unloading in a calm, on panel, 7" x 12½" (signed bottom left)
Dunwich, water-colour, 7" x 11", signed J.S. Cotman 9/7742
John Joseph Cotman, 1814-78
A river landscape with tower, on panel, 9" x 7"
John Crome, 1768-1821
Sandling's Ferry, Norwich, on panel, 17" x 14", a subject noted as exhibited in Crome's Exhibition, 1805. (The frame bears the actual blue label of John Thirtle, Magdalen Street, Norwich, the painter and contemporary of John Crome.)
John Berney Crome, 1794-1842
A mountain riverside by moonlight, on panel, 8" x 6", signed and dated 1821
Moonlight river scene with waterfall, on panel, circular, 10"
Thomas Gainsborough, RA, 1727-88
Woodland landscape with peasants and cattle, 11½" x 17½", oil on paper, signed
The Cottage Door, on canvas, 24" x 19½"
The Cottage Door, oil on panel, circular, 6"
Woodland scene with gipsies and a camp fire, oil on board, 11¾" x 10½"
David Hodgson, 1798-1864
Old houses near Norwich, oil on paper laid down, signed, 16¼" x 13½"
John Middleton, 1828-56
The cornfield, water-colour, 8½" x 12½", signed under largest stook
Edward Robert Smythe, 1810-99
A cottage family, on panel, 9" x 12½", signed (ex Parker Gallery London)

Thomas Smythe, 1825-1906
A snowstorm with a market cart and waggoners, oil on card, 3¼″ x 5″, indistinctly signed and inscribed
Portrait of a horsewoman taking a fence, oil on board, 11″ x 14¾″, signed
A cottage with a peasant woman returning from market, oil on board, 7″ x 11″ (another picture verso), signed
James Stark, 1794-1859
Woodland scene with gipsies camping, oil on board, 10½″ x 14½″
Stannard
Portrait of the fish auctioneer on the beach by Yarmouth Pier, on panel, 18½″ x 12″

19th Century
W.H.B.
Turkey and the Russian Bear, a political cartoon entitled 'Tightening the Grip', sepia drawing, 10″ x 7″, signed, Dec. 1877
Thomas Barker (Barker of Bath), 1769-1847
The attack on Scio by the Turks, oil on board, 9¼″ x 12¾″, described on old label verso (a sketch in preparation for his famous fresco painting on the wall of Doric House, Bath)
The Woodman, oil on canvas, 12½″ x 10″
Basil Bradley, 1842-1904
The Escape, oil on canvas, 13″ x 7¾″, signed with initials
Alfred de Breanski
A Highland loch with travellers resting, oil on canvas, 11½″ x 17½″, signed and dated 1879, pencilled on stretcher 'Gruinard'
William Blair Bruce, 1859-1906
A climbing lizard watched by native boys along a wall, oil on canvas signed with monogram, 13½″ x 18″
Edwin Byatt RI, 1888 –
A female nude seated as model, oil on board, 12″ x 9¼″
Adelaide Claxton,
'Courting', oil on board, 13″ x 18″, signed and dated 1860
Josiah Conder,
A Japanese pavilion with figures and barges, bridges across a lake, oil on canvas, 11¼″ x 19½″, signed and dated 1879 (Probably one of the very first topographical paintings done in Japan by a European)
David Cox, 1783-1859
Salmon fishers on a rock above the river, on canvas, 22″ x 19½″, signed and dated 1849

The Parson's Pony, on panel, 6½" x 9", signed
David Cox (Junior), 1809-85
A half-timbered farmhouse, water-colour, 11" x 12", signed and dated 1841
W.C. Cooper
A distant conflagration, black-and-white drawing, 5½" x 7½", signed and dated 1830
Joseph Crawhall, 1861-1913
Jack ashore with his chained monkey, 7¾" x 5¾", signed with monogram bottom right
Amelia Curran, (died 1847)
Portrait of Shelley, 23½" x 20" (one of several portraits of Percy Bysshe Shelley, 1792-1822, c.f. Nat. Gallery portrait no. 1234., National Portrait Ex., 1868, No. 153, 24" x 20", lent by Sir Percy Shelley. New Gallery (Guelph) 1891, No. 212, 24" x 19", lent by Lady Shelley)
Francis Danby ARA, 1793-1861
'The Curfew Tolls', on board, 8¾" x 11½" (ex. collection of Edward Bird RA)
William Etty RA, 1787-1828
Iris, water-colour, 9" x 6", inscribed on old label verso
A Greek maiden spinning wool, oil on card, 6½" x 4", signed on stone bench (top right)
Study of nude with basket of fruit, on canvas, 24" x 18", signed
A bathing nymph on a rocky shore, posed against a rainbow, on canvas, 30" x 23", signed
Thomas Faed, 1826-1900
At the Fountain, a peasant woman with her children drinking, oil on canvas, 16" x 12½", signed
Sir William Russell Flint, 1880-1969
'At the Marchesa's Boat-house', MSS letter dated 22 July 1967
Stanhope Alexander Forbes RA, 1857-1947
Setting the eel-traps, on canvas, 12" x 17½", signed
Harry Furniss, 1854 (Wexford)
Lord Salisbury, pen-and-ink drawing for *Mr Punch's Puzzleheads*, 10" x 8½", signed and dated 1889
James William Grant, 1829-66
The Itinerant Cherry Vendor, on canvas, 9½" x 8", signed with monogram and dated 1861
Walter Greaves, 1846-1930
Boat Race Day, oil on canvas, signed (indistinctly inscribed verso in

charcoal: 'Done for Mr Whistler')
E. Haycock
The expulsion of Hagar and her child, on panel, 7½" x 6", signed
James Holmes, 1777-1860
Portrait of Lord Byron, signed with initials, on panel, 12" x 9" (c.f. miniature at New Gallery Guelph exhibition, 1892, No. 1269a, owner Isaac Falcke)
Sir Edwin Henry Landseer RA, 1802-73
Scottish washer-women, oil sketch on board, 8¼" x 13½", clearly signed on rim of chair below seated woman
John Frederick Lewis, 1805-76
The Chinese Pagoda at Kew, oil on canvas, 15¾" x 7¾", signed
Henry Liverseege, 1803-32
'Good Resolutions', on panel, 8½" x 7¼" (a sketch for the larger picture engraved and published in *Memories of Liverseege*)
William Mulready RA, 1786-1863
A Game of Leap-frog, on panel, 5¼" x 4¼", initialled with monogram on right, quarter inch from edge
Samuel Palmer, 1805-81
Moonlight over the Darenth valley, water-colour on card, 7½" x 10½", signed with initials in lozenge on road before bridge
Mediterranean scene with a muleteer taking the cliff-top path to a monastery, monochrome water-colour, 7½" x 12", signed
J.F. Pasmore, fl. 1841-66
A hedge-cutter in a summer landscape, oil on canvas, 11½" x 23¼", signed with monogram
Stephen Pearce, 1819-1904
The Martyrdom of a Saint, oil on board, 9" x 10", inscribed and signed verso: 'From the original by Paul Veronese in the Uffizi, Florence. Stephen Pearce.
George John Pinwell, 1842-75
A Dhow on the Nile, on panel, 14½" x 25½", signed with initials
Paul Falconer Poole, 1807-79
The Bather Alarmed, oil on panel, 10" x 18" (ex Collection of David Price sold at Christie's, 3 April 1875, Lot 245, for 17 guineas!)
John Anthony Puller (exhibiting 1821-56)
A travelling Cobbler outside a hostelry, oil on board, 11" x 8½", signed and dated (below chequerboard)
David Roberts, 1796-1864
The bridge at Ronda, water-colour 7" x 10", signed
George Samuel, 1785-1823

The Lime Burners, a team of women porters with a male overseer delivering chalk to the kiln, oil on paper, 5½" x 7½", signed bottom right

William Say, 1768-1834

The Price Family, oil on canvas, 13¼" x 19", signed with initials under 'Low Price'

Alfred Stevens, 1817-75

Pandora, 14¼" x 18½", a charcoal sketch

James Mallord William Turner RA, 1775-1851

Burial at Sea, oil on board, octagon of 11½" each side in 30" x 20" surround (a study for the famous picture)

Self-portrait of the artist sweeping his studio, the broom made of a palette nailed to a stick; on his smock is pinned the Légion d'Honneur medal, on panel, 13" x 11" (bought as 'portrait of a hostler sweeping'!)

Sir David Wilkie, 1785-1841

A Scottish Wedding, on panel, 17" x 22", signed (under the bride in the fold of dress, left side)

Thomas Woodward, 1801-52

Returning from Market, a mounted farmer with his dog, oil on board laid down on panel, 5½" x 8"

English School

Red-coated marines preparing fortifications by Cossack Bay, Balaclava, warships standing by, oil on panel, 8½" x 11¼"

A lifeboat rescuing shipwrecked survivors in a gale, oil on canvas, 19" x 26"

English School (naïve)

London Street Traders, oil on panel, 12½" x 52"(possibly from a fair booth or restaurant wall)

The clay pipe broken, on panel, 10½" x 12½"

Gloucester riverside scene, on panel, 11" x 19½"

Rustic village scene with cattle and cowherd, on panel, 13" x 18"

English Colonial School

Portrait of a steamer-sailer, oil upon a shell interior, 6" x 7"

20th Century

Edmund Dulac, 1882-1953

Four drawings for *The Graphic*; illustrations of a Sicilian *banditti* trial, in one frame, described on old label verso, each 8" x 11"

Bernard Walter Evans, born 1848, Birmingham

A Street Scene with Hansom Cabs, oil on vanvas, 9½" x 6⅜", signed and dated 1905

Leonard John Fuller
The Bathing Party, 8½″ x 18″, gouache, signed.
Augustus Edwin John, 1878-1961
Self-portrait, oil on panel, 12″ x 9″, signed
Portrait of Mrs Lascelles, oil on canvas, 16″ x 14″, signed, inscribed on an old label verso
Laura Knight RA, 1877-1970
Study of a ballerina, water-colour, 14¼″ x 9½″, signed with initials
Sir Alfred James Munnings PRA., KCVO, 1878-1959
Reading the news, a gipsy camp, oil on canvas, 8″ x 12″, signed
The Meet. Hounds and Riders, oil sketch, canvas laid down on panel, 14¼″ x 18½″, signed near edge below left horse's haunch
The Horse Show, oil on canvas, 14″ x 18″, signed
Paul Nash, 1899-1946
The Avenue, Flanders, on panel, 9″ x 13″ (also bears another World War I sketch verso)
Christopher Richard Wynne Nevinson RA, 1889-1946
Seascape by Moonlight (inscribed verso 'Nr. Bournemouth Boscome 1920 2.30 a.am. by C.W. Nevinson A.R.A.' and also signed bottom left), oil on board, 12″ x 15½″
Walter Richard Sickert RA, 1860-1942
The Old Flower Seller, oil on board, 13″ x 8¾″, signed
Steven Spurrier RA, 1860-1942
The Bathing Party, charcoal and pen-and-ink drawing, 16″ x 24″, signed on left of left bench
A. Whitehead
Warships steaming in battle formation, water-colour on board, 9¾″ x 20″, signed
English School (naïve)
The Aircraft Carrier being launched, oil on canvas, 12½″ x 19″

American School
William Howard Shüster 1893 –
Mixed Flowers in Glass Vase, oil on copper, 11½″ x 8″, signed
George Catlin 1794-1872
A Red Indian Tribal Scalp Dance, painted on carribou hide, 12″ x 16″
Unattributed
Indians Attacking a Wagon Train, oil on panel, 10½″ x 12½″

Dutch School
Rembrandt Harmenz van Rijn, 1606-69
River landscape with bridge, village and boat with fisherman, oil on panel, 9¼″ x 15¼″ (24 x 39cm), signed with initials on mooring-post (Bought in Birmingham, 1982 as 'Dutch School with numerous figures in background, 9¼″ x 15″, on panel'. C.f. version in Amsterdam Rijksmuseum (Br. 440) 'Landscape with stone bridge', 29.5cm x 42.5cm. C.f. photo in A. Bredius, revised H. Gerson, 3rd ed., 1969, on Page 2 of Landscapes and note 440. HdG 939. Bauch 543.)
Adrien van de Veen, 1589-1680
Rembrandt, a contemporary portrait, pen-and-ink drawing, 6½″ x 6″, signed with monogram
Cornelis Pieterz Bega, 1620-64
Two Boors Drinking, on panel, 6½″ x 5¼″, signed C.B. bottom left
Balthasar van der Ast, 1590-1656
Flowers, lilies and narcissi arranged in vase, with a butterfly, on panel, 17½″ x 12¼″, signed and dated 1647
Tulips in a glass jar, on copper, 8″ x 5″, signed with monogram and dated 1623
Flowers on a ledge, on panel, 6½″ x 9½″, signed 'Van der Ast fecit 1649'
Dutch School, 17th Century
Still life with fruit arranged upon a table, 3¾″ x 6″
A Vase of flowers with a bird's nest on a marble ledge, on copper, oval, 7″ x 5″
Christ healing the blind, on panel, 6″ x 8″
Benjamin Gerritz Cuyp, 1612-52
Portrait of St Sebastian, on panel, 16″ x 12″
Jean Josefsz van Goyen, 1596-1665
Dutch shipping anchored on a lee shore, pencil and wash, 6¾″ x 10½″, signed bottom right
Josef Israels, 1824-1911
'Growing Old', 15¾″ x 12″, oil on porcelain panel, signed and stamped
Wouter Knyff, 1607-93
Frozen landscape with peasants skating beside a village and windmill, on panel, 7″ x 9″, signed at the bottom left of figure before windmill
Jacob Izaakszoon Ruisdael, 1628-82
A Norwegian Waterfall, on canvas 23″ x 17″

Philips Wouverman, 1619-68
The Fishmarket by the Seashore, on panel, 12″ x 10½″ (a less spectacular version of this is in the National Gallery, Cat. ill. no.880)
Adrien van der Velde, 1636-72
A snow scene with farm animals and a mounted peasant, on canvas, 12″ x 14″

Flemish School
Adrien Brouwer, 1605-38
Portrait of a bearded peasant lighting a candle, on panel, 9″ x 7″
Jan Sanders Hemessen (known as Jan van), 1504-66
Portrait of a travelling piper, oil on panel, 42½″ x 12″, signed with monogram bottom left
Gérard Jozef Portielje (Belgian school) 1856 –
At the Frontier, a haystack and sentry box with turkeys in a landscape, 12½″ x 22½″, signed and dated 1892
Aimé Pez, 1908-49
The smoker asleep, on metal, 11½″ x 10″, signed with monogram bottom right
Frans Pourbus II, 1569-1622
Portrait of a cleric, oil on canvas, oval, 6½″ x 5″, signed inside circle.
17th Century
The Raising of Lazarus, on panel, 21″ x 29½″
Rubens
Portrait study, oil on panel, 18½″ x 13½″

Italian School
Titian (Tiziano Vecelli), 1485 or 1488/9- 1576
Christ Crowned with Thorns, on canvas, 21″ x 12″ (related to the painting on wood now in the Louvre painted about 1542 and measuring 120″ x 71″, for which this is the sketch itemized as existing in the studio of Tintoretto and mentioned in his Will. Another large version is in the Altere Pinakothek
Sebastiano Bagolino, 1560-1604, '*peintre dessinateur et poète italien*', born at Alcamo, son of the painter Leonardo Bagolino of Verona who died at Alcamo in 1585
The Forge of Vulcan, 10½″ x 12″, on copper, signed bottom right (Vulcan's Forge was reputed to be on Mount Etna, Sicily. Drawings of Sebastiano are conserved at Alcamo and in the Public Library at Palermo, Sicily.)

Alessandro Magnasco, 1667-1749
The Angel serenading St Francis, on canvas, 11¼" x 7½"
B. Musi, 18th Century
Architectural study with figures and petitioners waiting, oil on panel,
8½" x 11¼", signed
Tintoretto (attributed)
Nativity scene with shepherds in adoration, on canvas, 13" x 10½"
Italian School
The Annunciation, on copper, 9¼" x 8"
Italian School, 17th Century
A reclining nude: half length fragment on canvas laid down, 14½" x
11½"
Portrait of a Pilgrim, on canvas, 18" x 14"
Italian School 19th Century (naïve)
Madonna and child, oil on panel, 12½" x 10"

French School
Jules Adolphe Aimé Louis Breton, 1827-1906
Reverie, Côte Bretonne, on panel, 10" x 14", signed
Charles Abraham Chasselat, 1782-1843
The Druid with the sickle-cut mistletoe, sepia drawing, 4½" x 3",
signed
Camille Jean-Baptiste Corot, 1796-1875
Dancers in a Forest Glade, oil on board, signed, 15¼" x 20", label of
a Paris exhibition verso
Fishermen angling from a boat under a wooded hillside, on board,
12¼" x 18", signed
Honoré Daumier, 1808-79
The Connoisseurs, oil on paper, 12" x 9", signed with initials
Charles François Daubigny, 1817-78
Landscape at sunset, on canvas, 7¾" x 12", signed bottom left
Narcisse Virgile Diaz de le Pena (Diaz), 1807-76
A Bowl of Anemones, on panel, 4" x 5", signed N. Diaz
Rest on the Flight to Egypt, on panel, 7¼" x 6", signed
Raphael Drouart, 1884-1972
Giessen 1917, signed and inscribed, oil painted on a card taken from
a World War I Rations Gift Box 'from Mrs F. Humphrey, 122
Victoria Street Westminster. S.W.' and reads verso: 'For Prisoner of
War in Germany c/o G.P.O. London. Lewis Renateau 2082, 13th
Batt. Compagnie No. 6 Barraque No. E.' The painting was probably
done in the prison camp, for the old label remains with the list of

grocery contents addressed to Gefängenen Lager, Giessen, Germany, despatched 15 August. Benezit records of Drouart: '*Il s'est parfois adonné à la sculpture, notamment en éxecutant le Monument aux Alliés mort en captivité a Gièssen Allemagne 1918*' and notes that he illustrated many books of the poets.

Louis Jules Hora (exhibiting in the Salon 1839-45)
Outside the Bull Ring at Ronda, on canvas, 16″ x 8″, signed

Gaston de Latouche, 1854-1913
A naiad by a stream, oil on board, 13″ x 9″, signed

Jean-Baptiste Le Prince, 1734-81
Fishermen drawing nets below a towered castle, pen and brown ink drawing, 13″ x 9″, signed and dated 1771

Adolphe Joseph Thomas Monticelli, 1824-96
Reclining nude with a mirror on canvas, 12¼″ x 16″ signed

Camille Pissaro, 1830-1903
Urban canal scene with towpath, figures, horse-drawn carriages and a steam barge, on panel, 9½″ x 15½″, signed

Victor Louis Mottez, 1809-97
A village landscape with post mills, oil on canvas, 14½″ x 17½″, signed V. Mottez under right of large tree and dated 1845 below yellow ochre root

Claude Joseph Vernet (known as *Joseph Vernet*), 1714-89
A priest and survivors receiving the shipwrecked on a rocky coast with *unlit* lighthouse, on canvas, 17½″ x 23½″, signed with monogram on rock bottom right

Watteau, 1684-1721
L'Indifférent, oil on panel, 9½″ x 7½″ (related to the Louvre picture, 10⅓″ x 8″, said to be 'in ruinous condition with an air of convalescence' and a drawing in the Museum Boymans van Beuningen, Rotterdam, in excellent condition but with the figure in reverse pose)

Georges Rouault, 1871-1958
The Clown's new costume, on panel, 19″ x 10½″, inscribed verso, '*Mauvais peinture faut etre destruire Roualt*' (bought at Sotheby's, Pulborough, at about the time of their take-over from King and Chasemore; the loose panel, unframed and unattributed, was ignored, mine being the only bid, at £1)

Simon Vouet, 1590-1649
Mediterranean Harbour with peasants, on canvas, 21″ x 36″, signed bottom left

French School, 17th Century

The Magdalen in a landscape, oil on relined canvas, 18½" x 14½"
French School, 18th Century
A classical landscape with figures and a garden, on panel, 4¼" x 4"
French School, 19th Century
A portrait of Sarah Bernhardt, indistinctly signed and inscribed verso, oil on panel, 16" x 8"
Riviera scene with a solitary pine tree, oil on canvas, laid down on panel, 15" x 11" (indistinctly signed bottom left)
An Arabian girl trying on an ear-ring with maidservant in attendance, on canvas, 28" x 19", signed P. Gauguin and dated 1902
Iles Sanguinaires Corsica, water-colour, inscribed, 2" x 5¼"
French School, 19th Century (Naïve)
Pair of portraits of a Count and a Countess, on panels, each 7" x 6½"

Spanish School
Alonso Cano, 1601-67
Souls in Purgatory with the Patron Saint interceding, canvas laid down on panel, 18" x 15" (purchased in a junk shop in Granada)
Velázquez (attributed)
A soldier marching in procession beside his horse, canvas laid down on panel, a fragment, 9¼" x 7"
Spanish School 17th Century
St Francis at Prayer, on canvas, 17½" x 13"
Death of Joseph with Christ and Mary present, on canvas, 18½" x 15"
The Christ Child and the Infant St John with St Thomas, oil on canvas, oval, 23" x 19"
St Francis and the Infant Christ with the Scriptures, oil on panel, 23" x 17½"
The Good and the Evil Angel vying for the Soul of a Child, on canvas, 21" x 27½"
Francisco José de Goya y Lucientes, 1746-1828
A Spanish Procession at Fiesta Time, 7" x 11½", on canvas
Sanctuary invaded, An incident during the French occupation, oil on board, 2" x 5½", signed with initial
Study of a Saint, a portrait sketch on leather, probably cut from a larger picture, 5¼" x 3¾"; verso bears label of J & W Vokins of Grt. Portland St. London
Servando del Pilar, 20th Century
A vase of mixed flowers on a ledge, oil on panel, signed, 7" x 5"
Picasso imitation!
Import from Hong Kong on silk, 22½" x 30"

Greek
Icon of Christ with the Scriptures, on panel, 13″ x 11″

Russian School
Icon. Portrait of a Saint, inscribed, 12″ x 10½″ on panel, (the gilded silver overlay has been picked away by devotees)
Icon. The Virgin and Child, on panel, 14″ x 11½″
Icon of the Madonna and Child, 19th Century, on panel, surmounted with elaborate copper riza, 8″ x 6½″
Pavel Fedorovitch Korovanov, signed with initials and inscribed verso, 25 April 1787, on panel, 5½″ x 5¼″
Russian School,
A landscape with a willow tree beside a pool, on canvas, 26″ x 16½″ signed and dated 1886
Russian School, 19th Century
A market scene with peasants and a one-horse sleigh in foreground, oil on copper panel, 14″ x 17½″
A. Dimitriev
A Russian roadside village in snow, on panel, 11″ x 24″, signed and dated 1916
Russian School, World War I
Portrait of a four-funnelled steamer warship with a mine-clearance service (old-style Cyrillic lettering on the ribbon below), on canvas, 11″ x 16″

Albanian School
A Turkish palace scene with a view of Durres, on panel, 12″ x 17″ (signed on the wall of the well)

German School
Felicien Joseph Victor Rops, 1833-98
Serpents and Seducers, pen-and-ink sketch on paper, illustration for a bookplate, 9″ x 7″, signed Felicien Rops
Hubert von Bülow (after)
Eve picking the Apple, on panel, 11½″ x 4½″, inscribed 'nach Hubert von Bülow'
Moïse Kisling, 1891-1953
Portrait of a young girl, a black chalk drawing, heightened with colour, 13″ x 9½″, signed
The Viennese Animal Painter (18th Century)
Daniel among the Lions, oil on panel, 18″ x 23½″

Unattributed
The Confession, oil on canvas, indistinctly signed, 10" x 13"

Austrian School 18th Century
Nessus and Deanira, oval on oil panel, 18" x 14"

Swedish
Wertmuller, Adolph Ulrick, 1751-1811
Portrait of a Swedish smoker seated at a table with a glass and wine flagon, signed, oil on copper, 7" x 5½"

Prints and Engravings Etc
Hiroshige 1797-1858
River and orchard landscape with peasants and wood-cutters, Japanese colour print, 13½" x 9¼", signed and inscribed
Chinese
The Opium Dealers, water-colour, 7¾" x 11½"
George Morland
Mrs Morland, in colour, oval, 3¼" x 2½"
19th Century
Coloured print inscribed 'The Royal Nuptials and Concert. Dresden' 10" x 6"
Charles Edward Holloway, 1838-97
Old Chelsea Church, signed etching, published by the Art union of London, 1890
Adrien van Ostade, 1610-84
The Dance at the Inn, 9½" x 12½", engraving, 8th State (949)
Lucus Vostermans, 1595-1675
Styled *Caleograpus*, self-portrait, engraving, 10" x 8" (A pupil and friend of Rubens, in 1624 he came to England to be employed by Charles I and his counseller Arundel. He was associated with Van Dyck.)
Gottfied Kneller (after)
Portrait of Sir Robert Walpole, print, 12½" x 10", 'G. Kneller Bart. pinxit J Faber 1733.'
Nicolas Lavreince (known as *Niklas Lafressen*), Stockholm, 1737-1807
Le Tendre Entretien, colour print, circular
Portraits of *George Robey*
A black-and-white print inscribed 'Simply George, in other words

Robey' and 'Pen sketch and self portrait drawn for *L.R. Nightingale*', 15½" x 10½"

Sculpture
English, 16th Century
Bronze relief of *Queen Elizabeth*, 12" x 8½"
William IV, portrait bronze, 5½", inscribed 'Published as the Act directs, Jany. 9 1831, by *Saml. Parker* 12 Argyll Place London'
Italian School, 17th Century
Head of Pan, with bust ornamented with vine branches and grapes
Raffaell Uccella, 1884-1929
Circus performers, a pair, bronzes, heights including socles, 6" and 5¼"
Russian School
A Muscovite bellringer seated upon a cushion mounted upon the bell over a socle decorated with beaded rims and floral leaves, 6½", bronze
Bronze *Russian* incense-burner of circular form, pierced openwork neck and pierced cover, 9"
Bronze *Turkish* lantern, with cast ornament, glazed panels with pierced decoration, 16", probably from a mosque
Spanish
Cast metal figure of Don Quixote challenging, 8", purchased in Granada
Spanish
Baked clay and painted figure of Sancho Panza, 6½", also bought in Granada
Spanish School, 17th Century
A sea-god in relief, wood carving on panel, 9½" x 11¼", probably part of an old sea-chest or ship's cabin wall panel, purchased in Cadiz
Peruvian
Pottery head, blinking eyes, red glaze decoration, 4½"
Japanese
Bronze figures of Oni
17th Century
7", mounted on a drum
18th Century
7½", mounted on a wood socle
Scandinavian
Bronze cutters with dragon head and bird design, 8"

Modern bronze plaque of the Phoenix arising, 10″, probably an Insurance Co emblem, mounted on panel

Miscellanies

The many additional collectables – coins, china and furniture – which have added themselves to the author's collection over the years are not listed; ranging as they do from trivia to important artefacts, they have become, to quote the recurrent phrase of the old-fashioned auctioneer's cataloguer, 'too numerous to mention'. Interesting items I could select as worthy of more notice are: the ancient silver vessel '*The Tale of Troy*'; the Argentine silver parrot cup and tea-infuser made of platinum; the English hall-marked silver George II cruet, George III tea-pot and 'Kaiser's tea-pot' (William IV), the antique Russian heavy silver caviare dish and cover, the Russian gilt silver cake basket, the Bedouin silver Kohl bottle from the Saharan oasis, the two Admiralty-issue antique silver bosun's whistles, the silver grape scissors and the cast vines on the wine coaster, the carved shepherd's crooks from Greece and the carved Turkish shoe-horn from Janina. The collector's fever seizes me as I write with the urge to note them all, and I must break the list!